The Vatican Prophecies

Also by John Thavis

The Vatican Diaries

JOHN THAVIS

The Vatican Prophecies

Investigating Supernatural Signs,
Apparitions, and Miracles in
the Modern Age

VIKING

VIKING
An imprint of Penguin Random House LLC
375 Hudson Street
New York, New York 10014
penguin.com

ISBN 978-0-525-42689-9
Printed in the United States of America
1 3 5 7 9 10 8 6 4 2
Set in Adobe Jenson Pro
Designed by Francesca Belanger

To my parents, Alice and Richard

Contents

Then some of the scribes and Pharisees said to him,
"Teacher, we wish to see a sign from you."

—THE GOSPEL OF SAINT MATTHEW

The Vatican Prophecies

Introduction:
At the Crossroads of Reason and Wonder

The Mexican man fidgeted in a wheelchair, waiting for a blessing from Pope Francis. It was Pentecost Sunday in May 2013, two months after Francis's election, and there was already extraordinary public enthusiasm for the new pontiff. The pope's down-to-earth and unpredictable style had captured the world's attention, and TV cameras followed his every move. Like his predecessors Francis ended his liturgies by personally greeting a line of the sick and their caregivers. On this day they had assembled in a shaded corner of Saint Peter's Square. Among them were pilgrims with cancer, cerebral palsy, multiple sclerosis, muscular dystrophy, and other serious infirmities.

The young man from Mexico, Angel V., did not suffer from any common illness or disability, however. He was convinced that he was possessed by the devil. For years exorcists in Rome had tried, unsuccessfully, to cast out his demons. One of them believed that Angel was possessed by no fewer than four evil spirits; ridding him of them would require a prodigious spiritual effort. But where ordinary exorcists had failed, perhaps a pope could succeed—especially a pope like Francis, who in his first weeks had shocked listeners by describing the devil as a real force in the modern world, and warning Christians to guard against Satan's cunning ways. After repeated attempts, Angel's clerical friends in Rome had finally received permission to bring him to the papal Mass. For the Vatican he was just one more sick person in a wheelchair, but for a small group of priests seeking to revive the exorcism ministry, he was an important test case.

Pope Francis was unaware of all this as he made his way down the line of the ill and impaired, greeting each sufferer and leaning in to offer a few words of comfort. When he came to Angel, he laid his hands on top of the man's head. Angel began to writhe and breathe heavily. His mouth opened wide, emitting a strange howling sound, and then he slumped in his chair. Vatican security guards quickly blocked the view of the professional photographers who were present and moved the pope along.

Had Pope Francis just performed an exorcism? The media headlines and YouTube postings suggested that he had, and several priests who routinely did exorcisms agreed. If not the full-blown exorcism rite, they said, Francis had at least recited a prayer of liberation from Satan, and the dramatic effect of the pope's intervention was there for all to see. A few hours later, however, the Vatican spokesman, Father Federico Lombardi, categorically denied that Pope Francis had conducted an exorcism. The pope had simply said a generic prayer to relieve suffering, which he often offered to the sick. For the Vatican, the case was closed.

This episode, described in greater detail in the fourth chapter of this book, is a striking example of the Vatican's extreme sensitivity to any suggestion of the existence of real-world demonic manifestation. The devil may be acceptable as a theological reality, but not as a personality who makes people howl, levitate, speak in unknown languages, and exhibit superhuman strength—all classic signs of possession, but far too Hollywood for modern Vatican tastes.

In a wider sense the "exorcism" of Angel V. highlights a growing tension between the Vatican's more intellectual approach to faith, heavily skewed toward philosophical and doctrinal assertions, and the popular thirst for something more tangible. In an age in which Christianity is supposed to be the faith of reason, many are still fascinated by the possibility of miracles, apparitions, encounters with the devil, and other signs of the supernatural.

Balancing these two aspects of faith is a task that has increasingly occupied the Vatican's time and resources. In recent years its offices have issued a series of instructions aimed at controlling devotional and mystical experiences whenever they threaten to disturb the church's beliefs and practices. In a sense the Vatican is engaged in vetting the supernatural and filtering "wondrous" experiences, to minimize anything it judges unorthodox, superfluous, excessive, or bizarre. At the same time, of course, officials in Rome cannot be seen as placing limits on divine inter-

vention, including the possibility of God's intercession in everyday life—
that would be viewed as betraying the church's oldest traditions.

The diverse forms of the supernatural—miraculous events, apparitions, healings, prophecies, and demonic interference—have been essential
elements of Christianity from the moment God said "Let there be light"
in the Book of Genesis. The wonders of creation brought about by the
word of God were followed by numerous Old Testament accounts of
divine favor or retribution: the Nile River turning to blood, one of the
ten plagues of Egypt; the withered hand of King Jeroboam, who tried to
silence a prophet; the diviner Balaam's donkey, who spoke to his master
in a man's voice; or the revelations received by biblical prophets like Daniel, who foretold events from his own time to the End Times. The life of
Christ was marked by an even more intense flurry of supernatural activity. Jesus raised the dead, healed the sick, restored sight to the blind, cast
out demons, changed water into wine, fed the multitude with a few
loaves and some fish, and walked on water. The New Testament records
thirty-seven miracles of Christ, but as the Gospel of John states, "There
are also many other things that Jesus did, but if these were to be described individually, I do not think the whole world would contain the
books that would be written."

According to scriptural accounts the Apostles continued to perform miraculous wonders after Christ's death. They cured the ill and
the lame, rid men and women of evil spirits, caused prison gates to
burst open, and experienced prophetic visions. Saint Peter's spiritual
powers were so great that even his passing shadow was said to have
healed the sick. Miracles came to be seen as an important indicator of
sainthood, and in the eighteenth century the Vatican established formal criteria for validating miracles as part of the canonization process.

In a very physical way, pieces of human bone and other relics came to
preserve the link to the early Christian evangelizers and saints, and their
supposed supernatural potency made them fixtures in churches in Europe and, in later centuries, on every other continent. In the Middle Ages
relics retrieved from the Holy Land assumed greater importance as communities began to rely on their patronage and protection. Sometimes

even small towns would honor a whole pantheon of patron saints, each of whom specialized in overcoming a particular type of disease or adversity. Prayers answered by saintly intercessors were often memorialized with ex-voto offerings, new shrines, or the construction of major churches.

Apparitions of the Virgin Mary were a later development in the church's history. In some areas of Christendom they began occurring frequently by the late Middle Ages, and were sometimes tied to annual processions or other events. Many towns in Mediterranean countries venerated their own particular "miraculous" images of Mary—typically, weeping icons or bleeding statues—which were objects of prayer and invocation. Over the last two centuries messages from Mary, delivered directly to chosen visionaries, have increased dramatically. The most famous of these apparitions have attracted worldwide followings, and some have won the Catholic Church's official approval. But hundreds of others have never attained more than local notoriety, and in many cases church authorities have avoided an official pronouncement on the visions or the prophetic messages that accompany them.

The other side of the supernatural coin, demonic influence, has always compelled Christians. The struggle against malignant magic and sorcery very much engaged the early church, and for centuries it was acceptable for both clergy and laypeople to drive out evil spirits by invoking the power of Christ, the saints, and the angels. Exorcism eventually became a recognized sacramental in the Catholic Church with its own rite, which was last revised in 1999.

From the beginning, then, Christians have relied on a web of supernatural connections in prayer, worship, and daily life. In early times there was not much controversy over these displays of divine power; they were accepted, at least by the Christian community, in the spirit of wonder and gratitude. For many centuries, in fact, the church hierarchy had no official set of procedures to investigate and authenticate such phenomena. The dangers inherent in private revelation, however, came to the fore in the fifteenth century, when the fiery and popular Italian Dominican preacher Girolamo Savonarola prophesied a series of scourges to be sent by God to purify a corrupt church in Rome. Alexander VI, the Borgia pope, took note and, after continued defiance by Savonarola, had the friar hanged and his body burned in his native Florence in 1498. The threat to authority posed by prophecies, and their ability to stir the masses, alarmed the Vatican, which began to insist on closer vigilance over all forms of supernatural signs and communications.

Today, with global media attention focused on every new claim of the miraculous and Internet pages dedicated to the latest "divine" messages, the Vatican is ever more sensitive to the potential damage, both internal and external, posed by false miracles, apparitions, and prophecies. Internally the risk is primarily that of sowing confusion and doubt among the faithful. The central Christian belief that God's public revelation ended with the New Testament leaves little room for dogmatic surprises and innovative prophesying by private visionaries. Nowadays no one is burned at the stake for heresy, but Catholic seers who do contradict official church teachings or invent new ones have been criticized, ostracized, and in some cases excommunicated.

Equally important to the Catholic Church is how it appears in the eyes of the world. In their ongoing campaign of global evangelization, popes and other Vatican authorities have emphasized that faith and human reason go hand in hand, and that the church has no desire to turn back the clock to the time before the Enlightenment. They argue that the church has been a thoughtful, if at times critical, force in the shaping of contemporary civilization, and as such rightfully merits a voice in the modern age. For that reason many Vatican officials wince whenever they hear about a new weeping Madonna, a healing relic, or a prophetic housewife taking dictation from God.

In the view of several experts interviewed for this book, the strain between the theological and devotional wings of the Catholic Church is real, and reveals itself whenever the hierarchy must pass judgment on apparitions, miracles, and private revelations. "Devotion to the saints and belief in the power of the saints sometimes borders on superstition," one Vatican theologian said. "On the other hand, 'superstition' is often used by the theologically enlightened to dismiss popular piety, because they don't appreciate the importance of these devotions."

But the demarcation lines are far from clear or complete. Even Catholic rationalists remain open to expressions of the divine, embracing a broader concept of reason and rejecting the idea that empirical science is the only path to truth. From the Christian viewpoint, material and supernatural realities coexist across a continuum in a world created by God and redeemed by Christ. They are not two separate realms; their points of contact are limitless. The Catholic understanding of the world is sacramental, in the sense that all things can be a medium of the divine and a means of grace, which helps explain why supernatural events have always been given wide latitude in the church. Even today many skeptics (including Vatican officials) may profess incredulity at the proliferation of apparitions and apocalyptic signs, yet will recount personal encounters and wondrous experiences that defy rational explanation.

The Vatican does not have a Department of the Supernatural, a central clearinghouse for all things miraculous or inexplicable. Instead, its various bureaucratic agencies, often operating with little coordination, attempt to evaluate and regulate a wide variety of extraordinary occurrences, though in most cases they throw responsibility for a verdict back to the local bishop. The Vatican's approach can be liturgical, doctrinal, or scientific, and the inevitable result is a series of mixed messages when it comes to otherworldly signs and wonders: One Roman Curia congregation may issue a document cautioning against "the mania of collecting relics" and superstitious belief in their powers, while another office will distribute small pieces of saints' body parts for veneration by the faithful. Likewise, while one group of doctrinal officials may be monitoring charlatan prophecies—including suggestions that Pope Francis is the antipope—other Vatican experts are writing books unlocking scriptural codes to the End Times. A papal commission investigates supposed Marian apparitions in the Bosnia and Herzegovina town of Medjugorje at the same time that cardinals are publicly disagreeing about the authenticity and value of the visions. The Vatican allows carbon-14 testing that dates the Shroud of Turin to the Middle Ages, but six months later a pope declares that the Shroud is "certainly a relic" from the time of the crucifixion. One Vatican office invites the submission of supposed miracles that demonstrate the power of saintly intercession, but then turns to medical science to reject about half of the miraculous claims.

The Vatican's efforts to be more objective and transparent about supernatural phenomena have sometimes backfired. A classic example came in 2000, when Pope John Paul II and top doctrinal officials divulged the third secret of Fatima, publishing a formal text and a commentary on the meaning of the Blessed Virgin's message to three Portuguese children in 1917. This initiative to set the record straight after decades of secrecy and ominous speculation not only failed to convince many Catholics, but ended up spawning a small industry of books and videos speculating about a Vatican cover-up. The third secret of Fatima was the Vatican equivalent of Area 51: any attempt at an official explanation was bound to ignite new conspiracy theories.

One central issue in the debate over mystical visions and prophecies is whether they are a matter of God's communicating directly with a devout individual, without the mediation of the institutional church—and if so, why? This is a question that Saint Ignatius of Loyola posed after his own mystical experiences in sixteenth-century Spain. Ignatius came down firmly on the side of the mystic, saying that spiritual exercises should "permit the Creator to deal directly with the creature, and the creature directly with his Creator and Lord." Ignatius was called before the Inquisition to justify his teachings, but unlike others who were branded as heretics, he was able to explain that a personal mystical relationship with God did not signify rejection of the practices and guidance of the established church.

Today one of Ignatius's modern followers, the German Jesuit Hans Zollner, is among a new breed of Catholic thinkers who are trying to build bridges between science and religious realities. Zollner, vice-rector of the Pontifical Gregorian University in Rome and head of its Institute of Psychology, is a theologian and a licensed psychologist. He studies phenomena like demonic possession with a wary and clinical eye and estimates that out of a thousand such cases, perhaps only one does not have a psychological explanation. "I would say, the more serious and the more reasonable a person is, the more he will concur that almost all these people need psychological help, and this will be the cure for them, not an exorcist," Zollner observed in a recent interview.

Yet Zollner added that scientists sometimes exclude belief in demons and miracles and apparitions simply because they don't fit into the prevailing empirical categories: "This is a major philosophical fault in many areas of science, because science has become a creed for some. They say things cannot be proven scientifically, but what they consider 'scientifically' is something that has been developed over the last one hundred and fifty years."

Between omniscient science and blind faith, Zollner said, some have proposed a third kind of reality, an outlook that is both philosophical and spiritual, and thus more open to religious and transcendent experiences. There is no doubt that direct experience with the supernatural is still very meaningful in the lives of many Christians, he pointed out: in fact, as Catholicism becomes a more globally diverse religion, it is being forced to embrace cultures where the dividing line between objective science and the supernatural is not so well defined. Some of these cultures have a deep attachment to the miraculous. "What is 'normal' by Anglo-Saxon and Western European standards," Zollner said, "is not necessarily normal in Papua New Guinea or in the jungles of Congo. That goes from how we greet each other to how we consider extraordinary phenomena."

Zollner observed that Catholic academics, like other intellectual elites, tend to share a bias against mystical visionaries and their prophetic revelations. The Catholic Church as a whole, he believes, needs to work harder to preserve a healthy connection with transcendent realities. This is all the more important today because Western societies are showing signs of a potentially detrimental schism between the rational and the supernatural—a growing disconnect between the scientific, hardwired world of people's daily lives and their private spiritual search. Established churches have not always responded to these aspirations, and, for many people, unguided spiritual exploration has replaced religious affiliation. Unmoored from the practices and traditions of faith, Zollner said, the appetite for the supernatural can manifest itself either in irrational and even destructive practices, like Satanic cults, or in a wide spectrum of fantasy seeking (for example, in popular films and literature) that reflects the fundamental human desire for transcendence. The church must reclaim the big themes of redemption and salvation, Zollner argues, and that means openness to the possibility of divine action in people's lives.

Navigating a modern approach to the supernatural is not easy, however. For one thing, the Vatican views signs and wonders as supplements to Scripture and doctrine, and never as a main theme. In addition the role of the miraculous has changed in increasingly pluralistic and secular societies. In Catholic cultures of past centuries, miraculous events and their commemoration strengthened the faith identity of local communities and often functioned as the interface between religious and civic life. The Vatican's priority was to make sure these devotions were doctrinally sound and that local enthusiasm for signs, relics, revelations, and prophecies didn't get out of hand. Today, however, such phenomena are frequently cut off from the traditional roots of Catholicism and devotional life and are instead treated as curiosities, gothic anomalies that pop up here and there on the spiritual panorama. If supernatural occurrences were once a sign of health in the mystical body of the church, the hierarchy now views them as free radicals, unstable elements that need to be better controlled.

Often, miracles no longer have a unifying role, even at the local level. Claims of supernatural phenomena today are just as likely to divide Catholic communities as bring them together. In some cases, when promoted aggressively by groups of lay Catholics, they are seen as challenging the clerical monopoly on spiritual authority. These are among the reasons why the Vatican has ramped up its oversight efforts and encouraged bishops to take a stronger hand in investigating any new "signs" from heaven that land in their diocese. In recent years the

Vatican has injected an uncharacteristic note of urgency in its instructions on how to manage eruptions of the supernatural. Rome has learned that in an era of instant global communications, it can no longer wait years or decades to reach a judgment. The supposed Marian apparitions at Medjugorje offer the perfect example (and, from a management point of view, a practically irresolvable problem). By the time the Vatican set up a commission to investigate the matter in 2010, the apparitions had been taking place for nearly thirty years. During that time dozens of books had been published to promote Medjugorje, movies about it had been released, and tens of millions of pilgrims had visited the Herzegovinian village. In effect Catholic devotees had already voted with their feet, making it politically difficult for officials in Rome to remove Medjugorje from the apparition map. The Vatican has also discovered that social media, uncontrolled and unfiltered by church authorities, are now routinely used to propagate claims of divine messages and prophecies. Facebook pages and blogs tout "Catholic End Times Prophecies," various apparitions of Mary, prayers against diabolical possession, and the private revelations of a number of Catholic seers. Not surprisingly, when the supernatural goes viral, it outstrips the Vatican's ability to investigate and verify.

On a personal level, too, modern mystics face new kinds of pressures. Historically humility has always been considered a sign of authenticity among those claiming to experience apparitions and miraculous signs. Today, however, these individuals are expected to take their turn in the media spotlight. The Vatican prefers that visionaries keep a low profile, but the world wants them to be celebrities—accessible, popular, and willing to engage in self-promotion.

When it comes to the supernaturally sacred, the news media love to depict the Vatican as desperate to preserve outdated practices and beliefs. If Rome sponsors a workshop on demonic influence, for example, the headlines will inevitably speak of a "revival of exorcism." If the Vatican puts the purported bones of Saint Peter on display, it represents a "return to relics." In reality a more subtle and complex shift is occurring, as the Vatican lets go of archaic elements that no longer make sense in the age of reason. Its overall emphasis has been to move away from supernatural events that contradict the rational world toward a more holistic approach, one that sees the connection to the divine as a constant in spiritual life.

That is a delicate task, however, and not without opposition, for Rome's desire to moderate the theatrical side of the supernatural is not always shared by the faithful in the pews. Local apparitions, weeping or bleeding images, healing relics, and enigmatic prophecies can still galvanize many Catholics in the twenty-first century, and there's inevitably a degree of resistance when the hierarchy tries to shut down these displays.

"These miracles should not be hidden," wrote one Catholic who signed a 2011 petition to reopen an investigation into reports of multiple weeping statues in the Saint Elizabeth Ann Seton Church in Lake Ridge, Virginia. For several months in 1992, the statues and other images appeared to shed tears or blood in the presence of a priest who was said to have the stigmata, the wounds of Christ's crucifixion. The events, known as the Seton Miracles, were witnessed by hundreds of parishioners. Diocesan officials investigated the matter at the time, found no particular significance or message, and silenced the priests involved. Nearly twenty years later local Catholics were still wondering why the Seton Miracles hadn't had more impact. Among them was Supreme Court Justice Antonin Scalia, who referred to the episode in a 2010 speech and asked: "Why wasn't that church absolutely packed with nonbelievers, seeking to determine if there might be something to this?" Scalia argued that it was not irrational to accept eyewitness testimony to miracles; what was irrational, he said, was to reject a priori, with no investigation, any possibility of miracles.

Multiply the Seton Miracles by several hundred or more across the international Catholic horizon, and one can understand why the Vatican has neither the capability nor the desire to monitor every reported apparition or wondrous occurrence. Instead, it issues strategies and procedures for local church authorities to follow. Increasingly the Vatican's policies have called for caution and closer regulation of the supernatural:

- Rules and guidelines for authenticating apparitions and supposedly divine messages now underline the limited importance of personal revelation and the need for vigilance by bishops—especially when apocalyptic prophecies identify the Vatican as part of the problem.
- Vatican officials have been particularly wary of visions that portray the Blessed Virgin Mary as a source of new revelation, a unique mediator, or a "goddess," or that press for a new Marian dogma.
- By revising the Rite of Exorcism and approving a church-sanctioned association of exorcists, the Vatican has actually increased its control over demon-hunting Catholic priests and curbed the activities of freelancers.
- In recent years, there has been a conscious effort to move away from cutting up saintly body parts for relics, a practice that one church official described as "obsolete."
- Even in the one area where the Vatican routinely proclaims scientific evidence for supernatural events, the verification of miracles for sainthood causes, change seems to be in the air. Pope Francis has waived the miracle requirement for several saints, and some argue that it's time for the church to move away from inexplicable healings in favor of a wider view of the "miraculous."

These are important trends, and often go unnoticed. There is, however, no master plan for altering the church's relationship with the supernatural. As in most Vatican affairs, forces sometimes push and pull in different directions. To give just one example, even as Vatican officials are limiting the distribution of corporeal relics, papal liturgists prominently feature saints' body parts in canonization Masses and other ceremonies. Opinions are likewise divided on the Shroud of Turin, the influence of the devil, and supposed messages from Mary.

One constant is that manifestations of the supernatural continue to simmer among the faithful, percolating up like hot spots on the global Catholic landscape. In response, the Vatican attempts to coolly examine the facts and exercise quality control, extinguishing any hint of fanaticism.

This book reveals the behind-the-scenes struggle to keep all this in balance. It tells the stories of recent miracles, apparitions, and prophecies from the diverse perspectives of key players: the true believers, the in-house skeptics, and the Vatican's diligent investigators. It describes the shock waves when a new pontiff like Francis starts to talk about the devil, or messages from Mary, or false prophets. It explains how public relations have influenced, and at times displaced, quiet discernment in mystical life. It offers assessments from the Vatican's field generals and theoreticians, and testimony from the *miracolati* who believe they've been saved by heavenly intercession. Finally, it examines the question that with increasing urgency Catholic thinkers and officials are trying to answer: In the church of the twenty-first century, can the miraculous and the reasonable peacefully coexist?

CHAPTER ONE

A Piece of Holiness

The religious souvenir shops that populate the Borgo neighbor-hood outside the Vatican are mostly family-run operations that have peddled the same goods to pilgrims for generations: rosaries, medals, crosses, and holy cards. The margin on sales of these items is so low that many of the smaller stores have closed in recent years. So when a popular new product comes along, the kind that will have peo-ple waiting in line to get inside the doors, it's an opportunity that the vendors cannot afford to miss.

In the fall of 2006 "relics" of Pope John Paul II went on sale in the Borgo and were an immediate merchandising triumph. The Polish pope had died only the year before, and his canonization cause was still in the early stages, but neither the Catholic faithful nor Rome's shop owners wanted to wait for an official Vatican declaration of saint-hood. Statuettes labeled "Saint John Paul II" had been selling briskly all year, and now people were lining up to purchase something even better: a small medal that enclosed a tiny piece of cloth, supposedly cut from a "papal habit." Signs in Italian, English, and Polish announced, "Relics of John Paul II on sale here."

As it turned out, the vendors were bending the definition of "relic," because the fabric in question had never actually been worn by the late pope. Instead, an enterprising Italian had taken a white alb down to the crypt of Saint Peter's Basilica and, when the guards weren't look-ing, quickly touched it to the tomb marker of Pope John Paul. He then cut the alb into thousands of minuscule fragments, enough to keep his cottage industry going for months. Touching objects to the tomb of a holy individual is a centuries-old tradition in the Catholic Church, but marketing such items as "third-class relics" crossed the line from devo-tion to exploitation. It didn't take long for Vatican authorities to demand an end to the sales, and shop owners—many of whom were tenants of the Vatican—promptly complied. The John Paul II "relics" disappeared.

But the story didn't end there. Officials of the Diocese of Rome, who were in charge of John Paul II's sainthood cause, officially denounced the profiteering aspect of this entrepreneurial venture but also recognized a growing appetite for mementos and relics of the late pope. They began distributing their own holy cards with genuine relics—minute pieces of a cassock that had, in fact, been used by John Paul when he was alive. These were "second-class" relics *ex indumentis* (from the clothing) and came with certification from the Rome diocese. The holy card was inscribed with a prayer "to obtain graces through the intercession of John Paul II." Because the item was available online, the tiny office in the diocesan headquarters was soon inundated with requests from all over the world. And thus a new problem arose: distribution costs. Although the holy cards and relics were available free of charge, the website began encouraging a "free-will offering" for postage and handling, which came back to haunt them when newspapers began reporting that the church was, in effect, selling the relics under the guise of a request for donations. The Diocese of Rome vehemently denied that these were financial transactions. "Relics absolutely cannot be bought or sold because they are sacred objects, they have no price. The problem of the sale of relics is widespread on the Internet, and let me say that this is a sacrilege," said Monsignor Marco Frisina, head of the diocese's liturgy office. But the damage was done. Despite Frisina's explanations, to the outside world the entire operation had the whiff of money about it.

The sale of relics has been a sensitive subject for the Catholic Church since the time of the Reformation, when the trade in relics and indulgences flourished. The Vatican eventually condemned the practice, and modern church law states straightforwardly: "It is strictly forbidden to sell sacred relics." Nevertheless, there are gray areas. For example, it's generally considered appropriate to charge money for a reliquary, a container holding the relics, which in some cases can be antique and very valuable. As a result, when buying relics online or at auctions, one often sees the proviso that the purchase price refers to the theca, a round metal locket, and not to the relic it contains—a disclaimer that many view as a ruse. Church officials have also stated that it is acceptable, even laudable, to purchase a relic in order to "rescue" it from mistreatment or desecration. But here, too, there are moral and practical problems. Rescuing a relic might help create a market for additional sales; or, if a relic is being auctioned, "rescuers" might only be bidding up the price against one another.

In the case of John Paul II, the monetary aspect of the relic distribution raised a red flag within the Vatican, where some officials had already been grumbling about the overeagerness of Polish clerics promoting the sainthood cause. "We're handing out his relics, and the paperwork for the beatification isn't even completed," one monsignor remarked in 2007. Even before Pope John Paul died, though, some of his closest advisers had been thinking about relics. As the pontiff lay in bed on the morning of his death, doctors took some of his blood for analysis. The pope's private secretary, Archbishop Stanisław Dziwisz, asked if he might have an additional vial of blood as a "remembrance," and the doctors happily complied, giving him two vials and adding an anticoagulant agent so it would remain liquid. Dziwisz, who was eventually named a cardinal in the pope's former archdiocese, Krakow, would later distribute the blood drop by drop to churches and dioceses clamoring for a John Paul II relic. John Paul's hair from his final haircut had been preserved. It and his blood were considered first-class relics, taken *ex corpore*, or from the actual body, and their importance increased when it became known that no bones or organs had been removed from the pope's corpse up to the time of his canonization. There would be no distribution of his body parts, and that meant the stock of first-class relics would be quite limited.

Long before John Paul's canonization ceremony in 2014, the offer of cloth relics disappeared from the Diocese of Rome's website. In fact, the entire sainthood campaign was soon moved to www.karol-wojtyla .org, far removed from the Vatican's own Internet site, where there had never been any offer of relics. The day he was officially proclaimed a saint, some of the holy cards with bits of his cassock were selling for close to $100 on eBay.

When the Second Council of Nicaea convened in 787, it decreed that every Christian altar should contain a relic. For centuries "a relic in every church" was indeed the norm, but the Catholic Church's expansion beyond relic-rich Europe made that edict harder and harder to maintain. The Second Vatican Council affirmed that placing relics under the altar was still a worthy practice, but said nothing about its being a required one. In the post–Vatican II liturgical renewal, which swept many sacred images from churches and minimized iconography, relics were increasingly forgotten. Traditionalist critics complained that with their disappearance, the church lost tangible reminders of the communion of saints. But for many Catholics, relics now began to be perceived as medieval holdovers. As the church modernized, the miraculous claims associated with some of its most famous relics seemed to invite ridicule. Along with the catalog of officially recognized body parts—the hand of Saint Teresa of Ávila, the finger of Saint Thomas, the head of Saint John the Baptist (claimed by several churches), the toe of Saint Francis Xavier, the foot of Saint Blaise, the heart of Saint Camillus, the tooth of Saint Apollonia, the nail clippings of Saint Clare of Assisi—were relics the church now downplayed or dismissed, most notably the foreskin of the circumcised baby Jesus, known as the holy prepuce. (The contemporary attitude was not too far removed from that of the Renaissance author Giovanni Boccaccio, who satirized the relic trade by having a fictional friar sell one of the angel Gabriel's feathers.)

The last thirty years, however, have seen a resurgence of interest in relics. Vatican officials account for this by citing the saint-making boom under Pope John Paul II, who personally presided over the canonization of nearly five hundred men and women from every continent. At every beatification and canonization ceremony, relics of the new saints were borne in procession and prominently displayed near the papal altar. This new visibility of relics, along with the increasingly multicultural population of saints and blesseds, led to the resurgence of dioceses and parishes requesting relics for local veneration. Schooled in a religion that emphasized doctrine, sacraments, and Scripture, modern Catholics were rediscovering a potent devotional element: the charismatic power of the saints, communicated through their physical presence in the form of relics, a visible link between heaven and earth.

At the Vatican, where more tradition-minded clerics were being appointed to head various offices, the return of relics found the expected support, and more and more often relics began turning up at papal liturgies. To inaugurate the Year for Priests in 2009, Pope Benedict XVI prayed before the heart of Saint John Vianney, which had been brought to Rome especially for the occasion and exposed in a glass and gold reliquary. Benedict also urged Vatican archaeologists to retrieve potential relics of Saint Paul from an ancient tomb sealed beneath an altar in Rome's Basilica of Saint Paul Outside the Walls, and then rejoiced when bits of human bone were found. More recently, to close the Year of Faith in 2013, the bones of Saint Peter were displayed for public veneration for the first time in history—a move that sparked internal debate at the Vatican, because archaeologists are far from convinced that these were actual relics of the first pope.

Pope John Paul II found another use for relics: as peace offerings to separated Christian Churches of the East. Aware that many relics preserved in Rome or Italy had deep meaning to various Orthodox Christian communities, John Paul began returning the bones of their significant saints. In 2000 he presented the patriarch of the Armenian Apostolic Church with a femur of Saint Gregory the Illuminator, who converted Armenia to Christianity in the fourth century. When John Paul traveled to Bulgaria in 2002, he brought with him the right humerus of Saint Dasius, a Christian soldier in the Roman army who was martyred there during the Diocletian persecutions. In 2004 he consigned a portion of the relics of two of the greatest Orthodox saints, Saint Gregory Nazianzen and Saint John Chrysostom, to the Ecumenical Orthodox Patriarch Bartholomew of Constantinople; the Orthodox had long considered the relics to have been stolen from Constantinople during the Crusades, when they were taken to Rome. The Russian Orthodox Church, meanwhile, was the recipient of a unique relic of Saint Nicholas, whose remains had been "rescued" in 1087 from territory conquered by Turks and brought to Bari, Italy. In 2001 Patriarch Alexei received a container filled with a sweet-smelling liquid that oozes inexplicably from the saint's tomb; called the Manna of Saint Nicholas, it is held by many to be a cure-all for diseases.

Father Zdzisław Kijas, a Polish Franciscan in his midfifties, works in one of the back offices of the Congregation for Saints' Causes, at a desk decorated with holy cards, a ceramic angel, and a tin of Mac Iver cherry sweets. His youthful face breaks into a smile when he tells visitors how long he's worked at the Vatican ("three years, nine months, and nineteen days"). Kijas is the congregation's relics expert, and at an annual course for promoters of sainthood causes he lectures on the evolution of relic veneration, from biblical times to the modern age. He agrees that relics are coming back into vogue.

"The idea of having a relic in a church is still important, a sign that we have a link with the communion of saints. For a time after the Second Vatican Council, relics lost their appeal, in part because of ignorance, but I think we've moved out of that phase. Interest in relics is returning, and not only in the church. Just look at show business and the culture of celebrity, where 'relics' used by the stars are sold for incredibly high prices."

It's an argument often made by Vatican officials, who, when asked why the church venerates the miter of Saint Thomas Becket or a tunic worn by Saint Louis, are likely to mention the price fetched at auction by a Jackie Kennedy dress or an Elvis guitar.

"In fact, I would say that even as the church has tried to moderate the veneration of relics, society has taken it to new limits," Monsignor Kijas said. As Kijas explained it, the Vatican keeps a judicious eye on the removal and distribution of relics, whether they come from someone already proclaimed a saint or someone who has been beatified (in church parlance, a "blessed"), which is the stage before official sainthood.

Traditionally most relics have not been removed from the corpse at the time of a holy person's death, but only with the approach of beatification, when a tomb is moved to a more dignified location or during an exhumation to verify the burial place and examine the condition of the body. This latter ceremony, known by the Latin term *recognitio*, is still generally performed today, and once the tomb is unsealed, it's effectively open season on relics—in theory, at least. Each sainthood cause has an appointed postulator, whose job is to guide the cause to completion and to take care of the necessary documentation. It's generally the postulator who, with the approval of the Vatican's saints' congregation, orders the removal of body parts for relics. In past centuries such exhumations were the occasion of abuses, usually well intentioned but excessive by modern standards. To give just one example, when the tomb of Saint Teresa of Ávila was opened a year after her death in the late 1500s, the saint's spiritual director, Father Jerónimo Gracián, cut off her left hand and had it sent to a Carmelite convent—except for her left ring finger, which he removed and wore around his neck for the rest of his life. In subsequent years Saint Teresa's relics were dispersed piece by piece, including her heart, right arm, a foot, her left eye, and a piece of jawbone. Claims to the relics became the focus of a bitter conflict among various Catholic groups, and church officials sometimes cite the episode to illustrate the potential dangers of relic veneration.

That wouldn't happen today, Monsignor Kijas explained: "If the body is intact, you can take some bone. But there is a hygienic element in all this, as well as respect for the body. You can't just cut off parts at will. In some cases, there may be no relics removed."

In 1994 the Vatican quietly promulgated new rules that said small pieces of the bones or flesh of saints would no longer be given out to individuals but "only for public veneration in a church, oratory, or chapel" that made a specific request. One reason is that worshipping a relic in one's own home is no longer considered a healthy spiritual practice: Catholics should be coming to church to venerate the saints, not keeping relics to themselves.

Once the physical material is removed, it's carefully maintained and dispensed to pastors and church communities who follow the application procedure. Typically a local parish will submit a request for the relics of a saint when dedicating a new church in his or her name for placement under the altar. When the Archdiocese of Anchorage wanted a relic for the Saint Andrew Kim Taegon Church, dedicated to a Korean-born priest and martyr of the nineteenth century, they waited for two years before authorities in Rome finally FedExed a piece of bone from the spine of the saint.

The size of relics has been a matter of debate among Vatican experts. When it revised its rules twenty years ago, the Vatican recommended that relics venerated in churches be large enough to be recognized as parts of the human body. That policy seems to have been ignored, in part because most of the relics in circulation today are fragments, and also because the severing of a saint's arm or leg would strike many today as mutilation.

"What we say now is that a relic should be visible. In other words, that it's not powder, that it be visibly recognizable as a relic, something that can be seen or touched. In the past, we've had relics so small that you needed a magnifying glass to view them," Monsignor Kijas explained. Especially in recent years, the trend of drawing blood or cutting hair immediately after death has won favor precisely because it does not require slicing up a body.

But obtaining first-class relics has become more and more difficult, as their continued popularity has created a supply-and-demand problem for the Catholic Church, especially with regard to the remains of ancient saints. In Rome caches of bones are kept under lock and key in a number of churches, but their distribution has been limited in recent years.

In a convent attached to the medieval church of Santa Lucia in Selci, on the edge of Rome's old Suburra neighborhood, Augustinian nuns still carve up the bones of ancient saints for distribution by the Diocese of Rome. The remains of many saints ended up in Rome, and long ago these cloistered nuns were put in charge of organizing them and "packaging" them for the faithful. At one time a steady stream of pilgrims would make their way to the massive brick convent and ring a bell next to a metal grate. The grate would slide open, the shadowy visage of a nun would appear, and the negotiations would commence. Sometimes the request would be for a relic of an early Christian martyr, while others would ask for something more obscure—say, a bone fragment from the third-century bishop Saint Trophimus of Arles. The nuns would search their inventory of the remains of hundreds of saints, kept in carefully labeled boxes, and do their best to satisfy the supplicant. The price tag could range anywhere from the equivalent of a few dollars to more than a hundred. Payment was not for the relic, of course, but for the exquisitely wrought theca in which the relic was enclosed, often decorated with foil and gold wire.

Santa Lucia in Selci was once a well-known stop on the devotional underground route, but nowadays few relic seekers visit this forgotten convent. The Vatican's 1994 restrictions had a big impact. For a while the nuns at Via in Selci continued to distribute relics to individuals despite the Vatican edict, but eventually they fell into line with the new policy. All requests are now handled through Rome diocesan offices, by means of an official procedure that requires the signature of a bishop; the days of dispensing relics at the convent door are long gone.

On a recent rainy evening, Suor Elena, who manages the relic bank, walked slowly up the steep hill in front of the convent, leaning on a cane and guided by a younger Filipina sister. (As in many Rome convents, most of these cloistered Augustinian nuns today are from the Philippines.) Suor Elena, who had spent sixty-six years at this convent, spoke wistfully of the golden era of relics. "We still have them, but we're running low. There are only small fragments of the ancient saints, and we're not getting many new ones," she said. To make the most of their resources, the nuns have been equipped with a microtome, a high-tech instrument used to slice paper-thin segments of bone. Even so the raw materials must be used sparingly.

Along with the Augustinian nuns in Rome, other churches and monasteries hold relics of specific saints and parcel them out. A little-known storeroom at the back of Saint Peter's Basilica holds the bones of many early Christian martyrs, each boxful cataloged and authenticated with an official seal. Not every saint is available, of course, but the active roster of relics includes the remains of some surprisingly famous figures. The bones of Saint Francis of Assisi, buried nearly eight centuries ago, are distributed by Franciscan friars at the Church of the Twelve Holy Apostles in downtown Rome; they use material collected when the saint's tomb in Assisi was exhumed in 1978. The reopening of Saint Francis's burial place was undertaken to repair the grave site, and had to be approved by Pope Paul VI. Vatican officials are adamant that remains must not be exhumed merely in order to collect more relics—though when the opportunity presents itself, postulators are usually there to replenish supplies.

Increasingly officials are not taking bones from the tombs of those being canonized or beatified, said Monsignor Enrico Viganò, a Vatican liturgist. As a result, those asking for relics are more likely to receive an article of clothing or a prayer book used by the saint. In some cases the relic falls into a gray area. In 1999 the Saint John Cantius Parish in Chicago received a relic of Saint Padre Pio of Pietrelcina, a widely venerated Italian Capuchin priest who died in 1968, which consisted of a square of linen stained with blood from a laceration in the saint's side, a wound known as the transverberation of the heart—in mystical tradition, the piercing of a soul inflamed with the love of God. The Chicago parish proudly proclaims it a first-class relic.

The role of relics in religious practice is a sensitive topic among Vatican experts. "Relics still have a place in the church, but we need a better understanding of their spiritual value," explained Monsignor Kijas. "It all depends on a person's faith. If someone doesn't approach this with faith, it's just a piece of cloth or bone. There's no magic power in a relic. In a way, it does transmit the force of a saint's holiness, so it can stimulate the holiness of the person venerating it. But it doesn't work like a talisman, and people need to know this." For years, in fact, the Vatican has been tempering relic enthusiasm with caveats like "We don't worship relics, we venerate them," and "Relics don't perform miracles, God performs them through the intercession of saints."

Part of the controversy regarding relics arose because of the abuses in the relic trade that occurred in the Middle Ages. In the 1200s Saint Thomas Aquinas defended the veneration of relics, arguing that it reminded the faithful that saints are "members of Christ and friends of God." Because saints are our intercessors with God, Aquinas said, it's natural that Christians should want to draw close to them: "We ought to honor any relics of theirs in a fitting manner: principally their bodies, which were temples, and organs of the Holy Spirit dwelling and operating in them, and are destined to be likened to the body of Christ by the glory of the Resurrection. Hence God Himself fittingly honors such relics by working miracles at their presence." One wonders what Thomas Aquinas would think, however, were he to walk today into the former Dominican monastery of Sant'Eustorgio in Milan, where the saint's right thumb is displayed in a church museum, about four hundred miles from the rest of his remains in southern France.

Theologians will explain that relics also reflect Christianity's "incarnational" nature, as a religion centered around the belief that Jesus Christ, as man and God, definitively bridged the gap between human and divine. The Word was made flesh, and flesh and the material world were made "holy." In a particular way, veneration of the relics of saints recognizes that, first, Christ's role as redeemer involves the assistance of other mediators and, second, that God continues to work through them—even after they have died, through the agency of their bones, garments, and other objects related by touch. Among the New Testament accounts of Jesus's miracles is his healing of a woman who had suffered gynecological bleeding for twelve years. In Saint Mark's Gospel, she approached Jesus convinced that if she could just "touch his cloak" she would be healed, and when she did so, "Immediately her flow of blood dried up. She felt in her body that she was healed of her affliction." Jesus notes that it was faith that healed the woman, but his clothing became the conduit for the supernatural power that was kindled by her faith.

This tradition of miraculous healings or other transformations was carried on by the Apostles. In the Acts of the Apostles, we are told that miracles were accomplished through Saint Paul, so that "when face cloths or aprons that touched his skin were applied to the sick, their diseases left them and the evil spirits came out of them." Even the Old Testament contains some references to the supernatural power of clothing, like Elijah's mantle, and of relics. The Book of Kings describes how a group of Israelites, under attack by raiders, threw the corpse of a fallen comrade into the tomb of the prophet Elisha. When the dead soldier came into contact with Elisha's bones, he "came back to life and got to his feet."

The lesson of these accounts is that God reaches people not only through prayer or spiritual effort but also through the material world, which can be charged with sanctity. The problem, according to Vatican experts, is that such theological aspects of the power of relics are often poorly understood by Catholics, especially the most enthusiastic devotees of relic veneration. "For many people, it's almost like magic. They don't see the larger design of salvation at work, they just want to touch the relic," one monsignor observed. Wherever relics are routinely displayed these days, the faithful are usually reminded that the Mass and the sacraments are more powerful spiritual tools than relics. The packed churches in Naples on the occasions of the miraculous "liquefaction" of Saint Januarius's blood, for example, have prompted more than one priest to suggest that attendees might come more frequently to Sunday Mass. But such encouragement generally has little effect. The drawing power of a relic cannot be underestimated, even in the modern age.

The Vatican has taken steps to keep relics out of the liturgical spotlight—for example, by prohibiting their public veneration on an altar and keeping relic devotions separate from the Mass. But in recent years it has approved a number of relic "tours" that have brought saints' body parts and sacred objects to countries around the world. In late 2013 long lines queued outside Westminster Cathedral in London to venerate two relics of Saint Anthony of Padua, a floating rib bone and a piece of cheek skin. This tour commemorated the 750th anniversary of the discovery of the saint's incorrupt tongue—held by some to be a supernatural sign of his gift for preaching.

When the bones of the French Carmelite nun Saint Thérèse of Lisieux were sent around France in 1997, the exposition drew surprisingly large crowds, including many non-Catholics. More requests followed, and since then the tour has continued to include more than forty countries, including a stop in South Africa during the 2010 World Cup. Saint Thérèse's relics have traveled three times to the Philippines, where they have their own Facebook page, and one of her relics even journeyed into outer space aboard the *Discovery* space shuttle.

On Easter Sunday 2001 the relics of Saint Thérèse—a small casket containing a thighbone and foot bone—arrived in Ireland at the start of an eleven-week pilgrimage. Among those who turned out for the event was Don Mullan, a bestselling Irish author and media producer. Mullan had mixed feelings about the whole affair. Advance publicity for the relic tour had promised the arrival of an anonymous "she" who would be bigger than U2 and draw larger crowds than Madonna. When the "she" turned out to be the bones of a nineteenth-century saint, Mullan and others wondered if the organizers had lost their minds. They were predicting a million people might come to see the reliquary as it made its way across the country.

As it turned out, the relics drew nearly three million people. And Mullan, who from childhood had a deep interest in Saint Thérèse, was so impressed that he decided to produce a book about those who came to pray before her earthly remains. The tour attracted devotees, of course, but also doubters and cynics, many of whom nevertheless found themselves strangely and profoundly moved. More than one hundred of them submitted their personal accounts and reflections. The resulting book, *A Gift of Roses*, disoriented Mullan's previous readers. "I was gaining a reputation as a hard-nosed and impactful investigative journalist. Then I do a respectful book about a box of bones, and some saw me as losing my marbles," he said.

What struck Mullan was not only the size of the crowds that came to see the relics but also the atmosphere of prayerful reverence. There was no triumphalism about this relic tour, he explained, no "bishop bandwagons" on hand to proclaim victory over secularism—only thousands of people, whether the elderly, middle-aged couples, teenagers, or young children, lining up to pay their quiet respect. They would wait for hours, often in pouring rain or cold wind, in order to stand in front of Thérèse's reliquary for a few seconds. For many of them, Saint Thérèse was a figure planted long ago in their spiritual memory by their mothers.

Born in 1873 in northern France, Thérèse Martin had a difficult childhood. An excellent student, she was bullied in school and suffered from illnesses and emotional frustration. At the age of thirteen she had what she described as a conversion, a sudden sense that Jesus had come into her heart and filled her with purpose. She entered the local Carmelite convent a few years later, and became known for her many acts of kindness. She knew her human limitations, and from this awareness created a spiritual path—the "little way" of reflecting God's goodness in ordinary and everyday ways. Spiritual heroism was not required for salvation, she said. Small acts of charity were enough.

Thérèse died of tuberculosis at the age of twenty-four. She never performed great works, and her only published writing was a journal. But her reputation for holiness spread far and wide, precisely because of her simple and practical approach to spiritual life. Pope Pius X called her the greatest saint of modern times, and Pope John Paul II declared her a doctor of the church, a highly unusual recognition for someone with no academic credentials.

Most Catholics know Saint Thérèse as "the Little Flower," and associate her presence with roses. As she lay sick toward the end of her life, Thérèse could see the roses blooming in the convent garden. One day, she promised that she would continue to help people after she died. As she put it, "I will send a shower of roses from heaven." Shortly after her death, devotees began to find roses appearing in unexpected places. Sometimes a stray rose would be growing in the ground, sometimes a cut rose would be discovered lying on a doorstep. Sometimes rose petals would fall in the breeze. Sometimes people would simply smell the fragrance of roses.

Even Pope Francis, who has cautioned against searching for supernatural signs, has said he sometimes prays to Saint Thérèse and "almost always" receives a rose in response. The Argentine pope confided to a friend that six months after his election in 2013 he had prayed to the saint about a particular worry. The next day, he was strolling in the Vatican Gardens when, out of the blue, a gardener walked up and handed him a freshly picked white rose.

In Ireland many people brought their own roses and touched them to Saint Thérèse's casket, distributing the petals afterward to friends and relatives. In the testimonials collected by Don Mullan, several mentioned the roses as a sign of answered prayers. Among them were people who came for physical or emotional healing. But most were drawn by a vague wish to connect with someone in heaven.

Catherine Gerety went to see the relics in suburban Dublin after completing a round of weekend duty at a nursing home. Approaching the church, she felt a mixture of joy and grief. Her mother had died recently, and events like this brought back memories of her mother's suffering and funeral. But as she drew near Saint Thérèse's relics, she felt a warm peace. It was as if she were meeting the saint for the first time, Catherine said, and it filled her heart with compassion. It moved her to read more about the Little Flower:

"She believed in small things, and I do small things in my life as I can't do big things—like home help and helping the elderly in a nursing home. The message I get from her is to be happy and cheerful and contented in life, as life is short. She teaches me to love myself before I can love others."

The day after visiting the relics, Catherine went back to her job in the nursing home. As soon as she arrived, the nurse in charge exclaimed, "Oh, Catherine, what a lovely smell!" Catherine asked the nurse what it was she was smelling. "Roses," the nurse said.

While these relic excursions have been immensely popular, questions do arise about the authenticity of some of them. The supposed shinbone of

Mary Magdalene, discovered in a French cave in 1295 and today encased in a glass reliquary, visited thirty-six midwestern churches in thirty-one days in 2013, its third whirlwind tour of the United States in recent years. Claims for the genuineness of a relic from a contemporary of Jesus struck some as far-fetched, and skeptics scorned the exhibit, suggesting that the Catholic Church had taken a page from the writer Dan Brown (author of *The Da Vinci Code*, among other novels). Yet the display also resonated in unexpected places. In an article published by the *Daily Beast*, a former call girl described how seeing the relic confirmed her belief that Mary Magdalene, who is considered the patron saint of reformed prostitutes, could be a meaningful model for "today's multitasking, sexually experienced woman."

Doubts about the authenticity of relics have long vexed Catholic Church officials, and it's a topic that Vatican experts today would rather not discuss. When the relic trade was flourishing in the Middle Ages, body parts of saints came on the market in such numbers that ecclesial authorities had no doubt there were many fakes in circulation. Chaucer's Pardoner, who carried a glassful of "pigges bones" and passed them off as holy remnants, was a caricature of the fraudulent relic trader, but one that appeared to be drawn from real-life figures of the fourteenth century. Some of these relics were publicly unmasked as bogus, much to the embarrassment of Catholic communities. The supposed "brain of Saint Peter," which had been venerated for centuries in the cathedral of Geneva, was investigated in the 1500s and found to be a pumice stone. The arm of Saint Anthony, housed in the same church and kissed by the faithful on festive occasions, turned out to be the part of a stag. In his sharply worded tract "An Inventory of Relics," the Protestant Reformation leader John Calvin mocked the relics of Mary's breast milk, writing that "had the breasts of the most Holy Virgin yielded a more copious supply than is given by a cow, or had she continued to nurse during her whole lifetime, she scarcely could have furnished the quantity which is exhibited." Likewise the proliferation of "True Cross" fragments prompted Calvin to assert that if all the pieces of the cross were assembled, they would fill a cargo ship (a claim strongly rebutted by Catholic clerics of the time). Today relics of the cross are still proudly displayed in churches around the world, from Texas to the Philippines.

Saint Peter's Basilica in Rome also has pieces of the True Cross, along with two other relics of the Passion: the Lance of Longinus, used to pierce the side of the crucified Christ, and the Veil of Veronica, said to bear the image of Christ's face. All three were encased in balconies designed by Gian Lorenzo Bernini in the 1600s for their display and veneration, yet today they are barely mentioned in the basilica guidebooks. The relics are displayed once a year in a ceremony that is virtually unpublicized. Vatican officials don't like to discuss the basilica's "major relics." When an Italian scholar asked a basilica official in 2000 about the authenticity of Veronica's veil, she was told simply that no image could presently be discerned on the piece of cloth.

In past centuries the discovery of the ancient relics of a saint or a prophet was a major event, because it created a new link in the historical and spiritual chain connecting Christians to their earliest times, as well as opening a new trove of holy remnants for dispersal and veneration. In modern times announcements of similar discoveries by "relic archaeologists" have routinely made headlines, but the Vatican's experts have been cautious or skeptical of such claims. The saga of the James Ossuary is instructive. In 2002 an Israeli antiquities collector, Oded Golan, displayed a first-century ossuary (a limestone box used to contain bones for burial) that bore an inscription in Aramaic: "James, son of Joseph, brother of Jesus." That this box might have held the remains of a brother of Jesus Christ soon caught the world's attention—even though the concept of Jesus even having a brother was a novel one for most Christians—and news reports hailed it as one of the most important archaeological discoveries ever made. Only a year later, though, Israeli authorities arrested Golan for suspected forgery and found what they described as a workshop for creating fake relics in his home. Nine years after his arrest, however, Golan was acquitted of the charge, rekindling fresh media interest in the ossuary and leaving a question mark over its authenticity.

An archaeological find in Bulgaria in 2010 gave rise to similar headlines. This time the object in question was a stone box containing six human bones, alongside a Greek inscription that referred to Saint John the Baptist. Radiocarbon testing by Oxford University dated the bones to the first century, and soon researchers were hypothesizing that the Baptist's bones had migrated to Bulgaria from the Jordanian fortress of Machaerus, where he was famously beheaded by Herod Antipas at the request of his stepdaughter, Salome. Despite the interest generated by this discovery, the Vatican was wary, perhaps all too mindful that relics of Saint John the Baptist have been the subject of multiple conflicting claims through the centuries. Professor Fabrizio Bisconti, a member of the Pontifical Commission of Sacred Archaeology, announced that the Vatican would await a more thorough study of the findings, adding that there were "thousands" of purported relics of John the Baptist in existence. Among them, of course, are relics of the severed head of the Baptist, which are today claimed by two churches, a museum, and a mosque. The cathedral in Amiens, France, has his head on a gold plate. The Church of Saint Sylvester in Capite in Rome displays the saint's skull on a red velvet cushion. Munich's Residenz Museum exhibits what it says is the saint's cranium inside a jewel-encrusted fabric reliquary. And when Pope John Paul II visited the Umayyad Mosque in Syria in 2001, he prayed before a shrine that also supposedly holds the head of the saint, who is honored as a prophet by Muslims.

Does the authenticity of relics ultimately matter? The question was raised by an English bishop, and judging by the reaction, the answer for many Catholics was a resounding yes. Then-Archbishop Vincent Nichols of Westminster was commenting in 2011 on the British Museum's "Treasures of Heaven" exhibit, which featured pieces of the crown of thorns, splinters from the True Cross, and, yes, breast milk from the Virgin Mary. The archbishop encouraged Catholics to attend the exhibit, saying relics were both an expression of faith and culture, "in the way that people cling to a souvenir from a person they've loved or a place that they've been to." He added that "if that connection is made through an object which maybe forensically won't stand up to the test, that's of secondary importance to the spiritual and emotive power that the object can contain." The Catholic blogosphere quickly lit up with objections. It was disgraceful, one commentator said, for the archbishop to suggest that fake relics can be just as spiritually effective as genuine ones: "Of course it matters. The REASON why a piece of cloth has been revered for centuries is because it was believed to be, say, from the clothes of a saint, or the shroud that covered our Lord's body. If the piece of wood is not from the cross, but came from someone's desire to make some money selling it as a piece of the cross, why should we continue to revere it after we know the truth?"

The fact remains, however, that the Vatican doesn't really have a formal verification procedure for ancient relics, and has been perfectly willing to allow local Catholic communities to venerate traditional relics, even when their authenticity is in doubt. In 2012 nearly half a million pilgrims came to the cathedral of Trier, Germany, when it displayed its prize relic: the seamless garment of Christ, for which soldiers cast lots at the foot of the cross. Venerated at Trier for at least eight hundred years, the holy tunic is a reddish-brown patchwork of wool and silk, displayed in a hermetically sealed glass shrine. It didn't particularly bother anyone that another version of the same holy garment is routinely exhibited at a church in Argenteuil near Paris.

Church authorities are somewhat more concerned with relics—real and fake—being trafficked online. While sites like eBay have rules against the sale of body parts (with the exception of hair), the bones of saints—often categorized under "reliquary"—routinely slip through the eBay filters and are sold for impressive prices. In late 2013, for example, two bone fragments of Saint Martha, a contemporary of Jesus, were being offered on eBay at a "buy it now" price of $1,090, while a bone chip from the early Christian martyr Saint Theodore was going for $890. Both came with authentication letters signed by Cardinal Clemente Micara, who was, in fact, vicar-general of Rome in the 1950s and would have been in charge of distributing relics. Fraudulent documents also abound, however, often bearing the signature of an obscure bishop from the past. Sometimes the fakes are easily identified because of basic errors in Latin. Sloppy counterfeiters have also been tripped up by their chronologies, forging relic "authentication" letters from bishops who died long before an individual was declared a saint. Websites now offer assistance to those trying to ascertain that a relic is genuine before bidding on it. Still, it's not always easy to tell. One online auction sold a hair of the Virgin Mary for more than $1,800, accompanied by a letter of authentication signed by a Belgian prelate. The letter itself was genuine—for centuries, relics of Mary's hair circulated in Europe, sometimes with the blessings of popes, as part of a popular "cult of the holy hair." Even today a lock of Mary's hair is said to be preserved, though no longer displayed, in Rome's Basilica of Saint John Lateran.

At the Vatican, where officials were initially hesitant to send relics on global tours, these traveling exhibitions are now viewed as teaching opportunities. They are also a way to underscore its view that a saint's relics belong to the whole church, and should not be considered the sole possession of a particular parish, town, or religious order, a notion that marks a major shift in the church's devotional history.

For the first few centuries of Christianity, cults of relics were tied to a specific sense of place, usually where saints and martyrs were buried, and quite often in the Holy Land. In early times Christians went on pilgrimage, sometimes traveling long distances to reach objects of worship, which might have been a tomb, a piece of bone, or a sliver of the True Cross. As the historian Peter Brown has argued, this "possession of the holy" underwent a transformation in the Middle Ages, when relics were separated, made more portable, and transferred to an entirely new constellation of sites, mainly in the western Mediterranean. The arrival of relics in a town or city was a major event that inaugurated a relationship between a specific community of believers and a saint who acted as its protector and as an intercessor with God. Relics were prayed over and kissed, accompanied armies into battle, were the preferred witnesses of oaths and vows, and were beseeched as instruments of miraculous healings. One group of French monks allegedly dumped the relics of a saint into a vat of wine and then drank it in an effort to ward off disease.

Sensitive to the beliefs and traditions of local communities, Rome has little desire to step in and actually halt the veneration of sacred objects, no matter how far-fetched they may appear to the rational observer. The Vatican treads lightly, avoiding official pronouncements and stating simply that Catholics are free to venerate relics or not. As one Vatican official remarked, "This is one area where we don't tell people what they can and can't believe."

The supernatural power attributed to relics has ranged from personal healings to wholesale deliverance from calamity. Particularly in the Middle Ages, a time when war, disease, or natural disaster could bring sudden widespread ruin, towns and cities would venerate the relics of their saintly protectors and credit them when afflictions abated. Nowhere has this type of civic devotion been preserved more famously than in Naples, where the liquefaction of the blood of the city's patron, Saint Januarius, is interpreted as a sign of good fortune, and its failure to do so as a disturbing omen.

Januarius was a young bishop of Benevento, northeast of Naples, when he was arrested during the Diocletian persecutions in the early fourth century. According to Catholic tradition, the Roman authorities found that his execution—like that of many early martyrs—was more easily ordered than accomplished. When Januarius was thrown into a furnace, the flames refused to touch him; when he was dropped into an amphitheater full of wild boars, the beasts suddenly lost their appetite. He was eventually beheaded, but not before curing his own prosecutor from blindness and converting thousands of witnesses in Naples. The Christian community quickly gathered up his relics, and a woman named Eusebia was careful to collect some of the martyr's blood as well. By the fifth century the remains were held in the catacombs beneath the Capodimonte hill in Naples, where they were the object of popular veneration. In the Middle Ages, the saint's body was moved to various cities and towns, depending on which army had the upper hand in the region. But Christians in Naples held on to two important relics: his head and an ampule of his blood. In the fourteenth century Neapolitans began to exhibit these relics during special rituals. In August 1389, in the midst of a period of famine, a priest carrying the ampule in procession noticed that the dried blood it contained had begun to liquefy and bubble, "as if it were flowing from the saint's body," in the words of local chroniclers. A miracle was proclaimed, and soon the blood was liquefying on a regular basis on the saint's feast day, September 19. In 1497 the rest of Januarius's relics were located and brought to Naples, and another liquefaction began occurring annually to mark that event, on the Saturday before the first Sunday in May. Then, in December 1631, Mount Vesuvius suddenly erupted with fury, killing thousands in the countryside and threatening Naples with a destructive mix of lava, ash, and poisonous gases. The people of the city turned to Saint Januarius, as they had done during similar eruptions in the fifth and seventh centuries, carrying his relics through streets dimmed by volcanic dust, as women shrieked in invocation and Vesuvius roared and cracked in the background. Their prayers were answered: within twenty-four hours the volcano calmed, and the ash cloud disappeared. Naples once again proclaimed itself saved by its patron, and a third day of liquefaction of the saint's blood, December 16, was now added to the calendar of religious observances.

The miracle doesn't always occur, however, and on those occasions the city's populace fears the worst. Selective memory may be at work, but Neapolitans point to outbreaks of plague in 1527 and 1656, the beginning of World War II in 1939, and a deadly earthquake in 1980—all events, they say, that followed the failure of Saint Januarius's blood to liquefy, despite the insistent prayers of the faithful. A full list of non-liquefaction disasters would also include twenty-two epidemics, eleven political conflicts, three religious persecutions, three droughts, seven torrential rains, nineteen earthquakes, one Turkish invasion, and the deaths of thirteen archbishops of Naples.

Strangely, when the liquefaction fails to occur, the people of Naples tend to blame the saint, not themselves. On the days when the miracle is expected, Januarius is initially venerated, but if necessary hectored and insulted, always in Neapolitan dialect and usually by the *zie di San Gennaro*, a group of elderly women known as the saint's "aunts." If an hour or two of prayers doesn't bring liquefaction of the blood, the *zie* begin to punctuate their prayers with loud imprecations: "Don't be an idiot, Saint Januarius!" "Come on, let's go! Do the miracle!" Staring at the gilded silver bust of Januarius that sits next to the altar, portraying the saint in a red cape and pointed red miter, they treat him like a stubborn child: "Hey, yellow face, what's the matter, are you angry? How long are you going to keep us here?" "You don't want to protect us, fine, we'll get Saint Anthony!"

The ceremony in the Naples cathedral brings together a hierarchy of ecclesial and political leaders, including the mayor, along with members of confraternities and guilds, whose hooded cloaks come straight out of the Middle Ages. As the archbishop of Naples turns the ampule to one side and another, the prayers and lamentations multiply. It usually takes less than an hour for the dried blood to turn liquid and begin to bubble in the glass container. When that transpires, a man in a tuxedo raises a white handkerchief and waves it furiously as the archbishop announces, "The miracle has occurred!" and the crowd goes wild with gratitude and relief. But if it doesn't take place, if the ampule has to be returned to its vault, the congregation is sent home disappointed, and Saint Januarius is viewed as a fickle intercessor and a fair-weather friend of the city. On such occasions the patron saint is even subject to the muttered imprecation "traitor."

On one level, the rite appears to be an uncommon modern convergence of religious and civic fervor, a community event that transcends the petty worries and divisions of daily life. But the relationship between Neapolitans and their patron saint can be surprisingly personal.

On a Saturday in May 2014, a few hours before the Saint Januarius procession was to wind through the narrow streets of old Naples, fifty-four-year-old Furgiero Onofri stood in a tobacco shop and shook his head disdainfully. He wasn't especially enthused about the day's pageantry, he said, because it was all show and very little faith. But when asked if he believed in the powers of Saint Januarius, Onofri brightened up. "I believe well enough, because he gave me a miracle." Several years earlier, he recounted, he collapsed in the street near the cathedral. As he was taken to a hospital for what turned out to be a serious heart attack, he saw a figure appear above him. "He was wearing a tunic, and he held a bishop's staff that moved back and forth. It was Januarius, and I knew I was going to be saved." Ever since then, Onofri said, he goes to the cathedral regularly—not to attend Mass, but to pray to Januarius in a side chapel, in front of the silver bust of the saint. "Well, I suppose it's prayer," he said. "We look at each other and communicate telepathically, even if he's only a statue."

Many older Neapolitans tell similar stories. They are devoted to Saint Januarius not because he enlightens people in the faith, or shows the way to Christian hope, or helps people build a more just society— all themes of the archbishop's homilies on such occasions—but because he grants them favors and miracles. In a city where the promises of politicians and the assurances of the church carry little weight, Saint Januarius delivers.

Younger people in Naples are not quite as passionate about their patron saint. There's been a decided drop in participation in the ceremonies by those in their twenties and thirties, who tend to view it all as a quaint tradition, worth preserving but not worthy of true belief. One young female police agent, working in Via del Duomo on the day of the saint's procession, put it this way: "It's a popular omen. Saint Januarius is our good luck charm."

That's precisely the attitude the Vatican wants to avoid when it comes to the delicate topic of relics. Asking Vatican authorities about the blood of Saint Januarius is often met with a rolling of the eyes, followed by the explanation that the supposed miracle is strictly a Naples phenomenon. The presumption is that if you're from Naples, you can believe what you want about your patron saint and his relics' extraordinary powers. But in Rome, the cult of Saint Januarius is viewed by many church officials as little more than folklore.

Over the centuries, the Vatican has at times discouraged the public veneration of the ampule of blood, and insisted that the liquefaction be termed a "prodigy" and not a "miracle." After the Second Vatican Council, there was a proposal to drop Saint Januarius from the General Roman Calendar, along with other traditional saints for whom little historical evidence could be found. The church in Naples objected loudly, complaining that the Vatican wanted to demote their patron to the status of *Serie B* (the second division in Italian professional soccer). Graffiti on the walls of the city offered solace to the saint and scorn toward the liturgical masters in Rome: *San Gennà, futtetenne!* (in Neapolitan dialect, "Saint Januarius, don't give a damn about it!"). In the end Rome again relented, and Saint Januarius kept his September 19 feast day on the universal calendar of saints. Modern popes have generally avoided saying anything about the liquefaction "prodigy" of Saint Januarius, even during papal visits to Naples—although Pope Benedict kissed the reliquary containing the vial of blood when he went there in 2007, an act that drew more media attention in the city than his denunciation of local Camorra mafia bosses.

The contrast between Neapolitan fervor and Vatican reticence was on display when Pope Francis came to Naples in 2015. Although the papal visit did not coincide with any of the three liquefaction feast days, local Catholics were buzzing with anticipation over the possibility of an unscheduled miracle, which would be seen as an extraordinary sign of favor toward the popular pope from their patron saint. And sure enough, after the pope kissed the ampule containing Saint Januarius's blood, Naples Cardinal Crescenzio Sepe inspected it, then held it up in the packed cathedral and proclaimed triumphantly: "As a sign that Saint Januarius loves the pope, who is a Neapolitan like us, the blood is already liquefied halfway!" Applause and cries of "*Miracolo!*" arose from the congregation. It was, in fact, the first recorded occurrence of the saint's blood dissolving in the presence of a pope outside the normal feast days. But Francis did not join in the jubilation. Instead, he smiled and made a joke. "The bishop said the blood was half liquefied. That means the saint loves us halfway. We all need to convert a little more, so he'll love us more," he said. A few minutes later the blood had turned completely to liquid, but the pope never mentioned it again.

In general, the Vatican has learned not to mess with Saint Januarius.

The thinking, explained by one official in Rome, is that when it comes to local devotional practices—especially those with strong cultural and social roots—the wiser course is to live and let live. The problem today, he added, is that nothing is really "local," as the Internet has brought even the most obscure saints and relics to an audience of millions. Saint Januarius, for example, has Facebook pages in several languages dedicated to his history and feast day. But along with online enthusiasm have come online doubts and objections, some of which echo long-standing skepticism in Rome.

"If the Catholic Church obligated me to believe this, I'd go off with the Dalai Lama." Jesuit Father Giandomenico Mucci, a former professor of spirituality and a writer for the prestigious Catholic journal *La Civiltà Cattolica* (Catholic civilization), laughed quietly as he spoke of the cult of Saint Januarius in Naples, a city where he once taught. "The Vatican has never pressed for an investigation of this 'miracle' because there'd be a revolution in Naples. In Naples they believe more in the blood of San Gennaro than in the Holy Trinity."

Father Mucci has witnessed the liquefaction firsthand, and has no doubt that it is human blood and that it does become fluid on these occasions. But in Naples, he noted, there are several other saints whose blood traditionally turns liquid on their feast days. "Four different bloods! Saint Januarius, Saint Patricia, Saint Alphonsus de' Liguori, and Saint Aloysius Gonzaga. And it always happens on fixed dates, which should count against the authenticity of a miracle, because divine intervention is always unpredictable and doesn't follow a regular schedule," he explained. In fact, in past centuries the blood of more than a dozen saints was said to have liquefied on their feast days in various churches of the city, earning Naples the moniker "city of blood." There have long been suspicions that a secret recipe must have circulated in medieval Naples that made it possible for so many blood relics to exhibit this amazing quality. Modern science has offered some explanations. Father Mucci pointed to experiments that have managed to reproduce the liquefaction phenomenon, simply by taking human blood and adding iron-rich compounds found at the foot of Mount Vesuvius. In an article published in 1991 by the scientific review *Nature*, three researchers explained that these ferrous additives turned the blood into a "thixotropic" gel, one that changes to liquid when vibrated or shaken and that returns to a solid state when left standing still. They theorized that the Naples ceremony, in which the archbishop repeatedly inverts the holy capsule to check for liquefaction, is enough to stimulate the transformation.

Church authorities in Naples were unimpressed with this hypothesis, pointing out that if liquefaction was caused by chemical additives, the blood would always liquefy—which it doesn't. The researchers said the only way to prove or disprove their theory was to open the capsule and test the blood. That's something no archbishop of Naples has ever considered, as he knows he'd have a popular insurrection on his hands.

In 2001 a small group of Vatican officials and technicians gathered in the crypt of Saint Peter's Basilica on an unpublicized mission. Their task was a delicate one, and the crypt had been closed to the public that day. They were exhuming Pope John XXIII's body in a "recognition" ceremony, in anticipation of its transfer from the grotto to the main level of Saint Peter's. Cardinal Angelo Sodano, the Vatican secretary of state, and Cardinal Virgilio Noè, head of the office in charge of the basilica, watched as workmen raised the marble lid from the tomb, revealing an oak casket, which was lifted out and placed on the floor of the burial chapel. Modern papal tombs feature three caskets of cypress, lead, and oak, which are nestled inside one another Chinese box–style. As the top of the innermost casket was opened and a protective veil removed, a medical expert joined the cardinals as they peered down and looked into the face of the pope. What they saw impressed them: Pope John's *simpatico* visage was recognizable and appeared intact, with the eyes closed and the mouth slightly opened. This was a face that not even death could erase. The rest of the body was examined, and it, too, was found to have remained remarkably well preserved some thirty-eight years after its burial. His fleshy hands still held a cross. *He looks as if he died yesterday* was the thought that ran through Cardinal Noè's mind.

After one official recorded the group's findings in a detailed report, the corpse was sprayed with an antibacterial agent, and the coffin was hermetically resealed.

It took two months for the news to leak out, and when it did, it made headlines in Italy and the rest of the world. The body of Blessed Pope John XXIII, the much-beloved "good pope" who had been beatified the previous year, was said to have been found incorrupt. Before long people were saying it was a miracle. "When the body of a blessed or a saint is discovered to be uncorrupted, this is considered a sign, and is interpreted as an anticipation of the resurrection. So it is also a confirmation of sanctity," the popular Italian Catholic journalist Vittorio Messori wrote.

But talk of a miracle alarmed Vatican officials, who quickly tried to downplay any supernatural element. Cardinal Noè told reporters not to jump to conclusions, noting that Pope John's body, although never fully embalmed, had been maintained in a sealed environment, and that thirty-eight years was a relatively short time. He reminded them that the body and burial clothing of Pope Boniface VIII were found completely intact in 1605, more than three centuries after his death, but when the body was reexhumed in 1835 it had turned to mere bones.

The fascination with "incorruptibles" may strike many people as macabre, but for centuries it was an important element in the Vatican's saint-making process. In his five-volume work on beatifications and canonizations, the eighteenth-century Cardinal Prospero Lambertini, later Pope Benedict XIV, included two chapters on "the non-corruption of cadavers," explaining the circumstances under which lack of decomposition of a body might be considered a divine sign of a person's holiness. Lambertini advised church officials to proceed with great caution when pronouncing on such claims. Any body that had been embalmed or artificially preserved should be automatically excluded. To be judged incorrupt, he said, the corpse in question should retain a lifelike color and suppleness; a mummified or desiccated cadaver was not a sign of a miracle, he explained, because desiccation is simply another form of corruption. Associated with incorruptibility is the phenomenon of a "sweet odor" emanating from an exhumed corpse, another classic sign of holiness. Here, too, Lambertini warned that the church's experts must make certain that such an odor had not been produced by either preservative fluids or ointments. Lambertini's work, which was recently republished by the Vatican, remains the standard reference tool for experts in Rome. Although church officials today do hesitate to use the term "miracle," many still consider an incorrupt corpse a legitimate sign of holiness, a harbinger of the universal resurrection of the body at the time of the Last Judgment.

Even as Cardinal Noè sought to deflect journalists' questions about a supernatural explanation for John XXIII's well-preserved body, he couldn't help but express his own conviction that it was "a providential coincidence, a sign of divine favor and of holiness." Among those listening was one Vatican expert who had a much more prosaic view of bodies and bones, having exhumed more than his own share of saints in the service of the Holy See.

"People come and ask me what it was like when John XXIII's casket was opened. They tell me: 'You witnessed a miracle!' I tell them, no, no, no. All you need to do is go to a cemetery sometime and talk to the people who work there and move bodies around. Do you know how many bodies are well preserved? A lot of them! It's no miracle."

Nazzareno Gabrielli was warming to a topic that always sparks his interest, as well as a bit of exasperation. Elegantly dressed in a wool sports jacket, he sat at a desk in the Fabbrica office of Saint Peter's Basilica, where he holds the title of scientific consultant. With a crop of dark hair and a nimble frame, he looks much younger than his seventy-six years, something people often comment on at the Vatican, where he began work as a young man in the 1960s. After obtaining a degree in biochemistry, he was employed in the restoration department of the Vatican Museums and began working with pigments and cleaning solvents. In 1972, after a Hungarian-born geologist severely damaged Michelangelo's *Pietà* with twelve blows of a hammer, Gabrielli was part of a team that reassembled the statue with special glue and powder made from Carrara marble. In the 1980s he worked on the Sistine Chapel ceiling, helping to remove a centuries-old patina of soot from Michelangelo's frescoes. But from time to time he dabbled in another kind of restoration—the repair and renovation of the corpses of saints.

It all began with a call in 1975 from Franciscan friars in the Umbrian city of Gubbio. The friars are custodians of the remains of Saint Ubaldo, a twelfth-century bishop who is still very popular in the region and whose feast is celebrated with a giant candle race through the medieval town center. In a more contemporary vein, Saint Ubaldo has his own Facebook page and has become the patron saint of those suffering with obsessive-compulsive disorder. The friars and some of Gubbio's civic leaders had become troubled about the state of Saint Ubaldo's body. Local tradition had always held it to be incorrupt, but there was new concern about the effects of heat produced by lamps that lit the saint's casket. The friars wanted a *recognitio*, an official opening and verification of the state of a saint's remains, and they needed someone with the technical knowledge to reposition any body parts that might have slipped out of place. Who better than Gabrielli, the Vatican's top art restorer? "I'd never considered that kind of work," he recalled, "but I said sure, I'll come and take a look."

The *recognitio* was a much more formal affair than simply "taking a look," however, as it involved a full-fledged ceremony that combined medieval customs with modern forensics. The casket was X-rayed and then opened, and everyone breathed a sigh of relief when the saint's body was revealed to be still intact. But after the funerary vestments were removed, Gabrielli took a closer look and realized that the corpse was hardly incorrupt; in fact, it needed some serious work. "The body was in pretty good condition, but I could see that over time it risked turning into dust. Like all organic tissue, it needed to be rehydrated, to regain the moisture and the fatty acids it had lost," he explained. Fortunately Gabrielli was able to concoct a potion that used vegetable oils and glycerin to restore suppleness and flexibility—a formula not so different, he said, from that of the cream used by women to prevent wrinkles. By the time he was finished, Gabrielli recalled with pride, he could once again move the hands and fingers of the eight-hundred-year-old saint.

He did make one odd discovery, however: Saint Ubaldo was missing a finger, specifically the little finger on his right hand. The Franciscan friars immediately guessed where to find it. For centuries a holy digit had been venerated in the village of Thann in northeastern France. According to legend, Saint Ubaldo had told his servant, who was from northern Europe, that he could take his episcopal ring for himself after Ubaldo's death. The servant did just that, but when he tried to pull the ring off, the finger detached with it. The man hid the relic in the knob of his walking stick as he made his way back to his hometown in the Netherlands, and stopping one day near Thann fell asleep under a tree. When he woke, according to the legend, his walking stick was rooted to the ground, and the tree had begun to send up flames, attracting nearby villagers. The local count arrived on the scene, appropriated the relic, and promised to build a church at the site and dedicate it to Saint Ubaldo, or as he was known in France, Saint Thiébaut. The church at Thann became a pilgrimage stop, and was said to be the site of many medieval miracles. In modern times, not surprisingly, the story of Thiébaut/Ubaldo's finger was viewed in France as pious fiction. But when, more than eight centuries after the fact, news of the saint's exhumation and the missing finger arrived, the town enthusiastically celebrated the fact that the legend had been confirmed. There was just one detail that caused perplexity. In Thann the relic had always been venerated as the "holy thumb" of Saint Thiébaut, perhaps because of the shape of the reliquary that held it. The faithful, informed that it was really the little finger, quickly made the adjustment and changed the label.

Nazzareno Gabrielli soon began receiving other calls for exhumations, and with each new saint's corpse he learned something. Gradually he developed his own techniques and preservation methods. He studied the Egyptians' ingenious method of dehydrating corpses by immersion in a strong saline solution, but realized that mummification was not an ideal outcome for the bodies of saints, as their keepers preferred a treatment that would retain lifelike qualities as much as possible. Gabrielli approached these jobs as a scientist, respecting the religious sensitivities of local Catholic communities while accepting the fact that their claims of "incorrupt" corpses often were exaggerated. He found that some bodies were simply desiccated, while others were preserved by a process known as saponification, in which body fats are converted to a soap-like substance that resists decay. And like Ubaldo's, some corpses appeared more intact than they actually were. "When a coffin is opened, the body can look good, but you never know until you start testing the articulation. You put a hand on a shoulder, and it moves too much, for example." Because a corpse with too many moving parts risks breaking apart, Gabrielli developed a technique of wrapping the body in gauze dipped in liquid paraffin. Via that method, he explained, the corpse is fixed and can be maneuvered into place for restoration work; the wax is later melted away with a hair dryer. If he found that vertebrae or other bones were migrating out of place, he would firm them up with injections of liquid resin, which would then harden. Then he would turn his attention to the skin, which usually needed an initial disinfection, followed by a chemical treatment to prevent decomposition. Gabrielli applied the solution in layers of chemically saturated cloth, all the while keeping the body in a sealed capsule. His procedures were so successful that in 2001, when the exhumation of John XXIII was proposed, he was asked to show photos of one of his recent projects to Pope John Paul II. The Polish pope at that point was unconvinced that John XXIII's casket should be opened, but when he saw pictures of Gabrielli's preservation work on the body of Ukrainian Cardinal Josyf Slipyj, he gave his approval.

Gabrielli said he wasn't surprised to find that John XXIII's body was well preserved, because the funerary preparations of dead popes make decomposition much less likely. Popes used to be fully embalmed and, like the ancient Egyptian pharaohs, eviscerated, primarily to prevent decay during the exposition of the body and the papal funeral several days later. In fact, the hearts and other inner organs of more than twenty pontiffs—the "guts of the popes" in Roman slang—are still preserved in marble jars in the Church of Saints Vincent and Anastasius near the Trevi Fountain. The last pope to receive this treatment was

Pius IX in 1878; since then the Vatican's medical experts leave the inner organs in place but run a disinfecting fluid through the corpse. Once a pope's body is sealed inside the three caskets, Gabrielli explained, some of the fluid seeps out and creates a type of protective chemical fog that helps slow decomposition. It was this process that led to John XXIII's body being exhumed in excellent condition.

But Gabrielli still had work to do, as the Vatican wanted to move the pope's body to the upper main floor of Saint Peter's and put it on display in a new glass coffin. That, of course, presented a whole new set of practical challenges, beginning with the pontiff's face. "It was fine, if you knew him, you'd recognize him," Gabrielli said. "But it was dark, too, so it couldn't be shown like that." Technicians designed a flesh-colored wax mask with the late pope's features and gently fit it on his face. A more difficult problem was regulating moisture: humidity was fogging up the inside of the glass coffin. Gabrielli solved it with his own "invention." Traditionally bodies displayed in a glass coffin rest on a mattress, but Gabrielli knew that a cloth cushion would absorb moisture and become a breeding ground for bacteria. Instead, he designed a replica of a mattress made of Plexiglas, with multiple holes to hold de-hydrating salts—packets of silica gel, like the ones inserted in new electronic products to keep them dry. He loaded the structure with nearly twenty pounds of the desiccating granules, and then covered it with red silk. Visitors to the tomb have the impression that the body of John XXIII is reposing on a comfortable bed.

Proclaiming a pope's body "intact" creates problems when it comes to relics. Normally the *recognitio* is a perfect time to gather body parts for future distribution to the faithful. Even a single piece of bone can be dispersed widely once it has been thinly sliced in the microtome of the Augustinian nuns. Although removing pieces from a supposedly incorrupt corpse like that of John XXIII struck some Vatican officials as unbecoming, Cardinal Noè had small strips of skin removed from the hands of the pontiff before the coffin was closed. Those relics *ex corpore* would in future years become practically impossible to obtain, rare treasures for those with a special devotion to Papa Giovanni. One lucky community was an order of nuns serving in Naples, the Daughters of Charity, who had a particular connection to the late pope. In 1966, three years after the death of John XXIII, one of the younger nuns, Sister Caterina Capitani, was in a hospital dying of esophageal hemorrhaging. In a vision Pope John appeared to her and placed his hand on her stomach, telling her she need no longer worry. She recovered fully, and it was her otherwise inexplicable cure that was certified as the miracle that paved the way for Pope John's beatification in 2000. In 2002 Cardinal Noè sent Sister Caterina one of the small sections of the hand that had healed her.

When such episodes are recounted to Nazzareno Gabrielli, he shrugs his shoulders and tries to change the subject. "The idea that the spirit can work through relics reflects the fact that God was incarnate. The problem is that some people value them almost as magical objects."

In a similar vein, he said, people want to believe that their favorite saint's body will miraculously resist the natural process of decomposition. But like others at the Vatican, Gabrielli views reports of incorrupt corpses with a healthy dose of skepticism. The Vatican no longer recognizes an undecayed body as a miracle for the purposes of beatification or canonization, and claims of saints' physical incorruptibility are today considered pious local traditions rather than official church positions. Many of the incorruptibles date to the late Middle Ages. But even as early as the fourth century, Saint Ambrose exhumed the body of the martyr Saint Nazarius and reportedly found fresh blood and a head that, although severed three centuries earlier, had maintained its well-groomed hair and beard. Jesuit Father Herbert Thurston, in his classic work *The Physical Phenomena of Mysticism* (1952), noted that incorruption was associated with other posthumous marks of divine favor, including fresh bleeding, the absence of rigor mortis, and the presence of warmth in cadavers months or even years after death. Perhaps the strangest and rarest sign, Thurston wrote, was when corpses spontaneously raised their arms in benediction or, as in the case of Saint Philip Neri, covered their private parts with their hands when the body was being unclothed.

Thurston's book took the position that the high proportion of Chris-tian saints preserved from decay could not be a matter of mere coinci-dence. Nevertheless, the author was cautious about specific claims of incorruption, recognizing that natural causes might account for an ab-sence of decomposition. Cool and dry tomb conditions, for example, could favor preservation of corpses, some of which were partially or completely mummified. Sometimes bodies were embalmed and the rec-ords lost; such was the case of Saint Margaret of Cortona, whose body was venerated as incorruptible for nearly seven hundred years. An exhu-mation in the 1980s, however, revealed suture marks throughout her body; Saint Margaret, it was determined, had been eviscerated and arti-ficially mummified shortly after her death, her body filled with preser-vatives. In other cases, internal organs of holy persons were removed not only to ward off decomposition, but for veneration and distribution as relics. When Saint Clare of Montefalco, an Augustinian abbess in cen-tral Italy, died in 1308, nuns took out her organs and examined them for supernatural signs. They found three gallstones, which they interpreted as a symbol of the Holy Trinity, and scar tissue in the heart in the shape of a cross. The rest of her body was said to be incorrupt, and is still ven-erated in the Umbrian hill town of her birth.

For many people seeing is believing, and the bodies of incorruptible saints are on display in churches throughout the world. The problem is that visitors do not always know precisely what they're seeing. Often the physical remains are hidden beneath clothing or an "effigy" that's designed to look real, but is made of wax or other material. That is the case for the Lourdes visionary Saint Bernadette Soubirous, for exam-ple, whose face has been covered for decades with a wax mask—a like-ness that is routinely cited as proof of a miracle. Saint Bernadette died in 1879, and when her body was exhumed thirty years later the word went out that it was found to be in a state of perfect preservation. The detailed report of the exhumation, however, also described parts of the body that were sunken, others that protruded, and some that had turned slightly black. When her corpse was reexhumed in 1919, once again it was described by the faithful as "absolutely intact," yet the medical report cited areas of skin that had disappeared and others that had mildewed, and a body that had essentially mummified. By the time of the third exhumation in 1925, Saint Bernadette's face was so dark that church authorities commissioned a thin mask to be designed by the Paris firm of Pierre Imans, famous for its lifelike wax mannequins. Today Bernadette's body is displayed and venerated in a crystal coffin in Nevers, France, where hundreds of thousands of visitors come each year to pray. Many are moved by the almost surreal loveliness of her face, which seems to correspond so well to the spiritual beauty of this popular saint. The features are indeed remarkable. Scientifically, however, it is difficult to make the case that her body is incorrupt according to the classic definition: complete immunity from natural decay.

Nazzareno Gabrielli knows only too well that opening tombs carries a high risk of disappointment. In 2008 church officials in England wanted to exhume the body of the nineteenth-century Cardinal John Henry Newman, whose beatification cause was being studied in Rome. They planned to move his remains from a secluded cemetery to a more prominent oratory in Birmingham, where they could be more conveniently venerated. But when undertakers opened his grave, they found nothing, not even bones or teeth—his entire body had rotted away, and so had the coffin. All that remained were a few tassels from the cardinal's red hat. Fortunately the Birmingham oratory already possessed a few locks of his hair, prudently removed at the time of death, so some relics survived.

Earlier that same year Gabrielli was summoned to exhume the corpse of Saint Padre Pio, the popular Italian Capuchin friar who died in 1968 and whose intercession is credited by devotees with more than a thousand miraculous cures. Church authorities wanted to put the body on display in a crystal sepulcher, and Gabrielli was hired to make certain that it was fit for exhibition. By that point he had disentombed more than fifty bodies and was the recognized expert for such delicate interventions—in a very real sense, the "taxidermist to the saints"— but as he made his way to this saint's burial place in the southern Italian town of San Giovanni Rotondo, he felt the unique pressure of this particular assignment. Padre Pio had followers around the world, and more than five million people visited his grave site every year. They would be watching the exhumation and restoration very closely, and would not forgive mistakes.

Gabrielli found the corpse in relatively good condition, although far from perfect, and he was mystified when Italian media began reporting that Padre Pio's body was incorrupt. He spent nearly two months working on the remains, skillfully employing his arsenal of chemical preservatives and resins, interrupted all too frequently by the prayers of the Capuchin friars who hovered around the work area. The saint's face was still intact, and Gabrielli thought it could be left as it was, perhaps discreetly displayed behind a veil. But the local archbishop and the Capuchin custodians decided otherwise, and hired the London-based Gems Studio to create a lifelike silicone mask, with a mustache and full beard. "It wasn't necessary," Gabrielli said, shaking his head. "But people arrive with the wrong mentality. They expect him to look as if he were brought back to life. That's impossible. Time passes."

CHAPTER TWO

Mother of God?

Lisa Harris picked her way carefully along the rocky path of Apparition Hill, keeping an eye on her husband, who was ahead trying to find a place for them to sit down. Just below them a multitude of people had crowded around the Blue Cross, and by now there was no way to get anywhere near the actual spot where Mirjana would experience her vision of Mary. It was almost two o'clock when, suddenly, Lisa heard the crowd go silent, and she knew. "It's happening, it's happening!" she wanted to yell out to her husband. But he was too far away, and shouting to him would cause a scene. So she paused with two of her daughters and her son, just taking it in. Lisa waited for a distinctive fragrance to arrive and then, there it was. She turned to her daughters and said, "Smell! Can you smell the roses?" They could, and even her teenage son said he caught a little whiff of them. *It was a beautiful experience,* she thought to herself, even though, when she finally reached her husband and the spot he had found for them, she had to tell him the apparition was already over.

It was an unusually warm day in Medjugorje at the end of the mild Bosnian winter of 2014, and more than two thousand people had assembled on the hillside, the earliest of whom had arrived at sunrise in order to stake out prime viewing positions. They sat and waited, praying and singing religious songs, looking out toward the snowcapped mountains in the distance. Most were outfitted in the pilgrim's gear sold in local shops: Medjugorje hats, Medjugorje water bottles, Medjugorje folding chairs, and Medjugorje walking sticks to help navigate the uneven terrain. And, of course, everyone had rosaries—not just one, but purses and backpacks full of them, rosaries that would be passed on to others with the whispered phrase, "This was blessed by Our Lady during her apparition to Mirjana."

On that day, March 18, Mirjana Dragicevic-Soldo was celebrating her forty-ninth birthday, one of the days she claims to receive apparitions of the Blessed Mother. Mirjana is one of the six original Medjugorje visionaries who, as youths, professed to see Mary on this hill in June 1981. Their visions, and Mary's messages, continued on a daily basis for years, drawing an estimated thirty million people to the tiny town and turning the seers into spiritual superstars. Three of them still say they have daily apparitions, while the others are visited by Mary only on special occasions during the year. While most of the visionaries have moved away from Medjugorje, Mirjana has remained in the Podbrdo neighborhood at the foot of Apparition Hill and has become a celebrity for the busloads of pilgrims who crowd its narrow streets. In addition to her birthday, Mirjana also has visions on the second day of every month, which is a blessing for the souvenir shops that are now crammed into every corner of Podbrdo. To a large extent, their livelihood depends on these reliable supernatural events at the foot of the Blue Cross.

On this particular birthday Mirjana's arrival prompted a wave of applause, the crowd immediately recognizing the attractive blonde in her trademark blue sweater. Escorted through an area cordoned off by ropes, her mouth set in a wide smile, she knelt before the cross. With video cameras already rolling, a priest began praying the rosary through a loudspeaker, and the pilgrims responded in their own languages. Mirjana, a rosary wrapped around one hand, prayed, too. Then, after a few minutes, she suddenly gazed heavenward and folded her hands. That was the cue for the recital of the rosary to be halted, and a silence descended. For those close enough to see her face, Mirjana seemed to be engaged in a mute conversation. She drew deep breaths, moved her lips, and shook her head as if responding to questions. She looked at turns perplexed, amazed, and concerned, furrowing her brow. After about five minutes she made the sign of the cross, bowed her head, and wiped away a tear. It was over, and the priest resumed the rosary.

Pilgrims experience these moments in different ways. Some kneel and pray; others say they feel the actual presence of Mary. But there is an overall casualness about the apparitions that can often surprise visitors. Medjugorje is not a collective mystical experience, or an expression of mass hysteria—far from it. Most of the pilgrims are merely spectators, filming the event on their video cameras or cell phones. Some later remark, in an almost offhand fashion, that they noticed supernatural signs. "Addie saw the sun spinning, and so did Sam and Joey," said Lisa Harris, speaking of her children. "I did not. I had before but I did not this time, and that's OK. I was feeling a great sense of peace."

A few minutes after the apparition ended, the rosary was interrupted again, this time to read out a rough draft of Mary's message to Mirjana that day. Translated on the fly from Croatian into Italian and English, it sounded much like the estimated thirty thousand previous messages that Mary, known by the Croatian term "Gospa," has supposedly given the Medjugorje seers: "Dear children, I want to be a mother to you." "Put my son in the first place of your heart." "Cast out the darkness and shadow that tries to deceive you." "Pray for those who, out of the hardness of their hearts, do not follow me." When the Gospa spoke of darkness and shadow, Mirjana told the crowd, a fog seemed to enshroud her divine figure, an image that was a little unsettling. Within a few hours the message would be edited and posted online for the global Medjugorje network of devotees.

As Mirjana left the site, she paused to greet the lucky ones who pressed to get close to her. Other pilgrims quickly gathered around the Blue Cross, kneeling in the spot where Mirjana had knelt, touching holy cards and rosaries to the cross, leaving rosaries on the arm of a statue of Mary, and depositing flowers and envelopes full of prayer intentions. Whatever their particular expression of devotion, they all had come to Medjugorje for one thing: to witness a direct line of communication to the Mother of God. They knew that in their lifetime this was as close as they'd get to heaven.

Mirjana, who is married with two daughters, today runs a pilgrims' guesthouse near her home that provides much-needed income for her family and gives visitors a chance to speak at length with the visionary.

At least two of the other Medjugorje seers also manage accommodation facilities for visitors. While some have criticized this as a conflict of interest, no one in the town considers it strange, as virtually every family here has profited from the pilgrim boom by adding guest rooms or building hotels.

From the balcony of her new gated home in Podbrdo, on a winding street where birds sang in magnolia trees, Mirjana spoke to a group of about three hundred visitors. This appearance was unadvertised to the public, but it was well known to the network of tour operators who act as a liaison with the seers. Most of the pilgrims were Italian, and they had waited for more than an hour for Mirjana to appear, passing the time by singing hymns and holding their rosaries up to "Mamma Celeste," the Heavenly Mother.

Surrounded by several priests and tour guides, Mirjana recounted in Italian the story of the apparitions in what has become her standard narrative: On June 24, 1981, Mirjana, then sixteen years old, and her friend Ivanka Ivankovic went for a walk on the hill above their neighborhood. Ivanka noticed something in the distance and said to Mirjana, "I think that's the Madonna!" Mirjana responded with a touch of sarcasm, "Are you sure she has nothing better to do than to see us two?" But Ivanka, who had recently lost her own mother, insisted that she had seen a woman dressed in a long gray gown holding a baby. Mirjana was still skeptical, but when the two returned a short while later to the same spot, Mirjana saw the woman, too. In the days that followed, the apparitions continued and were witnessed by four other friends. Mary came into clearer focus and began to speak to them, telling the children not to be afraid. The Gospa said that what she had begun at Fatima, she would complete at Medjugorje—a reference to the famous Marian apparitions in Fatima, Portugal, in 1917. Mirjana told the pilgrims that at that time she knew nothing about Fatima, and so had no idea what the Gospa's words meant. Before long word of the apparitions had spread, drawing the attention of the local Franciscan priests and arousing the suspicion of local law enforcement. In 1981 Bosnia and Herzegovina was part of Communist Yugoslavia, and police soon called the children in for questioning and tried to prevent the increasingly large crowds from gathering on the apparition hillside.

The Italian pilgrims stood in rapt attention as Mirjana advanced her narrative to Christmas Day 1982. By that time, she said, she had received ten secrets from the Blessed Mother, and the daily apparitions ceased. In the years that followed she saw Mary only once a year, on her birthday. But in 1987 Mary also began appearing to her on the second day of each month, in connection with a mission assigned to Mirjana to pray for nonbelievers. In fact, Mirjana explained, the Gospa never used the term "nonbelievers," because that would be judging. Instead, Mary describes them as people who "don't yet know the heart of God." Each of the six visionaries was given a specific mission, focusing on the sick, youths, families, priests, and the souls in purgatory. Their assignment did not, however, involve social action or the mobilization of resources. "Mary just wants our prayers," Mirjana said. Indeed, a striking characteristic of the Medjugorje phenomenon is its simple spiritual prescription: "Just keep praying."

When Mirjana took questions from the pilgrims, she seemed more spontaneous and less self-assured. What does it feel like to see Mary? "Like I'm going to explode inside from emotion. I only see heaven and Mary. The hill and the Blue Cross disappear. When I'm with Mary, I forget I have children." What does Mary look like? "She's beautiful, with long black hair and blue eyes, about my height, maybe a little taller. She hasn't aged in all these years." What do you think about unmarried couples who live together? "They are nonbelievers because they don't know the heart of God—they couldn't possibly, if they do this. The white wedding dress should mean something." What should a woman do if her husband leaves her for another? "Well, we all know that men stop growing up at age fourteen. . . . I'm really just a seer. That's a question for a priest."

Many of the questions concern the ten secrets—so many, in fact, that Mirjana chided the group. "All you want to know about is the secrets! I shut up about the secrets!" But she and the other visionaries have offered hints about them in the past, generating excitement and apprehension about apocalyptic events to come. The secrets are essentially prophecies that will be fulfilled on the Gospa's timetable, and several of them apparently promise chastisement for those who fail to convert. The first two are said to be warnings. The third secret will be a "permanent sign" placed on Apparition Hill, as an emblem of gratitude to believers and a "last call" for nonbelievers. The pilgrims who congregated around Mirjana's house wanted to know more about this sign, and Mirjana assured them that there would be no doubt when it occurred: the world would sit up and take notice.

As the first visionary to receive all ten secrets, Mirjana said she had worried about forgetting some of the particulars. For that reason, she explained, Mary gave her a special parchment containing all the dates and details. What if the parchment should fall into the wrong hands? That would not be a problem, Mirjana explained, as the secrets were written in a mysterious code that only she was able to understand. Should people be afraid of what's coming? Not if they're prepared— but they had better pray! Mirjana said Mary asks her to pray continually for sinners, because "they do not know what awaits them."

Once Mirjana was given all the secrets, she said Mary told her to select a priest to whom she would reveal each secret in sequence, ten days before their fulfillment. He in turn would reveal them to the world a few days later. She chose Franciscan Father Petar Ljubicic, who has become an itinerant promoter of the Medjugorje apparitions. The first of the secrets, it was said in 1982, would soon be made known. Thirty-three years later even stalwart Medjugorje devotees are wondering how long they'll have to wait. Father Ljubicic said in 2008 that he had the impression that the secrets would come to pass "very, very soon." As the visionaries themselves grow older, some pilgrims ask whether all six of them will still be alive when the secrets are finally disclosed. The answer, according to the seers, is yes.

One odd aspect of the ten secrets is that, while the visionaries agree that they will all come to pass, some of the specific details regarding them have changed. Mirjana, for example, has said that the eighth secret frightened her so much that she prayed for mercy on humanity, and in response Mary "softened" the punishment. For critics of Medjugorje, that represents one more reason to distrust these apparitions. They bristle at the idea of the Mother of God as a temperamental negotiator, offering a concession on divine chastisement in exchange for prayers.

At the end of Mirjana's long soliloquy, she came down from the balcony to greet several sick people, who were accompanied by relatives or friends. Many miraculous healings have been claimed at Medjugorje, though none of them has been officially verified and recognized by the Catholic Church, a point often noted by critics. That did not seem to matter to those who waited in wheelchairs at the bottom of the stairs. They reached out for the one thing that gave them hope: Mirjana's touch.

Thirty-five years ago Medjugorje was a tiny hamlet in a region of subsistence farming. The apparitions of 1981 brought a stream of international visitors, but most people thought the sensation would end just as quickly as it began. It wasn't until several years later that locals realized it didn't have to end at all—as long as the apparitions kept occurring, the tour buses would continue to unload thousands of pilgrims each week. Banking on Mary to make daily appearances was risky, but by the late 1980s many families in Medjugorje had abandoned their tobacco fields and vineyards and invested in religious tourism. They added rooms to their homes to accommodate visitors, opened restaurants and souvenir shops, and forged connections with foreign tour operators who needed local logistical support. The fighting in Bosnia during the breakup of Yugoslavia in the early 1990s slowed the pilgrim traffic to a trickle, but when the war ended in 1995 the visitors returned in greater numbers than ever. Larger and more modern hotels were constructed, as foreign investors realized that Medjugorje visitors, especially those from the United States and western Europe, did not necessarily want to rough it. The boom continued until the global financial crisis of 2008, when the pilgrim traffic again slowed. Small-scale operators in Medjugorje had too many empty beds, and were having trouble repaying loans. Today, the numbers are back up to previous levels.

In a sunny courtyard just outside of Medjugorje, a tiny figure held a microphone close to her lips and, in a hoarse voice, implored her listeners to "water the heart with prayers, and see how it grows." Fasting was important, too, and the Blessed Mother didn't want to hear excuses on that score—as when people claimed they got headaches or didn't feel well after skipping meals. "That's just a lack of will. Our Lady wants a complete conversion."

Vicka Ivankovic-Mijatovic, the oldest of the Medjugorje visionaries, spoke emphatically in rapid-fire Italian, translated phrase by phrase into English for several hundred faithful. She was dressed in a worn checkered sweater, her hair pulled back in a manner that accentuated her thin and angular face. Flanked by four clerics on a wooden porch, she gazed wide-eyed at the crowd, occasionally blowing kisses in slow motion, like an aging movie star. The pilgrims waved at her, trying to catch her attention. At eight o'clock in the morning, some had been standing here for hours, waiting for this chance to meet her and listen to her words of spiritual wisdom. Vicka still claims to receive apparitions daily, usually in the privacy of her home, and every evening Mary's new message is relayed by telephone and broadcast to pilgrims at Saint James, the parish church in Medjugorje. Now fifty years old, Vicka has experienced health problems, and twice in recent years she withdrew from all public appearances following injuries to her shoulder and back, both apparently caused when she was jostled by overly enthusiastic admirers. To the delight of tour operators, she returned in 2014 to a regular schedule of encounters, on Mondays, Wednesdays, and Fridays. Organizers picked a place big enough to accommodate more than a thousand people, the walled grounds of a church-run orphanage. The setting might have suggested a connection between Marian prayer and the church's social activity, but in her hour-long "testimony" on this particular day, Vicka did not mention the orphanage's programs or any other good works. The Medjugorje message prescribes prayer, not humanitarian action or charity.

"The Gospa says Satan is very much present, trying to disturb our prayers and ruin our lives! To defend against Satan, it's a good idea to keep a rosary with you, or wear a small cross or medal," Vicka told the crowd.

Murmurs of assent arose from the courtyard, and some held their rosaries on high. The heart of Vicka's speech came when she recounted how Mary once took her and Jakov Colo, the youngest of the visionaries, on a tour of heaven, hell, and purgatory. This was not an epic Dantesque journey, however; the whole trip lasted only twenty minutes, Vicka recounted. Mary held their hands, and "there was just enough space to go through, we arrived in heaven in one second." She described heaven as "a huge space with a special kind of light, and small angels flying around." Everyone was dressed in red, yellow, or gray gowns, apparently because wearing individual street clothes would have been "too confusing." Mary urged them to look around and see how happy everyone was in heaven, which was a striking contrast with purgatory, where souls were suffering in a type of fog. As for hell, Vicka said, it was basically "a big fire" where people were transformed into animals—a result of their own bad decisions in life, as Mary was quick to point out.

As she neared the end of her address, Vicka announced a "moment of silence for meditation," and the crowd went dutifully quiet. She made the sign of the cross, folded her hands, and, closing her eyes, began whispering prayers. After ten minutes of the silence, people standing in the warm sunshine began getting impatient; after twenty minutes a high-pitched scream pierced the stillness—a child was apparently bored or frightened. As the silence persisted past thirty minutes, a man keeled over and remained on the ground and was soon followed by another. This phenomenon of collapsing, known as "slain in the spirit" in the Christian charismatic movement, did not seem to perturb others standing nearby.

When Vicka finally took the microphone again, it was to close her appearance with a Hail Mary. Then she waved and blew more kisses, accepting prayer petitions passed up through the crowd. "I pray for all of you!" she assured them, before disappearing inside.

The pilgrims dispersed, pausing at the roadside souvenir stands to buy a few more medals and rosaries before boarding their giant buses. Carlene Frickelton of Green Bay, Wisconsin, a repeat visitor to Medjugorje, took a moment to explain what brings her back. "It's just such a feeling of holy, it makes you feel special," she began, and soon she was describing how she'd seen the sun spinning and smelled the miraculous roses on Apparition Hill. Frickelton had been standing next to the man who fell to the ground in the courtyard. As a nurse, she said, she recognized this as a spiritual event and not a medical emergency. She had noticed that just as the man collapsed a bird appeared and stayed near him for about ten minutes. The instant the bird flew away, the man rose. She took it as a sign.

When she was a girl, Frickelton said, her mother had taken her to the Shrine of Our Lady of Good Help just north of Green Bay, where Mary is said to have appeared to a Belgian immigrant woman in 1859. In 2010 the shrine became the first officially approved Marian apparition site in the United States. It was practically in Frickelton's backyard. Yet she had traveled nearly five thousand miles, to a foreign country, to pray in Medjugorje. Asked to explain why, she responded without hesitation: "Mary's not in Wisconsin now. She's here. This is going on *now*."

The main street of Medjugorje was lively on a Sunday evening. The religious souvenir shops were doing a brisk business, selling almost anything that could be marked with a Medjugorje logo. The rosaries came in every possible color and style, and each store had several thousand of them on display. The locals were out walking, the women in high heels and sunglasses, virtually everyone smoking cigarettes. Restaurants featured Italian cuisine, mainly pizza, or fast food for pilgrims on the run. From a *birreria* loudspeaker, Tina Turner belted out, "What's love got to do with it?" Young men drove up and down the street in their black Mercedes, rosaries hanging above the dashboards from rearview mirrors.

Saint James Church, with its characteristic twin towers, is the institutional side of the Medjugorje experience. Its interior is unadorned and nondescript; behind the church, an outdoor amphitheater-style worship area has been added, seating several thousand people. When the apparitions began in 1981, the Franciscan pastors were concerned that Mary was appearing on the edge of town and not at the parish's place of worship. The priests soon moved the young seers into the church, and for years the apparitions took place there, in a side room or a choir loft before evening Mass. For the Franciscans it was important to show the world that Mary's message of conversion and prayer led people back to church—not just to a rocky hillside, but to a place where one participated in Mass and the sacraments. Today apparitions no longer occur at Saint James, but pilgrims still come here for what many describe as their most moving experience in Medjugorje.

There are more than thirty confessionals at Saint James, arranged by language groups in open-air atriums on either side of the church. The queues on this particular Sunday were at least fifteen people deep—the kind of lines older priests remembered from a bygone era of Catholicism. Eventually each penitent entered a small room about the size of a broom closet and sat face-to-face with a priest. For many of the pilgrims, it was their first confession in years, and the sessions lasted fifteen or twenty minutes. As the lines grew longer, other priests appeared on the scene and began to hear confessions on nearby benches, next to topiary bushes.

Julie Kraemer stepped out of a door marked "English," smiling. She had experienced an unusual confession, for the priest who heard it had not offered spiritual direction in the classic sense. Instead, he had delivered a message about Christ and God and challenged her to live it. It reminded her of how conversions are described in the Bible—someone speaks the truth, and someone else changes in response to it. The priest spoke about a variety of spiritual experiences, and gave her the blessing of the Holy Spirit. "I am looking to find peace, joy, and love, and he gave me a book and a mission to do that. It was really inspiring," Julie said.

Kraemer, who lives in Saint Paul, Minnesota, came to Medjugorje hoping for a moment of grace, yet was aware that, as she put it, "There have also been some spectacular fakes, where unbelievable holiness and signs and phenomena have fooled *everybody*." She acknowledged that she found the Medjugorje messages a little confusing, and that its "pray, pray, pray" theme seemed to stop short of advocating evangelical action. Nor was there much time for personal contemplation or reflection in Medjugorje. "This is more like boot camp than retreat," she said. "I've been marched up and down mountains, and dragged in and out of Masses where I can't understand the language." She was also wary of the many pilgrims who came seeking supernatural signs. Yet for all her caution, after a few days in Medjugorje, she said she was convinced that Mary was truly appearing here. As Kraemer explained, "I believe she can. I believe in a God who is powerful and can do pretty much what he wants to do."

That belief had been challenged years earlier when her mother died, Kraemer said. "I had to figure out whether I really believed all this stuff or not. Because I was like, you know what, if it's not really real, I'm not going to waste my time going to Mass." Those doubts led her to a deep study of the Bible, which she began to read in a different way. The episodes in Scripture seemed to suggest that God was using the biblical accounts of peoples and their experiences to tell a larger, transcendent story. To her they indicated a consistent author behind human events. This was a God who worked in human history, often through miracles. In the end she told herself that if you really believed in God you had to believe in miracles. "I was raised Catholic, so I always 'believed' in God. But this is where my brain started to believe it." For Kraemer and many others who visit Medjugorje, a proof of credibility is found in the spiritual "fruits" of the pilgrimage experience—the return to confession and Mass, the forgiveness of past wrongs, the rediscovery of prayer and fasting, the sense of inner peace.

That argument has so far failed to convince some members of the church hierarchy, including the former and current bishops whose territory includes Medjugorje. The opposition of local diocesan authorities is rarely mentioned to pilgrims, and when it is, the words used to describe their resistance are chosen carefully. A guide from northern Italy, addressing about thirty visitors near Saint James Church, phrased it this way: "The bishop doesn't believe Mary is working miracles here?

Well, that's his theory. The poor man. The devil tempts everyone, even the bishop. You can imagine how many people he's discouraged from coming here!" The pilgrims shook their heads ruefully, apparently wondering why a bishop would want to undermine such a beautiful experience. The guide continued, addressing the "absurd" notion that Medjugorje might be the devil's work. "The devil doesn't operate that way. The devil doesn't ask people to come here and pray and confess! Millions of people! What kind of strategy would that be—the devil, leading people back to God?"

The jagged rocks on the path up Apparition Hill have been smoothed and polished by millions of pilgrims' feet, but they are still sharp enough to cause serious injury or even death. In 2013 an Indonesian man stumbled, hit his head, and was pronounced dead on arrival at the local hospital; a German died under similar circumstances a few years earlier. More often people twist an ankle or break a leg, and go home in a cast. Yet few pilgrims to Medjugorje, no matter what their age, would forgo the steep and hazardous climb, which is considered part of the penitential routine. If the journey is strenuous, they tell themselves, imagine what it must have been like for the children who hiked up this hill barefoot in June 1981. Inevitably visitors say the ascent is worth the effort. For many of them, Apparition Hill is where they feel Mary's presence, and where miracles can happen.

The place of the first apparitions is a ten-minute hike above the Blue Cross, where the apparitions moved in 1982. The original location is marked today by a large statue of Mary, which, like most things in Medjugorje, has a wondrous story behind it. On a recent weekday about two hundred people were gathered around the statue as a local guide told the tale. For years the apparition site was indicated simply by a small pile of rocks. In 2000 a Korean woman arrived in Medjugorje with a deaf-mute son who had a number of other maladies. She ended up staying for three months, the guide said. Every morning she hiked up Apparition Hill and the nearby "Cross Mountain" to pray for her son's healing. The woman was quite religious, though her husband was not—in fact, he wanted nothing to do with this prayer petition. Your God, he told his wife, is the God who gave you a sick child. One morning, deep in prayer on the hillside, the Korean mother had a vision of Mary, who was suffering the pain of Jesus's crucifixion. The woman immediately saw her own suffering in a new light. She vowed to accept the "cross" of her son's illnesses and help him carry it. She would no longer pray for healing, she told herself, and headed down the mountain. When she returned to the Medjugorje guesthouse where she was staying, she heard other pilgrims singing. As she drew near, she was astonished to see her own son among them, smiling and singing an Ave Maria in a loud voice. In the face of this miracle, the woman's husband converted and insisted on bringing the statue of Mary to this hill, as a sign of thanksgiving. "This is where heaven touched earth," the guide concluded.

This is also the site where the permanent sign will be left by Mary once her ten secrets begin unfolding, the guide explained. He told the story of the secrets, the parchment with its mysterious writing, and how a priest would give the world three days to prepare for each one. A pilgrim asked whether the secrets foretold benign or dangerous events, and whether it would be a good idea to be here in Medjugorje at the time. The guide shrugged. "Let's put it this way," he replied. "You'll have three days to get to Medjugorje—or three days to get out!" The crowd buzzed with nervous laughter.

The guide left the pilgrims to pray, and the hillside turned quiet. They knelt or sat on the rocky terrain, gazing at the statue of Mary, or at a nearby crucifix, or at the panoramic scene of the town and the valley below. As always at Medjugorje, people seemed hyperattentive to signs of the supernatural. One pilgrim nudged his friend and looked up to the sky, and they both smiled and nodded. The contrails of two jets had formed a perfect cross.

What is essential to understanding Medjugorje—and what visitors rarely, if ever, receive—is a lesson in the region's religious history.

Franciscan friars were sent to Bosnia in the thirteenth century as part of a papal effort to eradicate a heretical sect called Bogomilism, which began in Bulgaria and spread throughout the Balkans. The Bogomils believed that the world was created by good and evil powers, with God the originator of the spiritual world and Satan the creator of the material world. In Medjugorje the dualistic creed of the Bogomils blended with local pagan customs, including traditional animal sacrifices designed to appease Gromovnik, the "spirit of thunder" that lived on the mountain overlooking the town. The Franciscans worked closely with the local people, Christianizing their traditions, educating their young, and introducing practical innovations in farming and construction.

When the Ottoman Turks overtook the region in the fifteenth century, the diocesan clergy fled but the Franciscans remained, earning the loyalty of the Christian community during more than four hundred years of religious persecution. Adept at mediating, the Franciscans eventually obtained from the Turks a degree of freedom for the Christian population. More than anyone else, it was the friars who kept the faith alive. After the Turkish hold was broken in the late 1800s, the Vatican moved to begin replacing the Franciscans with diocesan clergy—a normal process in the Catholic Church, but one that created a lasting conflict in Bosnia. The Franciscans resisted removal, and over the next one hundred years a succession of local bishops attempted in vain to convince the friars to share or relinquish control of Bosnian parishes.

In 1975 the Vatican issued a decree demanding obedience from the Franciscans, a move that had virtually no effect. In 1980 Bishop Pavao Žanić of Mostar, the diocese that includes Medjugorje, launched a plan to reorganize parishes and remove them from Franciscan control, prompting a rebellion among both the friars and many local Catholics. That same year the Yugoslavian leader Josip Broz Tito died, and nationalistic sentiments began to stir again in Croatia and among Bosnia's ethnic Croatian population. It was in this atmosphere of religious and political tension that Marian apparitions were first reported in Medjugorje in June 1981.

Bishop Žanić at first defended the young visionaries and the possibility that Mary was indeed appearing to them. He instituted an investigation commission and prepared to report the findings to Rome. But as the apparitions continued and the messages from Mary accumulated (recorded in some of the visionaries' diaries), it became clear that the Blessed Mother was siding with the disobedient Franciscans against the bishop. On more than one occasion, according to notebook entries made by the seer Vicka Ivankovic, Mary was "consulted" about the situation of two Franciscan priests who had been ordered to surrender control of parishes in Mostar. She had supposedly answered that the bishop was to blame, and that the priests could continue their ministry.

Bishop Žanić interpreted this as a clear sign that the visionaries were being manipulated, and that the apparitions themselves were false. He began to speak publicly about his doubts. In 1983 Žanić received a letter from another visionary, Ivan Dragicevic, claiming that Mary was demanding the bishop's "immediate conversion on the happenings in the Medjugorje parish before it is too late." The letter indicated that this was a final warning before the "verdict" of Mary and her son would reach him. Bishop Žanić was appalled. "I mailed the letter to the Vatican the same day," he said. "For me, the question was decided."

In 1984 Žanić published a statement challenging the authenticity of the Medjugorje events and denouncing the Franciscan friars who were promoting the apparitions. Specifically the bishop warned that Father Tomislav Vlašić, a priest in Medjugorje who had become a spiritual adviser to the visionaries, was a "manipulator and a deceiver." Two years later, Žanić sent a report to the Vatican's doctrinal congregation, headed by Cardinal Joseph Ratzinger, arguing that the Medjugorje apparitions were not genuine. The bishop publicly called for an end to church-organized pilgrimages to the site, and the Vatican supported him—though it also decreed that individual pilgrims to Medjugorje should be given pastoral attention and access to the sacraments. Although Medjugorje supporters tried to depict Bishop Žanić as a stubborn and unfair critic, and one who could safely be ignored, by 1991 the Yugoslavian bishops' conference had weighed in, declaring that "on the basis of studies conducted so far, it is not possible to affirm that supernatural apparitions are occurring" in Medjugorje.

While the long-standing feud between the Franciscans and their bishop cast a shadow of doubt over Medjugorje, many church experts had even deeper misgivings. Even those who were devoted to the Blessed Mother, and who strongly believed that Mary had appeared and spoken to the faithful at other times in history, sensed that the apparitions at Medjugorje did not fit the established pattern of authenticity.

For one thing, the multiplicity of Mary's appearances and messages, day after day for decades, raised the implicit question: What was the Blessed Mother trying to convey to humanity? In fact, when the apparitions at Medjugorje first began, the visionaries told local priests that Mary had no message at all. The Franciscan priests immediately saw this as a problem, which is clear in transcripts of their taped conversations with the visionaries. A week after the apparitions began, Franciscan Father Jozo Zovko, the pastor at Saint James Church, asked Vicka what it was, exactly, that Mary wanted to happen at Medjugorje. When Vicka replied that the Gospa didn't know, Father Zovko exclaimed, "What kind of Gospa is it who doesn't know? Then she is smaller than a child."

Moreover, Mary at first seemed disinclined to initiate any conversation; instead, she only replied to the children's questions. When they asked why she had come, the Gospa offered vague answers like "we must be together." In the months and years that followed, once Mary's messages at Medjugorje began flowing, they routinely focused on the same—some would say banal—spiritual prescriptions: surrender your hearts to my son, offer your sufferings as a sacrifice to Christ, remember that sin offends God, and "pray, pray, pray." For what was billed as her "last apparition on earth," Mary seemed to have little more than generic platitudes to offer.

To many Marian experts, these details stood in stark contrast to the apparitions that had been authenticated by the Catholic Church over previous centuries. In genuine apparitions of the past, Mary would arrive with a purpose, express clearly and succinctly her desire for a specific task or mission, and then, after a limited number of appearances, depart. A visitation by the Blessed Mother was therefore an extraordinary spiritual experience, not a lifetime vocation. One of the first things the Franciscans asked the visionaries was when the apparitions would end. The children put the question to the Gospa, and the answers were contradictory. According to some witnesses, after the first week more than one of the children said Mary would appear only three more times. In fact, the apparitions continued on a daily basis.

For critics another telltale sign was the conflict that initially occurred between the Franciscan pastors and the seers over the location of the apparitions. At Father Zovko's insistence, the visionaries agreed to conduct the apparitions in Saint James Church, at a designated hour. From the Franciscans' point of view, relocating the apparitions into the church not only gave them more control over the visionaries but also defused a security issue. The Communist authorities were harassing the thousands of faithful who were gathering to witness the apparitions in Podbrdo, but were less likely to object if the events took place within a place of worship. This relocation struck some Marian experts as strangely manipulative, a suspicion that was only reinforced when, in later years, the seers would effectively take Mary with them on tours around the globe. Unlike her previous apparitions in church history, Mary was no longer choosing where and when to appear, but was being stage-managed by visionaries and priests.

The image of the Blessed Mother that emerged from these visions was an unusual figure in other ways, too. She seemed to change moods, at times laughing and other times scolding. In 1984 she told local parishioners not to expect a message that day because her appearances were becoming too routine for them, attracting curiosity seekers and "only a really small number" who took her words to heart. The following week, however, she insisted that she had much more to say at Medjugorje, ordering the faithful: "You just listen to my instructions!" A year later the Gospa again threatened to withhold messages, saying she was appealing "for the last time" for spiritual renewal and prayer in the parish. This Mary also made occasional verbal mistakes. According to the children, when a woman asked if she could touch the Gospa, she responded: "There are always unbelieving Judases. Let her come near!" The visionaries' supporters would later amend that reference to "doubting Thomases."

Many of the Gospa's messages mentioned Medjugorje as "an oasis of peace," a characterization that seemed oddly disconnected to current events. As the region was engulfed by war in the early 1990s, the Blessed Mother seemed detached from the ongoing violence. In 1992, a year in which bloodletting between ethnic Croats and Bosnian Muslims reached a peak, Mary rarely referred to the conflict, and when she did, it was with typical blandness: "Only by prayer and fasting can war be stopped." It was fully in keeping with the almost total absence of social justice content in the tens of thousands of Medjugorje messages.

The messages, as repetitious as they were, only served to fuel the cult status of the Medjugorje seers. As the number of visitors reached into the millions, the meme of miraculous signs also began to gather strength among devotees. As early as the third day of the apparitions in 1981, one of the visionaries, egged on by the crowd in Podbrdo, had requested of the Blessed Mother: "Give us a sign which will prove your presence." Mary's supposed answer, "Blessed are those who have not seen and who believe," did nothing to diminish the desire for the miraculous. The most common "supernatural" sign supposedly witnessed at Medjugorje has been the spinning sun, in which the solar disk pulsates and changes color. It requires that the faithful stare at the sun for an extended period of time, a practice that remains quite common among pilgrims despite the real risk of retinal damage. The visual illusion of a sun that appears to throb and dance in the sky has been attributed to retinal distortion and other physiological changes caused by sun gazing, but Medjugorje followers dismiss scientific explanations. For them it's a God-given wonder and a reminder of the "Miracle of the Sun" that reportedly occurred during Marian apparitions in Fatima, Portugal, on October 13, 1917. While the Fatima phenomenon took place only once, before a crowd of nearly one hundred thousand people, at Medjugorje the sun miracle is a personal event experienced by individual visitors, and occurs virtually on demand.

One of the arguments frequently made in support of Medjugorje is that the global interest stirred by the apparitions is itself a divine sign, a movement that could never have been orchestrated. Yet there is no doubt that the popularity of Medjugorje owes a great deal to the promotional efforts of a Catholic movement known as the Charismatic Renewal, whose encounters feature praying in tongues, prophecies, faith healings, and other manifestations of "the gifts of the spirit." Over the years Catholic charismatic groups have functioned as a network of propagation for Medjugorje, organizing countless pilgrimages and spreading the Medjugorje messages through a capillary system of parish contacts. Among the charismatics was the seers' own spiritual adviser, Father Tomislav Vlašić, who in 1981 was working in the town of Capljina, just south of Medjugorje. At a major Charismatic Renewal meeting in Rome that year, Father Vlašić was said to have predicted that the Gospa would soon begin appearing in Yugoslavia. A month later, when the apparitions commenced in Medjugorje, he moved to the Saint James Parish. For three years Vlašić led the visionaries in prayer, gave them guidance, and acted as their public relations consultant. In 1982, when Bishop Žanić questioned Vlašić's role in Medjugorje, the seers took his case to the Blessed Mother, who supposedly praised him with the words: "Thank Tomislav very much for he is guiding you very well." In the late 1980s, however, it was publicly revealed that Father Vlašić had fathered a child with a Franciscan nun and then covered up their affair. Shortly after the scandal broke, he left Medjugorje to establish a mixed male-female religious community in Italy. According to one of the Medjugorje seers, Marija Pavlovic, Mary had endorsed Father Vlašić's Italian initiative with the words, "This is God's plan," but after the Vatican expressed its opposition, Marija issued a formal retraction, saying her earlier statement was false. In 2009, following a Vatican investigation for heresy and sexual misconduct, Pope Benedict XVI removed Vlašić from the priesthood and ordered him "under pain of excommunication" to refrain from making public comments about Medjugorje.

The wheels of ecclesial justice were turning for some of the other Franciscans who managed the parish and the seers, too. Father Zovko, who had been jailed for a year and a half by Yugoslavian authorities on charges of subversion in connection with the apparitions and was considered a saint by many Medjugorje followers, was suspended in 1989 from exercising priestly ministry in the Mostar diocese for insubordination, and by 2009 his Franciscan superiors had removed him to a monastery far from Medjugorje. These cases had a profound influence at the upper levels of the Catholic hierarchy, especially in Rome. Despite the supposed reflowering of the faith among pilgrims, in the eyes of many Vatican officials Medjugorje had become synonymous with disobedience.

Pope Benedict XVI did not like ambiguity. For nearly twenty-four years, as Cardinal Joseph Ratzinger, he had headed the Vatican's Congregation for the Doctrine of the Faith, where reported apparitions are investigated if and when they become too big for a local bishop to handle. Medjugorje had come to his attention in the 1980s, and the congregation's doctrinal experts opted to take the classic prudential approach: don't rush to judgment; wait it out. No one imagined that the apparitions in Medjugorje would go on for decades.

As one of the church's most respected theologians, Cardinal Ratzinger chose his words carefully when it came to apparitions. On one hand, he emphasized that no private apparitions or revelations could possibly add anything essential to the faith. For that reason the doctrinal congregation was always scrupulous about monitoring visionaries who claimed to disclose new truths to be held by all Catholics. As the cardinal himself would point out, even Marian apparitions recognized by the church were not required belief for anyone in the church.

Yet Ratzinger also seemed open to the idea that the increasing number of Mary's appearances represented a "sign of the times" and perhaps was a phenomenon that reflected God's plan for humanity.

"We certainly cannot prevent God from speaking to our time through simple persons and also through extraordinary signs that point to the insufficiency of the cultures stamped by rationalism and positivism that dominate us," was how he put it, in typical Ratzingerian fashion, in a 1985 book-length interview.

But as the millennium approached, the cardinal was seeing too many questionable "signs" on the Catholic horizon. A report by his doctrinal congregation noted a steady increase in "presumed Marian apparitions, messages, stigmata, sweating statues of the Blessed Virgin or Jesus Christ, Eucharistic 'miracles' of various kinds, etc." Some of these episodes proved embarrassing to the Catholic Church. In 1988, in the Italian city of Pescara on the Adriatic Sea, a woman who claimed she had seen Mary about five hundred times announced that at midnight on February 28 a special message from the Blessed Mother would be written brightly in the heavens. Supported by a local priest and tourist officials, the event drew a vast assembly of faithful and curious to the city, where seaside hotels were forced to reopen out of season. On the appointed day an estimated one hundred thousand people stared into the sky for hours, but nothing happened. The following day it was announced that the local priest would withdraw for a period of "psychological rest," and the Pescara seer dropped out of sight.

In early 2003 groups of Brazilian bishops visited Cardinal Ratzinger's office on their once-every-five-years trip to the Vatican, and almost every one of them had a report of local apparitions—often accompanied by new tensions in their dioceses. Some of the prelates, after ruling against apparitions or questioning their authenticity, were facing defiance by lay groups. Cardinal Ratzinger accordingly ordered his staff to review the Vatican's guidelines for judging presumed apparitions or revelations, which had been formulated in 1978, to determine if they could be clarified and strengthened. The Vatican was particularly concerned that modern means of global communication were making the church's cautious, considered approach obsolete. By the time local bishops or the Vatican could even begin to investigate apparitions, they had already become news all over the Internet.

In the case of Medjugorje, Cardinal Ratzinger was especially troubled by the acts of jurisdictional rebellion among the Franciscan pastors and the imperative tone taken by the young visionaries. Yet there was little he could do. As long as the apparitions continued, Medjugorje was considered a "work in progress," and making a definitive judgment about them would be seen as premature. Moreover, Pope John Paul II had a soft spot for Medjugorje, and he was unlikely to approve the suppression of a site drawing millions of people to prayer, confession, and conversion. Although the Polish pope avoided any official pronouncements on Medjugorje, the anecdotal evidence was clear enough. One story, related by Archbishop Harry J. Flynn of Minneapolis–Saint Paul, was widely circulated on pro-Medjugorje websites. In 1988 a group of eight American bishops was lunching with John Paul II at the Vatican when one of them blurted out, "Holy Father, what do you think of Medjugorje?" The pope took a sip of his soup before responding: "Medjugorje? Medjugorje? Medjugorje? Only good things are happening at Medjugorje. People are praying there. People are going to confession. People are adoring the Eucharist, and people are turning to God." Mirjana Dragicevic-Soldo has told pilgrims that she had a private meeting with John Paul II in 1987, and that the pope expressed his support with these words: "I know everything about Medjugorje. I've been following Medjugorje. Ask pilgrims to pray for my intentions, to keep, to take good care of Medjugorje, because Medjugorje is hope for the entire world. And if I were not pope, I would have been in Medjugorje a long time ago."

Cardinal Ratzinger was chosen as John Paul II's successor in 2005, and as Pope Benedict XVI he tried to ignore the matter. But late in 2009 a shadow appeared on Benedict's finely tuned doctrinal radar screen when Cardinal Christoph Schönborn of Austria made a highly publicized pilgrimage to Medjugorje, where he spoke favorably about the apparitions and met with at least one of the visionaries. That prompted a protest from Bishop Ratko Perić of Mostar, who, like his predecessor, Bishop Žanić, was convinced the apparitions were a fraud. Within days Cardinal Schönborn was summoned to Rome for a meeting with the pope, after which Schönborn dutifully faxed an apology to Bishop Perić, explaining rather unconvincingly that his visit had been intended to be "private." Meanwhile, Cardinal José Saraiva Martins, a longtime Vatican official, had weighed in with an interview casting doubts on Medjugorje. Cardinal Saraiva raised issues that were of concern to many Vatican experts: the economic interests behind the Medjugorje apparitions, the strange behavior of the seers, and the disobedience of the Franciscans. He contrasted these with the church-approved apparitions at Fatima in Portugal nearly a century earlier. That was perhaps a natural comparison for the Portuguese-born Saraiva to make, but it left the impression that the cardinals were fighting a proxy war between contending Madonnas: Fatima vs. Medjugorje.

Pope Benedict had heard enough. The divisions over Medjugorje were now making their way into the church hierarchy, and that could not be tolerated. Three months later he appointed a high-level international commission to study and evaluate the events at Medjugorje, and then to deliver a report to the Congregation for the Doctrine of the Faith. The commission included experts in theology, church law, psychology, psychiatry, anthropology, and spirituality. Under the helm of the aging Italian Cardinal Camillo Ruini, the panel began taking testimony from the principal protagonists at Medjugorje, including the visionaries, most of whom were now in their forties. But problems were immediately apparent. For one thing, the mix of the commission members—which included both theological skeptics and Marian experts who were sympathetic to Medjugorje—raised the strong possibility of a deadlocked jury. More challenging was the fact that the apparitions and the messages were still allegedly occurring, so how could any final verdict be rendered? As one Vatican official put it, "Suppose they declare that Mary is truly appearing in Medjugorje, and tomorrow she starts spouting heresy? That's a risk the church has never taken."

While the commission's work advanced in fits and starts, Pope Benedict ordered the translation and publication of the Vatican's revised procedural rules for verifying Marian apparitions. The 1978 guidelines had previously been available only in Latin, and exclusively to bishops, though few bishops had actually read them. Moreover, Vatican officials were now convinced that the boom in apparitions required better preparation at all pastoral levels, not only among the church hierarchy. The document advised that, given the speed of modern communication and the ease of international travel, church authorities might need to act more quickly and decisively when faced with an alleged apparition or similar supernatural occurrence. Despite such pressures, however, bishops were not to rush to judgment. On the contrary, the Vatican said, the potential for global attention made it all the more important to exercise caution and prudence. Bishops should first determine the true facts of the situation and also take into account the personal virtues of the visionaries, the possibility of psychological disorders or delusional behavior, doctrinal errors in messages, and the potential for economic exploitation. The document spelled out when responsibility for discernment should pass from a local bishop to regional or national conferences of bishops and, in rare cases, to the Vatican itself. Its strong recommendation was to handle such matters at the local level, because once the Vatican was involved, they became a burden on the entire church.

Though only a few pages long, the Vatican text was distilled from centuries of experience. During that time many apparitions had come and gone and been forgotten, which the document recognized might be a good thing. When an apparition is doubtful but not particularly disruptive, it said, a local bishop might simply allow it to "fall into oblivion." That strategy had generally worked well for the church, but in the contemporary world it required bishops to keep local enthusiasm in check and the media at bay—not an easy task.

The difference between having a bishop in support of an apparition and one opposed was illustrated by two unusual sets of events that occurred in central Wisconsin in the mid-nineteenth and mid-twentieth centuries.

Adele Brise was the daughter of Belgian settlers, the oldest of four children. The family worked a farm near Champion, not far from Green Bay, where immigrant farmers and lumbermen struggled for survival. One October morning in 1859 Adele, then twenty-eight, was carrying grain to a mill when she suddenly saw a woman clothed in white, standing next to the trail in the woods. The apparition quickly vanished but left Adele terrified. The figure reappeared the following day, as Adele walked to Mass, and she asked her parish priest for advice. He told her to ask the woman who she was and what she wanted. On her walk back home, Adele encountered the woman for the third and final time, and worked up the courage to ask her identity. "I am the Queen of Heaven," she replied and made two requests of Adele: to pray for the conversion of sinners, and to reach out to children "in this wild country" and teach them about salvation.

Although she had no church facilities at her disposal, Adele set to work immediately, walking from house to house and asking if she could help instruct children. She soon became a familiar and beloved figure in a region of rural Wisconsin that had few priests or catechists. Later she founded a small school, which was expanded and staffed by religious sisters, although Adele herself remained a laywoman. When she died in 1896, the apparition site was known as the Shrine of Our Lady of Good Help, and it had attracted a growing number of visitors.

As the decades passed, however, Adele Brise's story came to be treated more as cultural folklore than as an established apparition. That changed in 2009, when Bishop David L. Ricken of Green Bay launched an official investigation into the apparitions. After international Marian experts and other church authorities completed their work in 2010, Bishop Ricken celebrated Mass at the shrine and announced the apparitions "worthy of belief," making the site the only officially designated place in the United States where Mary is said to have appeared. No formal Vatican approval was necessary; all it took was an energetic bishop. What established this apparition on the Catholic devotional map was, above all, its simplicity: a vision, a message, and a life of holiness.

In contrast, the alleged apparitions in Necedah, a tiny village about one hundred miles west of Green Bay, created only headaches for the church. In late 1949 Mary Ann Van Hoof, a forty-year-old mother of eight who, with her husband, worked a dairy farm on the outskirts of Necedah, began reporting apparitions of the Blessed Mother. The visions continued for several years, drawing media attention and large crowds. At an apparition on August 15, 1950, the feast of Mary's Assumption into heaven, tens of thousands of people gathered in Necedah to witness a promised Miracle of the Sun. Some claimed to have seen the sun spin; most saw nothing.

Van Hoof continued to report alleged messages from Mary for many years, and their tone became increasingly apocalyptic and political. Van Hoof spoke of a threatened Soviet invasion, thousands of priests acting as Communist spies, and a plot using schools and government institutions to subvert the American way of life. It sounded a great deal like an ecclesial version of the Red Scare promoted by the Wisconsin senator Joseph McCarthy. Later, in the 1960s, Van Hoof would criticize the Second Vatican Council and the new Mass, and warn that the Catholic Church was full of traitors and heretics.

From the beginning, church authorities in Wisconsin were skeptical of Van Hoof's claims. A few months after the apparitions began, Bishop John Treacy of La Crosse had called them "extremely doubtful" and warned against publicizing them. He tried, unsuccessfully, to prevent Van Hoof and her followers from promoting the events. In 1955 the bishop formally declared the visions false and banned worship services at the Van Hoof farm. In 1975 Treacy's successor, Bishop Frederick W. Freking, placed Van Hoof under "interdict," a step just short of excommunication, prompting the seer to break with the Catholic Church and affiliate with the schismatic Old Catholic Church of North America. Van Hoof died in 1984, but the shrine at Necedah still operates, drawing sparse groups of elderly visitors. For Catholic Church authorities in the United States, Necedah still represents a worst-case scenario for Marian apparitions, as it contained all the ingredients for disaster: dubious visions and unorthodox content, massive publicity, defiance of the hierarchy, and potential damage to the faith of gullible devotees.

But Necedah was not unique. In the wake of the changes introduced by Vatican II, other apparitions were said to be issuing warnings against modernizing trends in the church. In Bayside, New York, in the late 1960s, for example, a Catholic housewife began claiming visions of Mary and the saints, relaying heavenly criticism of such practices as distribution of Communion in the hand, ordination of married men as deacons, and women wearing pants. In 1986 the bishop of Brooklyn finally declared that the apparitions lacked all authenticity and contradicted the church's teaching.

Vatican experts estimate that in modern times, the Catholic Church has investigated more than a thousand alleged appearances of Mary, of which only a handful have received official church approval. Of that select group, two stand out: Lourdes and Fatima. For different reasons and in different historical contexts, both caught the imagination of large groups of Catholics around the world, attracting millions of pilgrims each year. And both have earned support from the highest levels of the church hierarchy, including several visits from modern popes.

The story of Bernadette Soubirous is one of simple faith, and it's one that Vatican officials often point to as a model of authenticity. The daughter of an impoverished couple in Lourdes, a town in the foothills of the French Pyrénées, Bernadette was a sickly child who suffered from severe asthma. Shortly after her fourteenth birthday in 1858, while collecting firewood in a grotto on the banks of a local river, she had a vision of "a lady dressed in white" who held a rosary in her hands. Startled and somewhat afraid, Bernadette nevertheless returned to the spot in the days that followed, and the apparitions continued. She was soon accompanied by her friends and then by a growing number of townspeople. None of them could see the mysterious lady, however, and Bernadette came under pressure from civil authorities to recant her story. By now the apparition had begun to speak to Bernadette. At one point the lady asked the girl to take a drink from a spring in the grotto; there was no spring, but at that moment water began bubbling up from the ground. In the years to come the "miraculous" waters of Lourdes would draw thousands of pilgrims in search of healing.

Among the skeptics was the local pastor, Father Dominique Peyramale, a gruff man who thought the apparitions were a hoax and who refused to witness the events in the grotto. As a first step in his investigation, he told Bernadette to ask the "lady in white" what her name was. Bernadette returned a few days later with the strange response: "I am the Immaculate Conception." Mary's "Immaculate Conception" was a dogma that had been promulgated a few years earlier by Pope Pius IX, but it was a term that would have been unknown to an uneducated, semiliterate peasant girl who spoke only the local dialect. From that moment on, the astonished Father Peyramale believed that the Blessed Mother was truly appearing to the girl.

Bernadette experienced eighteen apparitions at Lourdes. Although Mary spoke very few words to her, the story of these encounters has attracted and inspired Catholics for more than 150 years. The fundamental message conveyed to the girl at Lourdes was divine favor for the poor and the humble, the promise of eternal happiness in the life to come, and a call for prayer and compassion for the sick. At the request of the Blessed Mother, a shrine was built at the site and drew unprecedented throngs. But Bernadette herself never really became a local celebrity, and in fact was subjected to derision by many of the townspeople. She eventually entered a convent in central France, where for years she endured the scorn and envy of some of the sisters. She was progressively weakened by disease, and when the sisters asked if she had heard about the miraculous healings at Lourdes, she said no. Bernadette reportedly accepted her own pain and suffering with the words, "You see, my job is to be ill." She died of tuberculosis in 1879, at the age of thirty-five, and was proclaimed a saint in 1933.

To church officials the humility of Bernadette has always weighed heavily in favor of her credibility. In evaluating apparitions the personal holiness of the seer is crucial. Likewise, innocence, unworldliness, and even inexperience in mystical affairs are seen as positive markers. Jesuit Father Giandomenico Mucci, a scholar in Rome who has written extensively about apparitions, said Mary has a history of appearing to people who are not highly educated, are less sophisticated, and are relatively unknown.

"If Barack Obama or Silvio Berlusconi says he's seen the Madonna, the church wouldn't give it much credence. The more a person is young, simple, and ignorant, the more the event is credible, because there's no cultural influence, no influence by theology or literature, no knowledge of the mystical experiences of others," Father Mucci explained.

Experts in spiritual mysticism sometimes distinguish between a vision and an apparition. A vision is generally understood as a private experience that results from a process of intense spiritual effort, reflecting, in a sense, a desire to see the supernatural. An apparition typically arrives unexpectedly, without warning, to people who are often spiritually unprepared to deal with it.

Apparitions usually occur in a public place. But what many people fail to understand, Father Mucci said, is that although they are in the "public domain," apparitions do not transpire in the objective material world, but in the subjective mind of the visionary. "At Lourdes, the Madonna was not really in the grotto. She was in the mind of Bernadette, who was touched by a special grace," he explained. That does not mean that an apparition is a mere fantasy, but it does explain why other witnesses fail to see Mary in the same way. This subtle distinction has been an important one for Catholic scholars through the centuries. Saint Thomas Aquinas made a similar point when he said that Jesus appeared to his disciples after his death not in his real body, but in a "visible form." Father Adolphe Tanquerey, one of the greatest modern experts on spiritual theology, applied the same principle to the Blessed Mother. At Lourdes, Tanquerey said, Mary's body was not present, but there was "a sensible form which represents her."

The differences between Lourdes and Medjugorje are telling, in the eyes of several church experts. For Bernadette the apparitions opened a chapter of suffering and led to a life of relative obscurity; the events at Medjugorje propelled its seers to fame and, in some cases, material gain. Bernadette reported simple and direct messages from Mary; at

Medjugorje the messages have been myriad and ambiguous. At Lourdes Mary appeared as a sympathetic protectress and a source of consolation; at Medjugorje she occasionally gave the impression of being demanding and impatient. Lourdes has been the site of sixty-nine healings judged miraculous by a Catholic medical panel; no such healing has been authenticated at Medjugorje.

Above all, the internal conflicts at Medjugorje have been of particular concern. Father Mucci, who believes that Mary did appear at Lourdes, explains the main reason for his skepticism about Medjugorje: "I find it hard to believe that the Mother of God reveals herself to children who are being directed spiritually by two Franciscans suspended from priestly ministry. We can't expect Mary to have a degree in canon law, but she should at least be aware of the general rules of the church."

Experts in Mariology often argue that apparitions don't take place in a cultural vacuum, and that Mary typically appears at crucial historical moments in the life of a people or a nation. From that perspective, the apparitions at Lourdes have been interpreted as a counterpoint to French positivism, the supposed triumph of empirical sciences over religion and metaphysics, which dominated the country's political and social development in the nineteenth century. Lourdes, for all its eventual commercialism, stood as a vibrant expression of Christian charity toward those suffering in body and spirit, attracting many people alienated or left behind by the increasingly secular drift of French society. Nearly sixty years later, another apparition of Mary would capture public attention, this time due to prophetic warnings about the fate of all humanity in the twentieth century.

The appearance of Mary in Fatima, Portugal, took place in 1917 as Europe was being devastated by World War I. The small village of Fatima, north of Lisbon, had been named after a Moorish princess, one of many signs of Arabic influence in a country that spent five centuries under Islamic rule. In a field owned by her family, Lucia dos Santos, ten years old, tended sheep with her younger cousins Francisco and Jacinta Marto. Their story actually begins in 1916, when the children experienced three visions of a young man surrounded by light. He called himself the Angel of Peace and asked them to pray with him. Unnerved and somewhat embarrassed, they said nothing to their parents or friends about these encounters. As it turned out, they were just the preliminaries.

On May 13, 1917, the children saw a flash like lightning in a clear sky and looked up to see a lady "clothed in white" and bathed in supernatural light. She told them she had come from heaven, asked the youngsters to sacrifice and suffer for the conversion of sinners, and promised that she would appear again on the thirteenth of each month for the next six months. Word quickly spread, provoking some interest but much derision among the local populace. On June 13 about fifty people showed up to witness Mary's promised appearance to the children. She encouraged the young seers to fast and to pray the rosary well, promised cures for some people, and asked the children to promote a particular devotion to her Immaculate Heart. With each new apparition, Mary's messages and instructions grew more complex. She also gave the seers three "secrets" that were said to predict the future.

Civil authorities reacted with alarm to the reported visions and the increasingly large crowds that had begun to gather on the thirteenth of each subsequent month. At one point they apprehended the young seers and threatened them with death if they did not disclose Mary's secrets; the children refused to comply and were released. The events reached a climax at the final apparition on October 13, 1917, the day when Mary had promised to perform a miracle "so that all may believe." Tens of thousands descended upon the field at Fatima, including reporters from secular publications that had ridiculed the children's story. Heavy rain fell throughout the morning, but at noon, the time of the apparition, the sun broke through the clouds in dramatic fashion. Lucia shouted, "Look at the sun!" Cries went up from the crowd: "A miracle! A miracle!" Many people—though not everyone—later claimed to have seen the sun dance and zigzag across the sky, turn colors, and spin wildly like a wheel on fire. They were convinced that Mary had, indeed, given the world a supernatural sign, one that soon became known as the Miracle of the Sun.

Life went on in Fatima after the apparitions ceased. The war ended in 1918, followed by the global influenza pandemic that killed at least fifty million people, including Francisco and Jacinta Marto. Lucia dos Santos entered a convent in 1925, and spent much of her life writing her memoirs. In 1941, at the request of the local bishop, Lucia disclosed the first two secrets supposedly given the children by Mary twenty-four years earlier. The first was a vision of hell and the horrible suffering that sinners endured. The second foretold the end of World War I and warned that a greater war would follow—a prediction seen by some as prophetic, and by others as suspect, given that World War II was already well under way when the secret was revealed. Part of Mary's second message focused on Russia, where the Bolshevik Revolution of 1917 had sent a shudder throughout much of Europe's ruling class. Mary allegedly told the Fatima children that if the pope consecrated Russia to her Immaculate Heart, the country would be converted; if not, the errors that had arisen in Russia would spread, and war and persecution of the church would follow.

Lucia did not feel the time was right to divulge the third secret of Fatima, which was rumored to predict a series of apocalyptic events. Naturally this spurred intense speculation among Catholics everywhere. Under pressure from Portuguese church authorities, she wrote down the final secret in 1944 and sealed it in an envelope to be opened only in 1960. At the Vatican's request, the sealed envelope was brought to Rome. The letter was indeed opened, not in 1960, but in 1959, by Pope John XXIII, who refused to disclose its contents. According to Cardinal Alfredo Ottaviani, a leading doctrinal official at the Vatican, John XXIII sealed the secret in another envelope and "sent it to be placed in one of those archives that are like a well where the paper sinks deeply into the dark, black depths, and where no one can distinguish anything at all." That only added to the conjecture, and for decades Fatima devotees asked the question: What is the Vatican hiding?

More than four decades later, during the jubilee year 2000, Pope John Paul II decided not only to release the text of the third secret but to offer, in a forty-three-page booklet, a detailed church commentary on its meaning. The move reflected the Polish pope's conviction that Fatima's final prophecy concerned his own life and pontificate, not the end of the world. By divulging the secret, the church could put to rest unwarranted fears and fantasies. Many Vatican officials disagreed with the pope's decision, which they believed illustrated the perils of digging too deeply into private revelations.

As published by the Vatican, the third secret, described in a mere three hundred words by Lucia, was a vision of a "bishop dressed in white," presumed to be the pope, going up a steep mountain toward a large cross with other bishops, priests, and nuns. "Before reaching there, the Holy Father passed through a big city half in ruins and half trembling with halting step, afflicted with pain and sorrow, he prayed for the souls of the corpses he met on his way. Having reached the top of the mountain, on his knees at the foot of the big cross, he was killed by a group of soldiers who fired bullets and arrows at him," Lucia wrote. In the vision all the church personnel are ultimately killed, and angels gather up "the blood of the martyrs."

The Vatican viewed this as a symbolic prophecy of the church's twentieth-century struggles under political oppression, in particular Soviet-era Communism, and the ultimate triumph of the faith. Pope John Paul gave the secret a much more personal interpretation. He was convinced that he was "the bishop dressed in white," and that Mary had saved his life after the papal assassination attempt on May 13, 1981, the feast of Our Lady of Fatima. It was while recovering in Rome's Gemelli Hospital following the near-fatal shooting that John Paul first asked his aides to retrieve the third secret of Fatima from the Vatican archives, so he could read it. In subsequent years, with the fall of the Soviet empire and the end of its persecution against the Catholic Church, Pope John Paul was even more certain that Mary was guiding him and the church through a delicate and risky phase of world history.

The Vatican disclosure and annotated commentary was, in a sense, intended as the final word on Fatima. Still, it left many people unconvinced and disappointed. Skeptics immediately observed that the third secret and the Vatican interpretation differed on a key point: In the Fatima vision, the pope was killed. John Paul II survived his shooting, which was carried out by a lone gunman, not "a group of soldiers."

When Cardinal Joseph Ratzinger, who helped write the Vatican commentary, was asked about the discrepancies at a Vatican press conference, he seemed to distance himself from John Paul II's mystical reading of Fatima. "There does not exist an official definition or official interpretation of this vision on the part of the church," he said. Ratzinger observed that the language of the third secret was symbolic and therefore open to interpretation, with a "margin of error." In the church's tradition, he explained, prophecy is not like a "film preview" of an exact sequence of events, but an offering of potentially helpful signs. He added that while the Fatima message could be useful to some, belief in such revelations was not obligatory: "No great mystery is revealed; nor is the future unveiled."

Cardinal Ratzinger's comments incensed Fatima devotees, for it was as if the Vatican was deliberately deflating the most prophetic Marian apparition in history. Many suspected the Vatican had not told the whole story. Where were the end-of-the-world scenarios? Where was the divine punishment for a world gone wrong? And if the third secret did not warn of the apocalypse or a global catastrophe like nuclear holocaust, why had the Vatican kept it secret for so long?

The coauthor of the Vatican commentary was Cardinal Ratzinger's assistant, then-Archbishop Tarcisio Bertone, who early in 2000 had made a confidential visit to Lucia dos Santos at her Carmelite convent in Portugal. Bertone reported that Lucia had approved the Vatican's interpretation of the secret and confirmed that the text, as published, was complete. That prompted critics to speculate that Bertone himself was the architect of a plot to dilute the real Fatima message, perhaps because—as some commentators had long believed, based on Lucia's other writings—it prophesied a terrible crisis *within* the Catholic Church, a time when church leadership would lose the true faith and the Antichrist would sit on the throne of Peter. In a book-length interview in 2007, Cardinal Bertone dismissed such accusations as "absolutely crazy."

But the skeptics, many of them Catholic traditionalists, have kept up their criticism, and to this day some claim that the Vatican continues to hide a "fourth secret" of Fatima. They say the Vatican's version has lulled the faithful into a false sense of security by suggesting that the prophesied problems are behind the church, when in reality the worst is yet to come. Far from ending speculation, the Vatican's revelation of the secret only spawned a new generation of conspiracy theories and accusations. For months afterward, there were rumblings in the Roman Curia, mainly directed at Pope John Paul II. As one veteran Vatican official put it: "This was a carnival act, and it made the church look foolish. The third secret was in the archives, and it should have stayed there. When it comes to things like apparitions and messages from heaven, the less we say, the better."

Father Salvatore Perrella didn't sit still for very long. Fueled by frequent deliveries of espresso on a weekday evening, he roamed his office like a cat, moving from one bookshelf to another in search of a particular volume, digging out one of his scholarly papers from an assortment of briefcases, or picking up the phone to ask a student why he hadn't shown up for class that day. Short of stature and barrel-chested, Perrella spoke in a clipped Neapolitan accent, delivering emphatic and precise answers to questions about Marian apparitions through the centuries: "Apparitions always speak to the people. Because people—whether their culture is primitive, or rational, or technological—cannot get along without emotion. As a church, we need to put together reason and sentiment. Apparitions can be useful in this regard. They remind us that God is present in human history, and they do it through the church's best image, Mary. But when it comes to the content of the faith—and people don't want to hear this—apparitions are not necessary. If Mary appears, she has nothing new to tell us. And if we overemphasize the importance of Marian apparitions, we are really damaging God's project and damaging the dignity of Mary."

The sixty-three-year-old Perrella, a member of the Marianist religious order, is the closest thing to a Vatican authority on the Virgin Mary. A prolific author on Marian topics, he has been a consultant to the Congregation for the Doctrine of the Faith and a key member of the Vatican's investigating commission on Medjugorje. He is dean of the Marianum Pontifical Theological Faculty, an institution that proudly traces its history to the seventeenth century. Situated on Rome's Janiculum Hill behind a crumbling brick gate lined with garbage bins, the Marianum has seen better days. Its students are few, its facilities are outdated, and its decor consists of potted plastic ferns and rudimentary mosaics of the Madonna. But inside Father Perrella's office, the energy level never abates. When he is asked about the bishops' role in judging the validity of apparitions, sparks immediately fly.

"For years many bishops didn't know how to react to claims of an apparition. That's why the Vatican decided to publish the norms. The bishops need to know these things! It's a problem for them, for the diocese, for the whole church! The first principle is prudence. The second is patience—to wait for an opportune time. The bishops' job is to let the cream settle, not to make whipped cream right away! And that means resisting the curiosity and the morbid interest of the mass media, which are infernal when it comes to apparitions," Perrella said.

Historically visions of Mary have been relatively rare, yet since Medjugorje became popular in the early 1980s, the Vatican has been tracking about forty other Marian apparitions throughout eastern Europe and Africa. Experts called it the "Marian corridor," and wondered whether it was a case of spiritual contagion or a genuine series of mystical events.

For some Catholics, Mary's maternal, comforting nature has made her a more approachable figure than Christ. She seems to fulfill a need among the faithful for a mediator, an advocate in heaven for their earthly causes, a role that has been underlined by her miraculous appearances in various countries and cultures. But because Marian apparitions are typically grassroots events, they are problematic for the hierarchy. On one hand, church authorities have to be open to the traditional concept of *sensus fidelium,* the sense of the faithful, which includes the ability of the "people of God" to intuitively recognize divine signs—with or without a stamp of approval from Rome. But, according to Father Perrella, modern claims of Marian apparitions often come from "uneducated people who let their feelings get the best of them" and who believe Mary is omnipotent. In many cases, he said, these are individuals who don't go to church regularly and who have an immature understanding of faith. For all these reasons, he said, the Vatican has to exercise caution and avoid "playing to the pews" by approving apparitions just to please large groups of Catholics.

"Remember, if the church has never pronounced on the authenticity of an apparition, then it's not a scandal if it turns out to be false," he said and offered a recent example. In late 2013, in a small church about four blocks from the Marianum in the Rome quarter of Monteverde Vecchio, worshippers reported that a white statue of Mary was turning reddish in the evening. The "miracle of Monteverde" soon made headlines and began drawing large crowds. Father Perrella, who acts as chaplain to the church, looked into the affair. The "miracle" turned out to be an effect of new interior lighting, and local residents quickly lost interest. A month later, however, the statue's cheeks turned decidedly red, and the excitement returned. This time, an investigation discovered that someone had rubbed the statue with lipstick, perhaps as part of a Halloween prank. Father Perrella denounced it as an act of vandalism or, at least, a joke in bad taste. Privately he said it offered a lesson: "When it comes to these phenomena, church officials cannot simply go along with the enthusiasm whipped up by news reports, or they'll end up in the nuthouse."

Small-scale Marian "miracles" like crying statues or bleeding icons are treated like brush fires by church superiors, who attempt to extinguish them before they can spread and incite popular enthusiasm. The Vatican itself generally tries not to get involved, but there are exceptions, as in the case of the Weeping Madonna of Syracuse, on Sicily's eastern coast. In 1953 a young Sicilian couple, Angelo and Antonina Iannuso, received a plaster relief of Mary as a wedding gift and hung it in the bedroom. Later that year Antonina became pregnant, and suffered from a life-threatening complication, eclampsia, which caused her to have convulsions. Early one morning she experienced a strong seizure that left her temporarily blind. Five hours later she regained her sight, and the first thing she saw were tears flowing from the image of Mary on her wall. Her astounded family also witnessed the tears running down Mary's cheeks and onto Antonina's bed. They tried to dry the face of the image, but it continued to weep, attracting huge crowds to the house. By now the image was displayed outside the small apartment, and excited pilgrims collected Mary's tears on pieces of cloth. Several people, including Antonina, were said to have been miraculously healed. The local archbishop soon sent an investigating committee, which removed the backing from the relief and found no evidence of tampering. Doctors were called in to analyze the liquid, and pronounced it to be human tears. Four days after it began, the weeping stopped. Soon afterward, the archbishop of Syracuse recognized the phenomenon as supernatural, a judgment confirmed by the bishops of Sicily at the end of the year. In 1954 Pope Pius XII added his endorsement, saying Mary's tears had spoken to the world in a "mysterious language." When Pope John Paul II visited Syracuse in late 1994, he said the purported miracle held deep meaning for the church: "The tears of the Madonna belong to the order of signs. She is a mother crying when she sees her children threatened by a spiritual or physical evil."

The words of the Polish pope caused some concern at the Vatican, where officials knew that most crying or bleeding statues, when inspected, turned out to be hoaxes. The Vatican was already having a huge problem with one such case in South Korea, where a Catholic laywoman, Julia Youn Hong-sun, had claimed to be receiving revelations from Mary after her statue of the Blessed Mother began weeping in 1985. The twenty-two-inch-tall plaster statue, which stood in the woman's home in the city of Naju, first shed human tears, then drops of blood. Well publicized by Julia and her advisers, the prodigy drew thousands of faithful, including some foreign priests and bishops. The tears ended after seven hundred days, but the messages from Mary continued. Relayed by the visionary, they took on an apocalyptic tone, warning that the devil was mobilizing priests to betray the church, that the world would be "reduced to ashes," and that only Mary could "turn away the wrath of God the Father." The events at Naju took an even more unusual turn in 1991. After receiving Communion one day, Julia claimed that the Eucharistic host had turned to flesh and begun to bleed on her tongue. In effect, her supporters declared, the Eucharist had changed into the visible flesh and blood of Christ. The alleged miracle occurred several times in subsequent years, and when it did, Julia was only too happy to open her mouth and exhibit the bloody evidence to astounded visitors.

In 1995 Julia Youn visited the Vatican as part of a Korean pilgrimage. The encounter was a classic ambush of a pope who routinely invited outside guests to morning Mass in his private chapel. During the liturgy, attended by about fifty people, Julia received Communion with the others. As she later described it, the host immediately began to swell in her mouth. After the Mass was over, Julia stood in a receiving line, filmed by a Korean video operator who was there to document the episode. When Pope John Paul approached her to give his blessing, she opened her mouth to exhibit what looked like a bloody piece of meat in her mouth. The pope flinched and drew back, while his aides, incensed at this staged spectacle, rushed in to move the pontiff away. The video and photographs would later be used by Julia's promoters to suggest that John Paul II had not only witnessed the Eucharistic "miracle" but also recognized and blessed it.

Two years later the Archdiocese of Kwangju, which had been closely monitoring the Naju visionary, declared that the events there were not supernatural and banned Catholics from participating in ceremonies at the Blessed Mother's Mountain, the spiritual center established by Julia and her handlers. In a 2008 decision backed by the Vatican's doctrinal officials, Julia Youn and her followers were declared excommunicated for promoting the apparitions and pretending that the hierarchy approved them. Julia and her supporters did not give up, however. Over the years they have continued to inundate the Congregation for the Doctrine of the Faith with letters urging a reversal of the excommunication.

One of the particular aspects of the Naju incident touched a theological nerve at the Vatican: Mary supposedly began referring to herself as "Co-Redemptrix" in her messages to Julia Youn—that is, she shared with Christ the role of redeemer. For the Catholic Church, Christ is the unique savior, an identity he shares with no one, not even his mother. This issue had also surfaced in previous apparitions. In the 1950s a visionary in the Netherlands reported that Mary was demanding that the Catholic Church declare her "Co-Redemptrix, mediatrix and advocate," titles that would be part of a fifth and final Marian dogma. (The four official Marian dogmas concern Mary's divine motherhood, her perpetual virginity, her Immaculate Conception, and her Assumption into heaven.) The Amsterdam apparitions were eventually dismissed by church authorities, but the notion of Mary as Co-Redeemer would not go away. In 1971 a Quebec woman who believed she was the reincarnation of the Blessed Mother founded the Army of Mary, which promoted the Co-Redemptrix role. After several years of the group's sparring with local bishops, the Vatican formally declared its members excommunicated. A "Mary is God" Catholic movement in the Philippines held that Mary was "the soul of the Holy Spirit"; it flourished for a while but was eventually shut down by church leaders. In the 1990s the issue was thrust into the media spotlight when conservative Catholics in the United States mounted petition drives urging Pope John Paul to declare the Co-Redeemer concept as dogma. This time the Vatican responded by convening a commission of theologians, who gave a resounding no to the proposal. Father Perrella acted as spokesman for the panel, explaining that Christ is the only redeemer and "we cannot decentralize his figure in favor of his mother." Indeed, the church teaches that Mary herself, although born without stain of sin, depended on Christ for redemption. Perrella said the petitions circulating in the United States were "theologically inadequate, historically a mistake, pastorally imprudent and ecumenically unacceptable." On a more fundamental level, there was something incongruous about the Mother of God appearing on earth in order to demand more ecclesiastical titles for herself.

In reviewing the Medjugorje apparitions, Father Perrella and others on the Vatican commission took a close look at two particular messages in which the Blessed Mother spoke of herself as "Mediatrix." In March 2012 the Gospa stated: "Dear children! I am coming among you because I desire to be your mother—your intercessor. I desire to be the bond between you and the Heavenly Father—your Mediatrix." For some theologians the statement was a little too ambiguous. Although "mediator" is an ancient title given to Mary and the saints as intercessors, the Medjugorje message appeared to hint at a new and more official role, a role that is completely unnecessary, in the view of Vatican experts. In their judgment the church doesn't need a mediator between God and man because it already has one—the Son of God, who gave his life on the cross.

Critics have argued that when it comes to judging apparitions and Marian messages, the Vatican today is setting the bar too high. Father René Laurentin, a French theologian who has strongly supported Medjugorje, complained in 2007 that the Vatican has adopted a predominantly dismissive attitude toward Catholic visionaries.

"Apparitions are not given much credit at present—they are seen very badly in the church. When the apparitions are historic ones, it's magnificent, and the Virgin can be honored in her sanctuaries. But when she appears now, this seems very dangerous, and one can't touch it," he said and cited Medjugorje as a prime example. "There are conversions there every day, but the bishop is against it. And when Rome protects and covers the bishops, one can't say Rome is in favor of the apparitions."

In the debate over Medjugorje, many of the church's experts long ago divided into two camps: those who believe Mary is truly appearing, and those who think the visionaries, consciously or not, are propagating a spiritual deception. There is a third possibility that is sometimes discussed in hushed tones at the Vatican, a hypothesis that, in the judgment of classic writers on mystical experiences, must always be taken into account: that what appears on the surface as the holiness of Mary is, in reality, the work of the devil.

From the earliest history of the church its leaders have warned that one of the most insidious traps for spiritual visionaries is Satan's ability to masquerade as a friend, an ally, or even a divine figure. Saint Paul said the devil can appear as an "angel of light," misleading the innocent with temptations—an admonition that was echoed by the great Spanish mystics Saint John of the Cross and Saint Teresa of Ávila. In Italy a classic case of this took place in the early twentieth century. Saint Gemma Galgani was a mystic whose supernatural visions were deemed authentic by the church. She once reported that she was visited by a beautiful young man, dressed in a white robe with a silver sash, who said he was sent as an angel from heaven. Only when he began to tempt her with shameful sins did she realize she was dealing with the devil.

Distinguishing between a divine apparition and a diabolical trick has always required careful discernment, focusing on the integrity of the seer, the content of messages, and the effect of apparitions on the wider community. Father Adolphe Tanquerey wrote in his classic work *The Spiritual Life* that it is easy for those seeking supernatural signs to "mistake for divine inspirations what is but the product of a feverish imagination, or even a diabolical suggestion."

The case for suspecting diabolical influence in Medjugorje has been summarized most convincingly by the English Marian expert Donal A. Foley in his 2011 book *Medjugorje Revisited*. Foley, who concluded that Medjugorje is most likely "an enormous religious fraud," found many suspect elements in the behavior of the young seers and the supposed messages of Mary—elements that suggested the devil, not the Blessed Mother, might be at work here. For example, according to the Medjugorje visionaries, Mary appeared with trembling hands, holding "something that looks like a baby," but which later she nearly drops. She can be touched, even caressed, but her robes are "like steel." Unlike other apparitions of Mary in church history, the Gospa has burst out laughing from time to time, for no apparent reason. When the pastors suggested that Mary move her apparitions into Saint James Church, in the presence of the Blessed Sacrament, the seers said Mary appeared to resist the idea. At the beginning of the apparitions, she made no attempt to initiate conversation or deliver a message but instead simply allowed the children to become accustomed to her presence—as if the Blessed Mother had come with no specific purpose. This was a Mary who responded to some questions in the manner of an oracle, and who did not hesitate to side with Franciscan priests in their dispute with the bishop. Sowing division in the church is the devil's goal, critics say, and Medjugorje has not only exacerbated long-standing conflicts but helped create new ones. This was also a Mary who from time to time expressed rather unorthodox opinions, such as the idea that all religious faiths are equal before God, that people in heaven are present in both body and soul, and that those in hell are there because they have committed sins so grave that they are unforgivable by God.

Even the Franciscan pastors, in the first days of the apparitions, questioned whether the children might be seeing the devil in disguise. Father Jozo Zovko, in a taped interview with Mirjana Dragicevic, asked the seer directly: "Aren't you perhaps afraid that Satan can pretend and say: 'I am the Blessed Virgin Mary?'" Mirjana dismissed the possibility. Interrogating another visionary, Ivanka Ivankovic, Father Zovko objected that the crowds that gathered at the apparition site were less than pious, and that cursing was frequently reported. "Can't you see that Satan is present there and not the Gospa? At Lourdes people do not curse," he reminded her. A few days later, after the visions moved into his church, Father Zovko overcame his skepticism and he became one of the strongest supporters of the Medjugorje apparitions. Oddly, two years later, in 1983, Mirjana reported that she had indeed seen the devil, a dark and hideous figure who appeared instead of Mary one evening, laughing and taunting. After a while Satan departed and Mary emerged, assuring Mirjana that the incident was a "trial" and would not happen again.

Some analysts have found tantalizing signs of diabolical influence in a phenomenon that has occasionally been described by pilgrims to Medjugorje: a sense that evil was suddenly very present. It is not all that uncommon, for example, to come upon a pilgrim writhing on the ground on Apparition Hill, held down by others, apparently engaged in a convulsive struggle with the devil. Episodes of possession, exorcism, and deliverance are also frequent occurrences at Medjugorje, according to priests who escort groups of visitors there. They claim that the demons that accompany pilgrims become enraged at the high level of holiness at Medjugorje and manifest themselves in guttural cries, snarling, and cursing. At other times, however, even when there is no evidence of possession, visitors may unexpectedly feel a certain malevolence in the air. Joan Ohnmacht, a Rhode Island Catholic who was visiting Medjugorje in 2014, said she had experienced many graces during her pilgrimage. But she also recalled a moment when the sky suddenly darkened, bringing with it a sense of foreboding. "That was a bad thing, not a good thing. There was something very bad happening. People ran in—it got dark, the wind started swirling, it was crazy. It was like something Satanic, some of that stuff. It was pretty bad."

The transformations experienced by the village of Medjugorje since the apparitions began—the influx of pilgrims, the economic expansion and decline, the terrible violence of the war years, the worsening conflict with church authorities—have left many villagers with an uneasy feeling of apprehension. According to Donal Foley and other researchers, this can only be understood in the context of the local population's "primitive spiritual universe," which has roots in the era of the Bogomils. Some experts say the Bogomils' heresy of dualism—the idea that both God and the devil are deities engaged in an ageless battle— is reflected today at Medjugorje in the persistent concept of a "middle field," a realm where the balance between good and evil can sometimes be disturbed. In this view, the apparitions are not simply a pious gift of grace, but a dramatic chapter of a struggle in which the devil is always a key protagonist.

The devil's possible "strategy" at Medjugorje has been outlined by critics of the apparitions. First, convince many of the faithful that the apparitions are authentic. Next, aggravate the divisions among church leaders over the authenticity of the apparitions and messages. When the hierarchy issues its negative judgment, persuade devotees that the "real" faith is found in Medjugorje, not in their local parishes or at the Vatican. Finally, when Medjugorje is ultimately unmasked as a fraud, tempt its disillusioned followers to abandon the faith entirely.

No one at the Vatican has stated publicly that the devil is behind Medjugorje. But one outspoken retired Italian prelate and longtime exorcist, Bishop Andrea Gemma, made headlines in 2008 when he called Medjugorje "an absolutely diabolical event." Bishop Gemma said it was obvious that financial interests were behind the apparitions, which he characterized as a "gold mine" for the sponsors. The disobedience and misconduct of the local pastors was only another scandalous indication. As for the visionaries, they were "playing the devil's game," Gemma declared. "These people claim to be in contact with the Madonna, but in reality are inspired solely and exclusively by Satan."

No doubt Bishop Gemma and other critics would be numbered among the betrayers of the faith, those denounced by the Gospa in one of her early messages: "There are many," she reportedly warned. Those who see the devil at work in Medjugorje retort with the authority of Scripture, citing Jesus's warning to his disciples about the proliferation of fraudulent visionaries in the final days: "False messiahs and false prophets will arise, and they will perform signs and wonders so great as to deceive, if that were possible, even the elect."

In early 2013 Ivan Dragicevic was preparing for public events in Argentina and Uruguay, a continuation of an on-again, off-again world tour that had taken him to several countries. The previous year he had made nineteen appearances in the United States, where he now spent most of his time. For Ivan, Medjugorje had become a moveable feast. The centerpiece of the events was always the Gospa's apparition, as Ivan, impeccably dressed in suit and tie, prayed and gazed heavenward before crowds that typically numbered in the thousands. Ivan would then give an inspirational speech about one of his favorite topics: the importance of the family, the need for world peace, or the dangers of the modern media. To his audiences those issues were inevitably less interesting than the revelations he received from Mary. In particular, people wanted to know about his two guided visits to heaven, where, Ivan explained, there are "angels and people walking and singing, and all are wearing long dresses."

Ivan was scheduled to appear three times in Buenos Aires, on March 4 through 6, and then twice in Montevideo, the Uruguayan capital, on March 8 and 9. But in late February, at a time when the entire world was focused on the resignation of Pope Benedict XVI and the preparations for a conclave to elect a new pope, the events in Uruguay were suddenly canceled. Organizers said that despite the fact that all the local permissions had been received, the Vatican's Congregation for the Doctrine of the Faith did not consider Ivan's public appearances to be "prudent." The Vatican's move caused immediate consternation among Medjugorje promoters, who wondered if Ivan's Argentina events would also be called off. Strangely they were not, and Ivan reported that when he arrived in Buenos Aires, he was welcomed warmly by the city's archbishop, Cardinal Jorge Mario Bergoglio, who hugged him and invited him to stay in Argentina as long as he wanted in order to spread Mary's message. Ivan's two appearances in Buenos Aires drew an estimated ten thousand people, and his visit was considered a great success. Cardinal Bergoglio, meanwhile, left for Rome, where on March 13, the second day of the conclave, he was chosen as Pope Benedict's successor.

The election of Pope Francis triggered jubilation throughout the global Medjugorje community, especially the Franciscans in Bosnia. They recounted that Bergoglio had welcomed Medjugorje priests to Buenos Aires as far back as the late 1990s, including the controversial Father Jozo Zovko. In an interview with a Croatian newspaper, Father Zovko reported that he and Bergoglio had spent a long time conversing. "We prayed together, and at the end he asked me for a blessing. I touched one fine and good man. He is a good choice," Zovko said from his monastic exile.

One of Pope Francis's first official actions was to consecrate his pontificate to the Virgin Mary. Six months later, at a Vatican ceremony attended by more than one hundred thousand people, he entrusted the world to the Blessed Mother. Representatives from Saint James Parish in Medjugorje were happily surprised to find themselves invited to the Vatican event, where they were seated in a VIP section near the papal platform. It seemed that the winds of change in the Catholic Church were blowing favorably toward Medjugorje.

Then, in an abrupt shift in tone, in mid-November 2013 Pope Francis delivered one of his off-the-cuff sermons at the morning Mass in his Vatican residence. His theme was how Christians should follow the spirit of wisdom in their lives, avoiding an unhealthy "spirit of curiosity" that seeks signs, messages, and supernatural prognostications.

"There is a group of Christians without Christ: those who look for rarities and curiosities that come from private revelations," the pope said. Like the Pharisees who pestered Jesus with questions about the future, these people desired "the spectacle of a revelation, to experience something new."

"Curiosity pushes us to want to hear that the Lord is here or over there, or it makes us say, 'Well, I know a visionary who receives letters from Our Lady, messages from Our Lady,'" Francis said. "But, look, Our Lady is the mother of everyone! And she loves all of us. She is not a postmaster, sending messages every day."

In Medjugorje those words stung, while in the Catholic blogosphere debate raged over whether Pope Francis had effectively given an indication of a forthcoming negative judgment on the apparitions at Medjugorje.

The same month, the Vatican's Congregation for the Doctrine of the Faith once again turned its attention to the Marian road show of Ivan Dragicevic. In a letter that was instantly circulated on websites, the congregation warned U.S. bishops that a series of planned public appearances by Ivan—whom it referred to as "one of the so-called visionaries"—could cause "scandal and confusion" in the parishes that had invited him. The Vatican reminded the American bishops that in 1991, their Yugoslavian counterparts had concluded that it was not possible to affirm that there were, in fact, any apparitions or supernatural revelations at Medjugorje, and added: "It follows, therefore, that clerics and the faithful are not permitted to participate in meetings, conferences or public celebrations during which the credibility of such 'apparitions' would be taken for granted." Privately Vatican officials were even more blunt, stating that the tour, which featured Mary turning up all too conveniently on Ivan's schedule, risked turning into a circus. Ivan's appearances were canceled, and his speaking engagements put on indefinite hold.

In January 2014, after nearly four years of interviewing witnesses and evaluating the written record, the Medjugorje commission appointed by Benedict in 2010 turned in a final series of reports to the doctrinal congregation.

The commission's work had been hampered from the onset by deep disagreements. Some of the panel's key members, convinced that no real judgment could be made while the alleged apparitions continued, had stopped coming to the meetings long before the inquiry ended. The transition to a new pope in 2013, meanwhile, had brought into question the entire project. Neither Benedict nor the doctrinal congregation had been considered "friends" of Medjugorje, and Vatican officials in general were known to mistrust the Franciscan priests who managed the seers and promoted the supposed Marian messages, so when Benedict resigned the papacy in 2013, many in Medjugorje breathed a sigh of relief. Perhaps the commission's work would be quietly shelved by a new pope, and judgment day would be averted. Pope Francis's election only raised their hopes: here was a pontiff so dedicated to Mary that his first official act was to pray before an image of the Blessed Mother and dedicate his pontificate to her.

At this point some began to question the wisdom of having appointed the commission in the first place. While Pope Benedict's goal of providing clarity was well intentioned, the available options all seemed to create more problems than resolve existing ones. Sources quoted by Italian media said the commission's experts had essentially concluded that while no obvious evidence of fraud was discovered, it did not seem possible to offer a final verdict on Medjugorje. Therefore, a positive judgment authenticating the apparitions as truly supernatural appeared out of the question; there were simply too many lingering doubts and disagreements on what had happened at the site over the past thirty-three years, and no possible way of determining what the visionaries might say or do in the future.

Because the commission had not found any proof of deliberate deception, however, a completely negative judgment would also appear unwarranted, and risked alienating all those true believers who had found holiness and rekindled their faith at Medjugorje.

Commission members who supported Medjugorje favored a jurisdictional change. Under this plan the site would be removed from the Diocese of Mostar-Duvno and established as a semi-independent shrine under the control of a separate church authority. This would implicitly recognize that Medjugorje was an international entity that required a different kind of management, one that transcended the age-old tensions between the Mostar diocese and the Franciscan friars, and that guaranteed the necessary pastoral care for visitors. But that proposal struck some Vatican officials as a very bad idea, one that would erode the governing ability of local bishops everywhere. In effect, it would send the message that busloads of pilgrims outweighed a bishop's legitimate authority to evaluate apparitions.

There was a fourth possible course of action, one that appealed to Vatican officials but alarmed the promoters of Medjugorje. While a definitive judgment on the apparitions could, and probably should, be delayed, the visionaries could in the meantime be put on a tight leash. The curb on Ivan Dragicevic's public appearances around the world would be extended to all the seers, including those in Medjugorje. That would mean an end to meetings with pilgrim groups, public visions on Apparition Hill, and daily announcements of a new message from Mary. The visionaries were the chief publicists for Medjugorje and, in the opinion of its townspeople there, silencing them would devastate the religious tourism trade. In the view of church authorities, however, such restrictions would be a good test of obedience for the visionaries and their handlers. At the very least, it would quiet things down.

The Vatican, of course, had a final option: to do nothing. The commission's report could be relegated to one of those archives described by Cardinal Ottaviani as "where the paper sinks deeply into the dark, black depths." The problem was that this particular commission, unlike others sponsored by the Vatican, had been highly publicized. Expectations had been raised for a final judgment on Medjugorje, and inaction would be seen as weakness.

In June 2015, the pope again signaled his sentiments when he critiqued Christians who seek after supernatural novelties. "They say, 'Where are the visionaries who can tell us exactly what message Our Lady will be sending at four o'clock this afternoon?' he joked. "They lived by this. But this is not Christian identity." The reference to Medjugorje was unmistakable.

As Pope Francis considered his alternatives, one Vatican official described the dilemma facing him. "This is a pope who is very devoted to Mary. That actually gives him more credibility, if restrictions need to be placed on Medjugorje. On the other hand, closing it down would be next to impossible, even for Francis. Too many years, too many people, too many messages—it's hard to put the genie back in the bottle. I only hope it's a clear verdict. People look at this and wonder why the Vatican has been so ambiguous. Because if these apparitions are false, why are we afraid to say so? And if Mary is really speaking to the world at Medjugorje, who are we to censor her?"

CHAPTER THREE

The Sacred Image

In one of his last decisions before he resigned in 2013, Pope Benedict XVI approved a special one-day exhibition of the Shroud of Turin, the fourteen-foot-long piece of linen that many believe was the burial cloth of Jesus. The display in the Turin cathedral was arranged to celebrate the Vatican-sponsored Year of Faith, and the German pope also authorized a ninety-minute television broadcast of the Shroud—only its second TV appearance ever, and the first in nearly four decades. The Holy Saturday transmission in March would be introduced by the pope himself, but when Benedict signed off on the project, he knew that task would fall to his successor. In a strange way the cloth bearing the faint image of a crucified man served as the emblem of transition between two pontificates.

Given the furor over Benedict's resignation and the excitement over the election of Pope Francis, the Shroud's brief appearance might have seemed almost a footnote to more historically notable events. But both popes were surely paying attention. Despite his personal and theological aversion to claims of signs, apparitions, and private revelations, Benedict had long considered the Shroud in a different category. As a cardinal he once described it as "a truly mysterious image, which no human artistry was capable of producing." Leading a Way of the Cross procession at Rome's Colosseum shortly before his election in 2005, he said the Shroud offered visual evidence of the "incredible cruelty" of the crucifixion. Benedict steered clear of the scientific debate over the Shroud's authenticity and was careful to refer to it as an "extraordinary icon" and not as a relic, which would have implied that it had surely wrapped the body of Christ. But Benedict's language did seem to reject the arguments of critics and skeptics, who maintained the Shroud was merely a pious counterfeit manufactured in the Middle Ages. Now, in a final gift to the church, the departing pontiff was offering an unplanned glimpse of what he once called an image of "the suffering Son of God."

Pope Francis spoke in similar terms when he inaugurated the display with a video message, stating that the Shroud's image reflected not only human suffering but "the power of the Risen One." His talk and the TV broadcast, which quickly migrated to YouTube, coincided with publication of a sensational new book in Italy that revived the debate over dating of the Shroud. *Il mistero della sindone* (The mystery of the Shroud) by Giulio Fanti and Saverio Gaeta reported that three new tests had placed the cloth in a time frame that coincided with Jesus's death. Fanti, an engineering professor at the University of Padua, analyzed fibers from the Shroud with infrared and spectroscopic instruments and dated them to 33 BC, give or take 250 years. Those results contradicted the carbon-14 testing of similar fibers in 1988, which had dated the cloth to the fourteenth century. Fanti said he was submitting his findings to a peer-reviewed scientific journal, but in the meantime, his book was selling briskly.

The Shroud was coming of age in the digital world, too. On Good Friday, the day before its exhibition in Turin, iTunes released a new app called Shroud 2.0 that displayed the cloth's full-length, front-and-back image in high definition, giving viewers a chance to zoom in on particular details of the image it contained, like the punctured wrists and feet, the swollen right cheek, and the wounds on the shoulders and back. Developed with the church's authorization, the app utilized 1,649 digital photographs of the cloth to create a single, twelve-billion-pixel image that could also be viewed as a negative, which offers more definition and detail—an aspect of the cloth that has long baffled scientists.

In April 2013 the Shroud was the focus of a science and faith conference at a pontifical university in Rome and a topic at a Vatican-sponsored series of TED talks. A few months later Pope Francis approved a new forty-five-day exhibition of the Shroud in 2015—ten years ahead of schedule—exciting Shroud enthusiasts around the world. Planning for the event spread on the multiple Facebook and web pages dedicated to it in every major language.

It was a remarkable comeback for a cloth that had been written off by many experts as a medieval forgery only twenty-five years earlier. The Shroud of Turin, with its mysterious and arresting image that seemed to correspond so well to the Gospel account of Christ's Passion and death, had claimed a place on the new pope's agenda, had reignited journalists' interest, and was building a global fan base through social media. This was an image that would not go away.

The documented history of the Shroud of Turin begins in the late 1300s, when it was kept and occasionally displayed in a church in Lirey, France. It was believed to have belonged to a French knight, Geoffroy de Charny, who may have acquired it in Constantinople. An alternative theory is that it was created by an artist of that era. A letter written in 1389 by Bishop Pierre d'Arcis, whose diocese included Lirey, claimed that a previous bishop had investigated and found that the Shroud had been painted and that the artist had acknowledged his work. The letter, often cited by Shroud skeptics, is dismissed by others, who say Bishop d'Arcis's accusation of forgery was unsubstantiated and was motivated by a feud with the clergy of Lirey. D'Arcis wanted to stop the exhibition of the Shroud, and his letter was addressed to the antipope Clement VII, but was apparently never sent. In any case, in 1390 Clement VII authorized the continued display of the Shroud as long as it was presented as a likeness of Christ and not as his true burial cloth.

The de Charny family began to have concerns about the Shroud's security in the Lirey church, and in the early 1400s Margaret de Charny, the granddaughter of Geoffroy, moved the cloth to a nearby castle and then took it with her on various moves through Europe, putting it on display from time to time. By the mid-1440s Margaret had apparently bequeathed the cloth to the Savoy family in exchange for property. The Savoys carried the Shroud with them from castle to castle until in the early 1500s it was given a more permanent home in the Royal Chapel of Chambéry Castle. In 1532 a fire broke out in the chapel's sacristy, and the intense heat melted part of the silver reliquary that held the Shroud.

Two Franciscan friars saved the cloth by rushing inside and pouring water on the reliquary, but it was permanently damaged with a series of parallel scorch marks.

In 1578 Cardinal Charles Borromeo planned to walk from Milan to Chambéry to venerate the Shroud, an act of thanksgiving for Milan's escape from an outbreak of plague. To spare Borromeo the arduous journey across the Alps, the Savoy family ordered the Shroud brought to Turin, where it was exhibited several times that year to increasingly large crowds. It would remain in the city until the outbreak of World War II, when it was secretly moved to southern Italy for safekeeping, returning to Turin in 1946. In 1983 Umberto of Savoy died, and his will bestowed possession of the Shroud to the pope, who at the time was John Paul II. Despite pressure to move the cloth to Rome, John Paul decided to leave it in Turin and to name the archbishop there its custodian.

Over the centuries millions of people have seen the Shroud during its various exhibitions. While few would admit to it, its visual impact is often disappointing. The reason is that in direct light, the image of the body is so faint that it can barely be distinguished from the sheet of aged linen. What made the Shroud famous, and what opened the era of scientific analysis of it, was a series of photographs taken in 1898 by an amateur Italian photographer, Secondo Pia. This was the first time the Savoy family allowed the Shroud to be photographed, and it took Pia several attempts to get the lighting right. While developing the plates in his darkroom, Pia discovered to his amazement that the negatives revealed an incredibly detailed positive image of the man in the Shroud. The face, in particular, was strikingly natural, a likeness that seemed to come out of nowhere. When the photo was published, it caused an immediate sensation, with some calling it miraculous and others accusing Pia of fraud. More than thirty years would pass before a professional photographer confirmed the findings of Secondo Pia: that the Shroud of Turin is, at least in great part, a negative image. To see it clearly, one had to invert the lighter and darker shades. Proponents of the Shroud's authenticity immediately seized on this discovery, arguing that no medieval artist would have had the necessary knowledge to create such an image. In fact, scientists are still trying to solve that mystery. Despite many efforts, no one has yet been able to convincingly produce the type of image that is found on the Shroud.

Not surprisingly the Shroud debate has generated countless books, documentaries, and international conferences, as well as an entire "Face of God" Catholic devotional movement. With notoriety have come dangers. In 1972 an unidentified man climbed over the roof of the state-owned Royal Palace in Turin, broke into the chapel, and tried to set the Shroud on fire. It survived intact, thanks to asbestos panels that protected the site. Security was increased, but in 1997 arson was suspected in a more serious fire that broke out in the cathedral. Firefighters saved the cloth by using a sledgehammer to break through the four layers of bulletproof glass that protected it, and then carrying it to safety from the burning church.

Scientific interest in the Shroud also exploded in the twentieth century. The cloth's enigmatic imprint drew the attention of specialists in imaging, chemistry, physics, and other fields, including radiocarbon dating. In 1988 church officials authorized carbon-14 testing by three independent laboratories on a few tiny pieces of the Shroud, and the results consistently dated the cloth to between 1260 and 1390. That appeared to bolster claims that the Shroud was a medieval artifact. But over the last twenty-five years, criticism of the carbon-dating methodology and the way samples were taken—according to several experts, the threads came from a repaired or contaminated area of the cloth—have cast doubts on those results.

Of all the investigations of the Shroud of Turin, the largest and in many ways the strangest was carried out by a group of American scientists in the late 1970s. The Shroud of Turin Research Project, or STURP, was a thirty-member team, assembled by word of mouth, that included experts in photography, chemistry, physics and biophysics, mathematics, optics, and forensic pathology. Several members worked in nuclear weapons research. One of the prime movers was John P. Jackson, a physicist working as an Air Force instructor in Albuquerque, New

Mexico. Jackson's interest in the Shroud reflected both scientific curiosity and deep religious faith.

In 1976 Jackson and fellow Air Force instructor Eric Jumper went to see a new instrument at the Sandia National Laboratories in Albuquerque. If fed the right information, the VP-8 Image Analyzer was capable of converting light and dark image density into topographical relief. Operating on a hunch, Jackson and others brought a photo of the Shroud—the same negative photo that in 1931 had confirmed the details of the image—and placed it in the analyzer. They were excited to see that the device created a three-dimensional relief of the Shroud's human form. In a normal photograph the bright or dark areas depend strictly on the amount of light reflected onto film, in what is a fairly random pattern. But the varying intensity of light and dark on the Shroud seemed to correspond to the body's distance from the surface of the cloth. In Jackson's view that meant the image itself contained precise spatial information, which would appear to rule out a painting or other artistic origin. The image would have to have been created while the cloth was draped over a body, even in places where the cloth had not come into direct contact with the body.

Jackson and his colleagues believed they had found a new way to examine the Shroud and were eager to perform imaging and chemical tests on the cloth. They soon convinced other scientists to join them in their quest, including top researchers from the Los Alamos National Laboratory in New Mexico, the U.S. Air Force Academy in Colorado, and the Jet Propulsion Laboratory in Pasadena. Collectively their experience tended toward weapons and rockets, but their expertise in radiation, spectral analysis, and thermal imaging made the Shroud a very tempting research target. Several key members of STURP were devoted Christians, but some were Jewish, and a few were nonbelievers. What brought them together was the science, not the religion. They saw the Shroud's image as a code to be cracked.

The scientists were able to borrow some of the more expensive equipment, but had to pay for most of their activities out of their own pockets. After obtaining rare permission from Italian church authorities, the

STURP team flew to Italy in September 1978 and set up their equipment in Turin's Royal Palace. The experts worked on the Shroud around the clock for five days, conducting tests from every imaginable scientific angle. They photographed the cloth in diverse light, X-rayed it, and ran ultraviolet and infrared experiments. They investigated bloodstains and examined the hidden underside of the cloth, which had been covered for centuries. They removed samples from the Shroud's surface with sticky tape for later analysis. Their findings, published in the years that followed, added an immense amount of data but also raised new questions. Essentially, the team agreed that the image was not the work of an artist and was encoded with unique, three-dimensional information; but how it was produced remained a mystery.

For many of the STURP scientists, the Shroud investigation was a fascinating parenthesis; they returned to their jobs and went on with their careers. Others wrote highly technical papers on their research, most of which were ignored in the growing public discussion of the Shroud's origin. But for two members of the STURP team, the 1978 trip to Turin proved to be much more than a passing scientific assignment. In the years that followed, the enigma of the Shroud would consume their lives.

The Turin Shroud Center of Colorado, which bills itself as "among the world's foremost scientific research and education centers on the Shroud," is not easy to find. Its address in Colorado Springs is given out on a need-to-know basis. Housed in a two-story, low-budget complex next to a hairdressing salon, it has no signs or markers to indicate the presence of a research facility. Its anonymity can make things confusing for visitors, but that's the way its founder and director, John Jackson, wants it.

When Jackson arrived at the center on a winter morning in 2014, he paused before turning the key. From his shirt pocket he pulled a small silver-plated nameplate that read "Turin Shroud Center" and attached it to the door with a strip of Velcro. He would remove it when he left the building later in the day. "There are a lot of strange people around," he explained with a chuckle.

That kind of cryptic remark is typical of Jackson, who for years worked on secret projects at the Air Force Weapons Laboratory in New Mexico. Lanky and soft-spoken, dressed casually in a sweater and jeans, Jackson, now in his late sixties, took a seat on a wooden stool. In the middle of the small, windowless room, eighteen chairs were arranged before a whiteboard, on which Jackson had scribbled mathematical formulas. Positioned close to the peach-colored walls were cardboard and Styrofoam models of the man of the Shroud, along with a life-size replica of Christ on the cross. A painting of the Last Supper hung above a glass display case, which held a crown of thorns and a plaster model of foot bones with a long iron nail driven through them. Giant photos of the Shroud, negative and positive, were everywhere. The ambience was part laboratory and part shrine, a balance that accurately reflects Jackson's faith-based approach to science.

In Jackson's view the "science" of the Shroud began in the empty tomb on Easter morning, as related in the Gospel of Saint John. "John was making observations. He was looking at what was there. And he says what was there. He saw the cloths lying there. It was clear that the body wasn't there. John says, and he's talking about himself: 'He saw, and he believed.' Seeing is an act of science. Believing is an act of faith. And the way I see it, Saint John is relating science and religion together, no less than at the tomb of Christ. If he didn't see anything—no science—there'd be no way to link faith with the world we live in. If we can't do that, there would be no church. No Christianity. If we think that we can have these theologies that are so esoteric and don't root themselves in what science can offer, I think we're fooling ourselves."

The church's discomfort with science is one aspect of the problem, Jackson explained. The other is scientific aversion to religious faith—specifically, the categorical rejection of the idea that God can work in the real world, sometimes through miracles.

"This is a miracle," he said, looking at a backlit photo of the Shroud. "There are all kinds of 'naturalistic' explanations put forward that try to say this is just one of those things that happens from time to time in our natural world. There are a lot of researchers on the Shroud who only want the science part of it. They're intimidated by faith—really, they do not want to go there."

Calling the Shroud a "miracle" would give many experts pause, but Jackson is very comfortable with that concept. He is willing to state openly what several researchers have only hinted at: namely, that the best explanation for the image on this cloth is that it was created by Jesus's Resurrection. Of course, Jackson can't prove that, but he is convinced that it's the strongest hypothesis, and that none of the other theories about the origin of the Shroud's image holds up to scientific scrutiny. In scientific terms what Jackson has proposed is that the image was formed when the Shroud collapsed into and through a radiating body, a body that had suddenly become transparent to its physical surroundings. It was the radiation emission that discolored the cloth. Jackson acknowledged that the idea of a disappearing body challenges the conventional laws of physics but argued that the Shroud makes a valid case for rethinking certain concepts of modern science.

To demonstrate how the radiation-collapse theory answers the key questions about image formation, and to refute other explanations like painting or rubbing, Jackson turned to the exhibits in his research center. His 3-D cardboard cutout models, which brought Jackson a degree of fame more than thirty years ago, were created using the brightness map of the Shroud photo obtained through the VP-8 Image Analyzer. Essentially Jackson scanned the photo in several hundred thin horizontal layers, then used an instrument called a microdensitometer to apply a mathematical value to the variations in light intensity in each scan, and finally converted the data to a three-dimensional graph represented by layers of cardboard, which were stacked one upon the other. The result was a topographical model of the man of the Shroud. As he explained this process, Jackson crawled beneath a table in a corner of the room to adjust a lamp in order to obtain the most dramatic lighting on the cardboard model, which allowed the figure to emerge in clear relief.

Jackson turned to a low table and placed his hand on a Styrofoam model of a reclining man. "This is Larry," he said. "Larry" was patterned after a volunteer who matched the height and build of the man of the Shroud. To test whether the cloth could actually cover a body at the correct contact points, Jackson wrapped the volunteer, front and back, with a full-scale replica of it. He found that the Shroud's image aligned perfectly, and that the distance variations between the cloth and the volunteer's body corresponded with the intensity of the image on the Shroud. As he reenacted the test on Styrofoam Larry, gently wrapping the Shroud around its head and feet, Jackson remarked, "You'd be surprised how many people who have researched the Shroud have never done this."

In the view of most experts, the most unusual feature of the Shroud image is that it is well defined yet superficial, only about two microns deep in the outermost fibers of the cloth. Jackson calls it a "surface shadow" and argues that it is consistent with the theory of image by radiation, which would have been absorbed primarily by the top and bottom surfaces of the cloth. Jackson said the shallow nature of the image rules out painting, because paint would have penetrated the cloth more deeply in a capillary flow. The image appears almost as a scorch mark, but attempts to duplicate it through heat scorching or by draping a cloth over a "hot statue" have been unsuccessful, resulting in a poorly defined image and deep discoloration of the cloth. Jackson is convinced that radiation scorching, on the other hand, would discolor the linen precisely in the yellow-brown pattern seen on the Shroud. Having conducted experiments to test the theory, he said he believes the body image was photosensitized by radiation onto the Shroud, and then the image darkened with age.

One of Jackson's most intriguing hypotheses is that the Shroud may contain imaging of internal body structures like bones, which would have emitted a higher dose of radiation than other tissue. Specifically, he said, the elongated fingers, which appear to be visible well into the palms of the hands, might actually be images of the finger bones, just as are seen on a modern X-ray of a hand.

The carbon-14 dating of 1988, which assigned a medieval date of origin to the Shroud, took the steam out of a lot of Shroud research. Jackson has been among several scientists who question the accuracy of the dating results, however, and had his own theory: that carbon monoxide contamination might have affected the outcome. In any case, he said, he considers the radiocarbon test result an outlier that has to be weighed against other evidence. Even if one does presume a medieval date for the cloth, Jackson said, it still leaves the main question: How was the image created? "A craftsman or a hypothetical someone in the fourteenth century would have had to be able to do this. The question is, what technique would he or she have used? It's not enough to just have a radiocarbon test that says, 'Here's the date, take it and choke on it.'" In other words, Jackson said, the Shroud's date is only one piece of the puzzle. Any truly scientific hypothesis has to be able to explain its other unique elements, like the high resolution of the image itself and the geometrical information it contains about the body.

In the thirty-five years since STURP delivered its findings, Jackson has carried out his personal investigation of the Shroud with quiet determination, generally avoiding the media spotlight and publishing relatively little in popular books or articles. As the avenues of scientific research have been exhausted, Jackson and his wife, Rebecca, have turned to historical and theological aspects of the Shroud. It was the Shroud, in fact, that brought the two together. Rebecca, who was raised an Orthodox Jew in Brooklyn, saw Jackson on a TV documentary about the Shroud in the early 1990s. What impressed her about the Shroud's image was that the figure looked Jewish—just like her grandfather—and she thought the Shroud researchers should be aware of that. So she tracked Jackson down in Colorado Springs, where she was living at the time, and the two began to meet to discuss the Shroud's mysterious properties. Two years later they married. As John Jackson remarked, "Our whole marriage has been built on doing this with the Shroud."

The Jacksons began researching the Shroud's possible connections with Catholic liturgy and came up with a unique theory: that the 14.3-by-3.7-foot linen cloth may also have been used as a tablecloth at the Last Supper of

Jesus and his twelve Apostles. That day was the Jewish day of preparation for Passover, and Rebecca Jackson believes the Shroud is consistent with the tradition of a tablecloth for the Passover meal. When it came time to wrap Jesus's body in a cloth the following day, the Apostles may have used what was already at hand. John Jackson conceded that there's no way to prove this theory but noted that the corporal, the small linen cloth on which the Eucharist is placed during Mass, has been seen as symbolic of both the tablecloth at the Last Supper and the burial shroud of Christ. In this sense, he suggested, the church's liturgy may be conveying a historical connection between the two.

Jackson thus views the Shroud as a witness to the first Eucharist and to the Resurrection, making it, as he says, a potential "Rosetta stone" for the Catholic Church. Yet he has found little enthusiasm for this theory in scientific or Catholic communities. Other researchers sometimes argue that Jackson has made the classic mistake of allowing faith to interfere with objectivity, in a way that diminishes the credibility of Shroud science in general. Church authorities have not embraced his claims, either. At the Vatican most officials have kept a prudent distance from Shroud enthusiasts. In 1981 Jackson and three others went to Saint Peter's Square for Pope John Paul II's general audience. At the end of the audience, they were to meet briefly with the pope and report on the conclusions of their Shroud tests, but as fate would have it, the pontiff was shot that day as he entered the square by a Turkish assailant, Mehmet Ali Agca, and the meeting never took place. No further invitation has come from the hierarchy in Rome, and the Vatican has had nothing to say about Jackson's idea that the Shroud was formed in a burst of resurrection radiation. "I understand the church doesn't want to hang its hat on that," he said with a sigh of resignation. "But the church did not hesitate to hang its hat on the Resurrection, which was a miraculous event."

About twenty miles west of John Jackson's Shroud center, on the other side of Pikes Peak and the Florissant Fossil Beds, Barrie Schwortz dug through a pile of books and magazines to find an old photo he took in Turin in 1978. Schwortz's expansive living room is also his office, a semi-organized landscape of imagery equipment, computers, and mementos from his glory days as a Shroud researcher. From this remote corner of Colorado, more than eight thousand feet above sea level and just out of cell phone range, he runs www.shroud.com, the most popular Shroud of Turin website, and heads the Shroud of Turin Education and Research Association. His redwood house, perched next to eleven giant solar panels, faces south toward the peaks of the distant Sangre de Cristo Mountains, visible on the horizon more than a hundred miles away. "I call this my monastery," said Schwortz, who lives here with his twenty-one-year-old cat, Pooh. "I'm convinced this is what God wants me to do."

Schwortz, a photographer and imaging specialist, is a one-man Shroud of Turin publicist and has lectured on the Shroud around the world. He's been interviewed for TV programs and documentaries on every major broadcasting and cable network, from Vatican Radio to Channel One Russia. He's written countless papers and coauthored a major book on the Shroud. All the while he's continued to conduct research, and was in Turin when the cloth was put on display in 2015. Like John Jackson's, Schwortz's life revolves around the Shroud in ways he could not have imagined thirty-five years ago. Like Jackson, Schwortz is convinced that the Shroud truly was the burial cloth of Jesus, and he makes the case for authenticity with detailed scientific evidence. But Schwortz does not believe the Shroud's image was caused by Jesus's Resurrection, avoiding that kind of religious perspective for a simple reason: Barrie Schwortz is Jewish.

In 1977 Don Devan, a computer image analyst at Los Alamos who helped put together the STURP team, phoned Schwortz and asked, "Barrie, what do you know about the Shroud of Turin?" Schwortz laughed and replied, "Don, I'm Jewish!" "So am I," Devan replied, "remember?" Eventually both men signed on to the project and made the trip to Turin. As it turned out, several members of the team were not Christian and some were not even particularly religious. Like Schwortz they expected to find that the Shroud image was a work of art.

What Schwortz discovered, instead, was that the image had several inexplicable properties, and showed no real evidence of having been painted. What intrigued Schwortz most was the spatial depth information that kept turning up in the photos he took and analyzed. "Looking at all the science, the only way that image could have formed was by some interaction between the cloth and the body. That eliminates the hand of an artist. There is no paint there. It was not a photograph. It was not made with a light-sensitive emulsion by Leonardo da Vinci." (Some have theorized that Leonardo may have secretly created the Shroud through a photographic process he invented, but as Schwortz pointed out, the Shroud was being displayed about a hundred years before Leonardo was born.) "It's not a rubbing, because look at the microscopy. There are people who have made rubbings, and compared the results side by side with the Shroud, and they're dramatically different. How about a scorch? That doesn't work, either."

When Schwortz starts discussing the Shroud, he's hard to stop. Buoyant and increasingly animated as he sat in a striped armchair, he went through all the arguments against the Shroud's authenticity and shot them down one by one, as he has done before innumerable audiences on the lecture circuit. His eyes sparkled behind big aviator-style glasses, and a smile frequently creased his graying beard. Behind his head, unkempt strands of white hair caught the light, creating a corona effect. He looked, for a moment, like a man on a messianic mission, explaining why the imaging mechanism of the Shroud had to be able to attenuate light over a short space of about four centimeters. But Schwortz also knows when to pull back on the scientific jargon and tell the story in layman's terms. The narrative he spins is largely about himself, seasoned with wisecracks and humorous asides.

Schwortz said it took him seventeen years of study before he was convinced that the Shroud was the burial cloth of Jesus. When he returned from Turin in 1978, he didn't abandon his professional life and begin obsessing about the STURP project. In the 1980s he worked in Los Angeles on children's video projects, editing, among other things, an award-winning *Rocky and Bullwinkle* home video series. Later he worked with universities and hospitals in developing video programs to teach new surgical techniques to doctors. All the while he kept abreast of Shroud theories and new findings. He felt certain the Shroud was not a hoax but had one nagging doubt, a doubt that arose when he and other scientists stood in front of the cloth in 1978. Why were the bloodstains reddish in color? Schwortz knew that blood darkens over time, turning brown or black. If these stains were really that old, why were they still red?

It was only in 1995 that he found a satisfactory answer, in the course of a casual phone conversation with Alan Adler, the STURP blood chemist who had analyzed scrapings from the Shroud. Schwortz mentioned to Adler that the color of the blood was a "deal breaker" for him when it came to the Shroud's authenticity. "Didn't you read my papers?" Adler asked and then explained that he had found an unusually high amount of bilirubin in the blood scrapings from the Shroud. At those levels, he said, bilirubin can cause blood to maintain its red color forever, despite exposure to air. A high bilirubin count could be accounted for by a number of factors, including illness. But one classic explanation for a flooding of bilirubin into the bloodstream faster than the liver can break it down is trauma: a man who was tortured and crucified, for example, would experience a high bilirubin level in less than thirty seconds. Schwortz suddenly felt the last piece of the jigsaw puzzle fall into place. "I trusted Adler. He was a world-renowned blood chemistry expert. And he was Jewish! I know that doesn't really matter, but he didn't have a horse in this race."

Any lingering doubts Schwortz had about the Shroud's being the burial cloth of Christ disappeared a few years later, after he reflected on a remark from his Jewish mother. His mother, who immigrated to the United States from a tiny Polish village at the age of seven, had only a high school education, and had raised their family in Pittsburgh, in what Schwortz described as an extended-family, *Fiddler on the Roof* milieu. After having heard her son lecture on the Shroud for the first time, she sat quietly, saying nothing, which made Schwortz nervous. He finally asked her, "Mother, what did you think?" "Well, of course it belonged to Jesus," she responded. Surprised, Schwortz asked her what made her say that. "Barrie," she answered with a sigh, "they wouldn't have kept it for two thousand years if it were anyone else, nobody would care." The more he thought about it, the more he was convinced that his mother was right. Moreover, Jewish law decreed that burial cloths must go into the grave, so there had to have been a compelling reason that this one was kept out.

Audiences lap this stuff up. In the court of public opinion, one Jewish mother trumps a dozen niggling scientific objections. Schwortz's popularity in the media and around the world reflects the fact that he understands public relations in a way that other Shroud scientists do not. From the beginning of the STURP initiative in 1978, the lack of media savvy undermined the team's efforts. The project had no one trained in PR, and its members were under orders not to give interviews. Schwortz recalled STURP scientists being chased down the streets of Turin by reporters, refusing to answer questions. "A *Rolling Stone* guy was there! We said we weren't allowed to talk to the media," Schwortz said, shaking his head. When STURP leaders finally agreed to designate a spokesman, they chose Kenneth Stevenson, a former Air Force pilot and evangelical Christian. "He's a dear guy, but he couldn't separate his faith from his role on our team," Schwortz said. "He gets up on *Good Morning America* and says, 'I believe this is an image of my Lord Jesus!' Representing us as a scientific team! It damaged our credibility instantly."

Schwortz said he remains good friends with some of the surviving members of the STURP group, including John Jackson, but he thinks Jackson's deep Christian faith does not necessarily help open people's minds to the Shroud. "John is a hard-core Catholic. I don't have that emotional connection. And that's one of the advantages I bring to the table. I never had that kind of attachment to Jesus," Schwortz said.

That helps explain why Schwortz finds Jackson's "resurrection radiation" theory unconvincing. He noted that Ray Rogers, a chemist and thermal energy expert on the STURP team, found that the image formation on the Shroud was a low-temperature event. "So it wasn't a burst of radiation," Schwortz said. "Remember, Rogers was a chemist at Los Alamos. What did those guys do? Nuclear weapons. They know about the effects of radiation on anything. And there was no way this could have been radiation. He said if this had been a radiation event, there'd still be a crater in Jerusalem a couple of kilometers wide."

So what *is* the best theory of how the Shroud image was formed? Schwortz believes it was some kind of natural interaction between cloth and body, and he finds persuasive a hypothesis put forward by Rogers in 2003. Part of the manufacturing process of linen in ancient times was soaking the fabric in a solution of *Saponaria officinalis*, known more commonly as soapweed. The treatment made the linen more flexible, but it also left a thin, starchy residue on the outermost surface of the cloth. Rogers wondered whether a chemical reaction of some kind might have caused that residue to discolor on the Shroud. He was familiar with a phenomenon called the Maillard reaction, a chemical browning effect well known in cooking. (It gives bread and beer their golden color, for example.) What could have caused a Maillard reaction on the Shroud? The theory was that amines—low levels of ammonia gas—secreted from the pores of the body as it began to decay interacted with the *Saponaria* on the surface of the cloth, causing the brown image. Schwortz liked this idea, because it explained why the image density would correspond to cloth-to-body distance. According to Schwortz, Rogers wanted to test the hypothesis, but he needed both a piece of linen manufactured in the ancient method and a fresh corpse. In 2005 he contacted Arpad Vass, a forensic anthropologist at the Oak Ridge National Laboratory in Tennessee who studied corpse decomposition and, in particular, body vapor emanation. "Rogers got in contact with this guy because he had access to fresh dead bodies. And you would need that to do this kind of experiment," Schwortz explained. But Rogers died before he had a chance to verify his theory.

As he travels around the world giving lectures and interviews, Schwortz insists that he's interested only in the science of the Shroud, and not in trying to convince people that it's genuine. "I don't care what you believe. That's between you and God. I'm not a rabbi, a minister, or a priest. I'm not proselytizing," he says. But if anyone indicates a doubt or raises an objection to its authenticity, Schwortz will gladly accept the challenge. He has debated skeptics—and there have been plenty of them—an exercise he seems to relish.

Walter McCrone, an American microchemist and a consultant to STURP, wrote a book that maintained the Shroud's image was a painting and the "bloodstains" were actually pigment. A book by Joe Nickell, a popular debunker of the paranormal and the supernatural, attacked Shroud claims with forensic data, and argued that medieval rubbing techniques could easily have produced the image. Within and outside the scientific community, one can find counterarguments for every pro-Shroud assertion or theory. The twill pattern of the cloth was either typical of the first-century Holy Land region or was a weave introduced in the Middle Ages. The reddish stains were either chemically degraded human blood or tinted tempera paint. The pollen found in a 1973 sampling from the Shroud's surface came only from plants unique to the Near East, or the pollen evidence was fraudulent and unconfirmed by later analysis. In 2014 researchers in Turin hypothesized that an earthquake that rocked Jerusalem could have released enough neutrons to cause image formation on the Shroud and to distort radiocarbon levels in the cloth; the theory was immediately dismissed by other geochemistry and radiation experts.

Schwortz stressed that, notwithstanding the myriad objections raised by skeptics, they have never been able to duplicate the Shroud image. "Now that doesn't prove anything. But we live in the most image-oriented age in history, where everybody has cameras in their pockets, and everybody has the ability to process images on their computers and their phones. With all that technology, we still don't know the mechanism that can make an image with these chemical and physical properties," he said.

The Shroud remains an enigma, a world-class mystery, and Barrie Schwortz is fine with that. He understands that, to a great degree, the public is fascinated with the Shroud precisely because it cannot be explained. And he suspects that Catholic Church authorities understand that, too. "The fact that it remains elusive plays in favor of the church.

As long as it's a mystery, it's going to get people's attention. The minute the mystery is removed—'OK, now it's not so interesting anymore. Next!' So I think the Vatican is playing their cards right by saying, We'll think about it."

It was Cardinal Anastasio Ballestrero of Turin who authorized carbon-14 dating of tiny samples of the Shroud in 1988, an initiative that greatly excited both the Catholic faithful and the mass media when it was first announced. The cardinal approved the testing in part to show that the church was not afraid of science. But when three independent laboratories dated the cloth to the Middle Ages, a chagrined Ballestrero had to disclose those findings to the world. The disappointment was most keenly felt in Italy, where Catholics criticized the cardinal for having entrusted one of the church's most treasured artifacts to the judgment of laboratory technicians. One priest addressed an open letter to Ballestrero: "Do you know what I advise you, Eminence? Put aside carbon-14, uranium and all the other modern pestilences. Keep the faith like a simple believer, tend to the substance, and leave relics alone. The supernatural eludes scientific investigation." Others called the scientific data a "mockery." Speaking on an Italian television show, the respected writer Italo Chiusano expressed the distress felt by many: "I suffered like a child who had never known the father and of this father had only one photograph, only to discover unexpectedly that it is false."

It didn't take long, though, before other church leaders shrugged off the carbon dating, which was later challenged by scientists as well. Six months after the results were published, Pope John Paul II was on a plane to Africa when reporters asked him what he thought of the Shroud and the test results. To the surprise of his advisers, the pope replied that the Shroud was "certainly a relic."

"If it were not a relic, one could not understand these reactions of faith that surround it and which are now even stronger after scientific test results," he said. As the journalists scribbled furiously in their notebooks, one of them asked if the pope believed, then, that the

Shroud really was Christ's burial cloth. John Paul realized he had waded into a science vs. faith controversy, and he briefly consulted with an aide before answering. In essence, he told the reporters, church authorities had wisely avoided stating whether the Shroud was genuine or not. For many people, the visual image alone was sufficient evidence that it had once held Christ's body. "The church has never pronounced itself in this sense. It has always left the question open to all those who want to seek its authenticity. I think it is a relic."

As one might expect, Pope Benedict, who was often called "the pope of reason," was much more circumspect on the subject. He, too, was interested in the Shroud and had stood before it as a cardinal. As pope he ordered the extraordinary exhibition of the Shroud in 2010. Benedict himself flew to Turin to venerate the cloth and gave a speech in which he described the Shroud as an "icon," a term that disappointed some of its devotees. In the code language of the Shroud, "icon" denotes just a holy image, while "relic" is the genuine object. But this was an icon with a capital "I"—literally, in the official text of the papal speech—which signaled some support for authenticity. Benedict added that the Shroud was "a winding-sheet that was wrapped round the body of a man who was crucified, corresponding in every way to what the Gospels tell us of Jesus." That appeared to reject out of hand the theory that it was a medieval artistic creation. The pope then went on to speak of the Shroud in dramatic and poetic language that moved many of his listeners: "The Shroud is an Icon written in blood; the blood of a man who was scourged, crowned with thorns, crucified and whose right side was pierced. The Image impressed upon the Shroud is that of a dead man, but the blood speaks of his life. Every trace of blood speaks of love and of life. Especially that huge stain near his rib, made by the blood and water that flowed copiously from a great wound inflicted by the tip of a Roman spear. That blood and that water speak of life. It is like a spring that murmurs in the silence, and we can hear it."

Like Pope John Paul before him, Benedict was speaking as a simple individual believer, not with the full weight of papal authority. Previous popes had made similar comments in public and in private, especially after Secondo Pia's dramatic negative-image photos were published in 1898. Pope Pius XI, who was a close friend of Pia's, became convinced of the Shroud's authenticity and would sometimes hand out small pictures of the image to schoolchildren. He arranged for the Shroud to be displayed during the Holy Year of 1933.

Six years later, with the outbreak of World War II, Pope Pius XII was asked confidentially by the Savoy family to protect the Shroud at the Vatican. Both the royal family and church authorities were afraid that Adolf Hitler wanted to steal it, their apprehensions having been raised the previous year when, during a visit by Hitler to Italy, Nazi officials posed unusual and insistent questions about the Shroud and its custody. Hitler was believed to have been obsessed about certain objects related to the life of Christ, including the Holy Grail and the Holy Lance of Longinus, and now he appeared to have his eye on the burial cloth.

The thinking was that the Shroud would be safer in the Vatican than in Turin. Pius XII, however, arranged for the cloth to be brought secretly to the ancient Benedictine abbey of Montevergine, a sanctuary nestled in the southern Italian mountains, where it was hidden under the main altar. The hiding place was almost discovered in 1943, when Nazi soldiers arrived and began searching the abbey premises. The monks gathered for prayer around the altar, and a German officer ordered his troops not to disturb them. The soldiers departed, never suspecting they were leaving behind a religious treasure. After the war ended, the Shroud was safely returned to Turin.

During World War II the image of the Shroud visage had begun to be featured on a medal worn by many Catholics, and in the 1950s the same image gave new momentum to the traditional devotion of the Holy Face of Jesus. Pope John XXIII, upon seeing photos of the Shroud, is said to have attributed a divine origin to the image with the Latin phrase *"Digitus Dei est hic!"* ("The finger of God is here!"). When the Shroud was displayed in 1978 for the first time in forty-five years, Cardinal Karol Wojtyla of Poland was among those who made a pilgrimage to Turin. A month later he was elected Pope John Paul II. In 1980, while visiting Turin, he called the Shroud a "silent witness" of Christ's Resurrection.

Yet despite the favorable disposition of popes, in recent decades most Vatican officials have said little or nothing about the Shroud, and have carefully avoided comment on the scientific research performed on the cloth. That reticence sometimes baffles the scientists who have invested so much of their own efforts in solving the Shroud's mysteries. One Vatican monsignor explained that the church simply does not want to paint itself into a corner: "It might seem tempting to point to the Shroud and say, 'See, there's the proof.' But the church will never make that kind of claim, and stake its credibility on a piece of cloth. They learned that lesson with the carbon dating."

While it is generally difficult to find Vatican experts to speak on the record about the Shroud, there's always an exception to the rule, and in this case her name is Barbara Frale. A paleographer at the Vatican Secret Archives, Frale has generated controversy with her published theories on the Shroud. In 2009 she argued in a popular book, *The Templars and the Shroud of Christ*, that the Knights Templar, the medieval crusading order, secretly held the Shroud in the thirteenth and fourteenth centuries and used it in initiation rituals. She claimed to have found a document that gave a detailed account of such a Templar ceremony in 1287. In an article published by the Vatican newspaper, Frale wrote that the document described how a Templar elder took a French initiate, Arnaut Sabbatier, into a room and "showed him a long linen cloth that bore the impressed figure of a man, and ordered him to worship it, kissing the feet three times." Frale said her research supported the theory, first proposed by the British historian Ian Wilson in 1978, that the Templars were once the Shroud's secret custodians. The idea is based on the argument of some scholars that historical descriptions of a sacred icon kept in Constantinople for hundreds of years before its disappearance during the Crusades in 1204 referred to the Shroud of Turin. Frale hypothesized that the crusading Templars brought the Shroud back with them to Europe, but kept it secret because of the papal order of excommunication for anyone involved in looting relics from Constantinople. That timeline would account for the "missing years" in the Shroud's supposed history before it turned up in the Lirey church in the 1300s. It would also refute the results of the carbon-14 testing on the Shroud.

Frale was back in the headlines later in 2009 with another book, contending that her study of photographs of the Shroud revealed a written death certificate for a "Jesus Nazarene." Frale based her conclusions in part on earlier research by Italian and French experts, who used computer processing to enhance the Shroud's image and claimed to have found "ghost lettering" on the surface of the cloth. Frale took a closer look and concluded that the letters corresponded to a report of Jesus's crucifixion, written in three languages—Aramaic, Latin, and Greek. The report would have been affixed to the body so that relatives could retrieve the corpse after a one-year period in a common grave, which was the Jewish burial custom in cases of a death sentence, Frale said. In this case, she theorized, the ink from the document seeped onto the burial cloth and left a faint imprint.

Frale's theories have been criticized by scholars, mainly because most experts believe there is no writing on the Shroud. Ghost lettering, they say, is either total nonsense or an example of pareidolia, the psychological inclination to detect something significant in random or vague images— the same type of misperception that leads people to see the face of Mother Teresa in a cinnamon bun. Another count against Frale is that she has chosen to publish in commercial books rather than academic journals, which could review and verify her research.

In an interview in a research facility of the Vatican Secret Archives not far from Saint Peter's Square, Frale defended her findings. A forty-five-year-old who sometimes wears jeans to work, she has never quite fit into the predominantly clerical environment of the Vatican. Frale said critics of her conclusions about the purported writing on the Shroud seem to have forgotten that the Holy Land was part of the Roman world, and "the Roman world was full of writings."

"They wrote birthday greetings for children on papyrus. There were horoscopes written, shopping lists, the Roman taverns had wooden tablets where the daily menu was written. They weren't illiterate. Romans were compulsive scribblers," she said.

More generally, she argued, the Shroud of Turin needed to be approached with a mentality that is open to both science and religion. From the scientific point of view, the Shroud is "an archaeological site," an object that contains diverse strata of information, deposited in different eras and chronologically datable with precision. But it is also an object that has been contaminated through the centuries, and science may not be able to solve the enigma of the formation of its image.

While researchers need to be objective, Frale believes they also have to recognize that the Shroud is a religious reality. Unfortunately, she said, there is a "rationalist current" in the Catholic Church and in the Vatican that is hostile to the Shroud and similar phenomena: "This rationalist current wants to separate mystery from religion. But if you try to strip mystery from religion, and remove the supernatural, nothing really remains."

At the Vatican Frale's findings have prompted widely divergent reactions. Favorable attention has come from the Vatican newspaper and Vatican Radio, which featured her studies prominently. But her own superior, Bishop Sergio Pagano, prefect of the Vatican Secret Archives, has sharply criticized Frale's thesis on the Templars and the Shroud.

"I don't approve of any of it, and I've said so publicly. She is imaginative. She takes documents and reads them in her own way. She wants to find the Shroud at all costs, and unfortunately she's been contradicted by others," Pagano stated bluntly. He sat at a long, polished wooden desk beneath a vaulted ceiling in the archives' headquarters, next to a stack of books and manuscripts.

"I don't think there are any real secrets about the Templars," Pagano said. "Like all the knights of the Middle Ages, they liked relics. They brought back relics from the Holy Land. This was normal. But there's no proof they ever had the Shroud."

The Shroud of Turin is sometimes referred to as the "thinking person's relic" because it invites quiet contemplation. When the cloth is put on display, the lines of visitors are almost silent, with nothing like the prayerful wailing that takes place in Naples when the blood of Saint Januarius is held up before the faithful for the ritual miracle of lique-faction. Nor, generally speaking, is there hope or expectation of a mir-acle in its presence. Vatican officials often point out that, officially at least, no miraculous cure has ever been attributed to the Shroud.

But in the middle of the last century, one poignant story of healing did make headlines in Europe. In 1955 Leonard Cheshire traveled through England in a bus, with a touring exhibition of photos of the Shroud of Turin. Cheshire, a highly decorated Royal Air Force pilot in World War II and a British observer to the nuclear bombing of Naga-saki, had become fascinated with the Shroud the year before while re-covering from tuberculosis. When Cheshire arrived in Gloucester, his exhibition caught the attention of ten-year-old Josephine Woollam, who was suffering with a severe bone disease. After seeing an article in the magazine *Picture Post*, Josie had the idea that if she could see the real Shroud, she would get through her health crisis. Her mother wrote a brief letter to Cheshire: "My daughter Josephine, aged ten, is very ill in hospital with osteomyelitis in the leg and hip and an abscess in the lung. The doctors have said there is no hope for her, and she has received the Last Rites of the Church. But Josephine has asked me to write to you, and says that if only she could see the Holy Shroud she will get better and walk again."

Cheshire wanted to help the girl but knew the Shroud was locked up in Turin, and exhibited only rarely. Josie was sent a small photo of the figure on the Shroud's face, along with a note explaining that her request to see the actual relic was impossible to fulfill. Five days later Cheshire received another letter from Mrs. Woollam with extraordi-nary news: After receiving the Shroud photo, Josie's condition had greatly improved. She was sitting up in bed and eating well, and as Mrs. Woollam reported, "the doctor could hardly believe his eyes."

Josie still wanted to see the Shroud itself, though, and believed that only then would she walk again. A month later Cheshire called on the Woollams at their home, where the girl was still recovering. Josie told him there had to be a way for her to see the Shroud, insisting, "I want to be blessed by it." Cheshire explained the difficulty to her mother: It would mean someone would have to take Josie to Turin and convince the aged Cardinal Maurilio Fossati to arrange a special viewing, a request the cardinal had turned down many times. But even as Cheshire spoke the words, he began imagining how he might bring it about.

But before going to Turin, Cheshire realized, they would have to obtain the permission of the former king of Italy, Umberto of Savoy, who still had legal ownership of the Shroud and who now resided in Lisbon, Portugal. While Cheshire handled the preparations for their complicated journey, Josie convinced her aunt in Liverpool to make her a "wedding dress" of white silk and lace, so that she would be properly attired when she viewed the Shroud. After weeks of planning and packing, Cheshire and Josie traveled by train to Lisbon and managed to arrange an audience with Umberto. The ex-king looked at Josie, dressed in her new white lace dress, and kept repeating the phrase, "Such a long way to ask such a question." He had no objection to granting her request, but he explained that any final decision would have to be made by Cardinal Fossati.

They next set out by train to Turin, with Cheshire carrying Josie or pushing her in her wheelchair. To his alarm Josie seemed to be taking it for granted that she would see the Shroud, and was already talking about where they could purchase some walking shoes. When they arrived in Turin several days later, they discovered that reporters were awaiting them: the story of Josie's unusual journey had come to the attention of the press, and Cheshire wasn't sure that would help their cause.

When they met with Cardinal Fossati the following morning, Cheshire handed him a letter of introduction written by Umberto, explaining Josie's request. Cardinal Fossati went to the far end of a large reception room to read it and confer with his aides. After a few minutes one of them came over to Cheshire and explained the difficulties involved. At that point Josie whispered: "I am going to show them my wedding dress." The girl, who looked tiny in her oversize wheelchair, was brought over to the cardinal and opened her battered suitcase. As she removed the beautiful white dress, the effect on Cardinal Fossati was remarkable, Cheshire later recalled. The cardinal placed his hand on her head, said he was very pleased with her, and walked over to the telephone to make a call. A few minutes later he returned to his guests and asked, "What time would you like to see it?" They were told to return that afternoon; the press was not to be informed.

Cheshire and Josie arrived at the cathedral at four o'clock and found Cardinal Fossati already there, praying. Josie, in her white dress, was wheeled close to him. The place was humming with ecclesiastical witnesses and other officials. Two priests climbed a ladder and, using three different keys, unlocked the series of grilles that protected the Shroud in its niche above the altar. They brought the casket containing it down and placed it in front of Josie, on a table draped with white fabric. The knotted red silk ribbons that bound the casket were cut, one by one. They then opened the lid, carefully lifted the Shroud out, and placed it in her lap. The Shroud was wrapped in silk, but Josie put her hands under the covering and touched the burial cloth. Three minutes later, the Shroud was returned to its casket, resealed with ribbons, and locked back in its cell.

Reporters inevitably learned about the special viewing and were interested in one thing: Had a miracle occurred? It was clear when Josie was wheeled out of the cathedral that she had not been instantly "cured" of her bone disease. But she did feel better and in the years to come she would say the Shroud had given her the courage to keep fighting every time she faced a setback. When they returned to England, her mother was waiting at Victoria Station and asked her daughter what she had received in Turin. Josie replied, "More than I went to ask for."

Josie never claimed to have been healed by the Shroud. Although the bone infection did not recur, her deformed left leg was useless and was amputated twelve years later, in 1967. She continued to have chronic chest problems but went on to live a relatively normal life, eventually marrying and having two children, and working as a barmaid, a printmaker, and a telephone receptionist.

In 1978, when the Shroud was officially put on display for the first time in forty-five years, Josie returned to Turin. Accompanying her was Leonard Cheshire. As always, the press was there to ask about a miracle, and as always Josie downplayed the notion: "I don't like it when people start shouting about miracles and cures and all that sort of thing."

More important, she said, was the fact that the Shroud was finally being exhibited publicly. At the Turin cathedral, tens of thousands of people were lined up to see an object she had once held in her lap. Josie, now thirty-three, said she was as eager as any of them for the viewing. It made no sense to keep this image hidden under lock and key, she told reporters. "If it is the precious relic that it's reported to be and that I believe it to be, then the world should see it."

CHAPTER FOUR

Full of the Devil

One morning in April 2012, Father Michael Maginot's Bible study group was meeting, as it did on every Friday, in his living room. They called his house "the rectory," but it was really just another rambler that blended into the middle-class neighborhood of Merrillville, Indiana, where Maginot had grown up in the 1960s and 1970s. Inside, the house was filled with knickknacks and artifacts of bygone years: a CD rack that featured Joan Baez and Jefferson Airplane, a collection of Marian plates above the fireplace, scale models of Saint Peter's Square and other architectural wonders, and photos of Maginot's years as a student in Rome, including one of him standing next to a youngish-looking Pope John Paul II. An assortment of Rubik's Cubes and other twisty puzzles, some unsolved, dotted the room. The five members of the Bible group had taken their places, some at a big coffee table, others on a couch or in reclining rocking chairs. Maginot himself loved to rock and was just settling into a comfortable rhythm when the phone rang. It was a call that would change his life.

The caller identified himself as a chaplain at the Methodist hospital, where Maginot sometimes helped out, and asked, "Can you come over and do an exorcism?" Shocked by the request, Maginot initially balked: before performing an exorcism, he explained, an investigation had to be conducted and a bishop's permission obtained. What was this all about? he asked. The chaplain paused, then said: "Several professional people have seen a boy walk up a wall backward." That got Maginot's attention. Have them call me, he said, and went back to the Scripture discussion, wondering what he was getting himself into.

In later interviews, Maginot offered a detailed reconstruction of the events that followed. Rosa Campbell and her daughter, Latoya Ammons, phoned him the next day, anxious to meet with the priest as soon as possible. Latoya's three children, a twelve-year-old girl and boys aged nine and seven, were being attacked by demons, they told him. The demons would typically jump from one child to another. Sometimes they would reveal their presence when the children began a kind of Satanic chanting, or growling in unnaturally deep voices, or rolling their eyes back in their heads and baring their teeth. The children would behave normally most of the time, but then would suddenly rage against one another or their mother, kicking and hitting. Occasionally the children had been thrown to the ground or against walls by an invisible force. Once, Latoya said, she heard her daughter scream and found the girl levitating above her bed. More recently the boys were going around as if under a spell, saying, "It's time for someone to die."

Child protection services had become concerned about the children missing school and ordered a visit with the family doctor. The doctor and nurses observed their aggressive behavior, which included guttural cursing at the physician, and thought they were dealing with frightening manifestations of delusion and hallucination. They then watched as one of the boys was lifted up and thrown against the wall without anyone touching him. At least, that's what they thought they saw. They ran out of the room and called 911. Several police cars and ambulances responded, and the children were taken to the Methodist hospital in Gary. It was there that a Department of Child Services case manager and a nurse said they witnessed the nine-year-old boy glide backward up a wall to the ceiling as his grandmother, Rosa, held his arms. He then flipped over her, landing on his feet. Both professionals quickly left the room. When they told a doctor about it, he came back and asked the boy to repeat the wall-walking feat. But the boy had no recollection of it, and said it was, of course, impossible.

By the time Rosa and Latoya spoke with Father Maginot, child protection services had already removed the children from their mother's custody. One boy was in a psychiatric lockdown facility, and his siblings were placed in a home run by Carmelite Sisters in Chicago. Maginot agreed to meet with them and see what he could do, but while he was eager to help, he immediately saw a number of problems.

For one thing, he had no experience in exorcism. He'd never been trained in the practice and had no idea where he would even procure the book of rites that would surely be needed. Years before, as an administrator in the Diocese of Gary, Indiana, he had handled a few "typical ghostly things," as he put it, with little fanfare. A simple house blessing or saying a Mass for the afflicted person always solved the problem. But when a few more serious cases arose, he discovered that his bishop had assigned them to another cleric. In effect, Father Maginot said, he'd been "shut down" on the demonology beat, and the diocese never called him again to handle such situations. That was a shame, he felt, because he'd always been fascinated with how evil works, and in pastoral counseling he sometimes would see cases of what he called "the devil's hand." Maginot firmly believed in the possibility of demonic possession. In fact, he was impressed with how enterprising the devil could be, and he thought the church should respond in kind. "You know, we have a good product, and they have a bad one, yet they seem to be very popular selling theirs. Give the devil his due, he's successful in what he does. Or *apparently* successful, I should say. It doesn't last." One thing the priest believed was that actual possession by a demon was never just an accident: the demon must have been invited in or sent to a person in some kind of ritualistic event. Getting the demon out would require a similar combination of ritual and cunning.

On Sunday evening Maginot drove to the house where Latoya and Rosa lived, an older two-story rental in a Gary neighborhood pockmarked with abandoned and foreclosed homes. Latoya, a well-dressed African American in her early thirties, spoke in a slight southern accent, calmly relating the details of her ordeal. Rosa, who didn't look that much older than her daughter, added more specifics that, if true, were rather alarming to the priest. After listening for several hours to the two women recount the strange events, Maginot began to suspect that the source of the problem might be Latoya's former boyfriend. To Latoya's surprise, the boyfriend had turned out to be married—something she learned in a phone call from his wife—and she had recently broken off their relationship. But even before then, she suspected him of taking things, including photographs of family members and a pair of her shoes. And he had once made a strange request, Latoya told the priest: he had asked for a pair of her panties to keep as a remembrance of their first night together. *Wow*, Maginot thought, *that's pretty weird.*

"We need to get to the bottom of this," Maginot told Rosa and Latoya, and as he did so the bathroom light down the hall began to flicker and buzz. They walked over to see what the problem was, and the flickering stopped. "I guess it's afraid of me," Maginot joked, at which the flickering immediately started again. A few moments later he noticed the rods on the Venetian blinds begin to sway, first in one window and then moving to the next, all through the house. Maginot was mystified but needed to return to identifying the cause of these strange occurrences. He sat the women down again and said, "Let's get back to the boyfriend." But they weren't looking at him. They pointed to wet footprints that had materialized on the hardwood floor of the living room. *Did I make those?* Maginot wondered to himself. But that was impossible; he had been in the house for three hours. He bent down and felt the prints, which were fresh.

Latoya suddenly looked ill. She complained of a headache and chills, got a blanket, and then said she was burning up. Maginot had a hunch and asked if he could place a crucifix on her head. When he did, Latoya began to convulse. He withdrew the cross, and she calmed down. "You have a classic sign, aversion to holy objects. That means *you're* possessed," he told Latoya. "I know," she responded sheepishly. He moved the crucifix over Rosa's head, but there was no reaction. "I'm fine," Rosa said. "It attacked me one time, but it never got into me like Latoya." In a way this discovery made Maginot's task simpler: whatever demon was harassing Latoya's children was operating through her, and so she would need to be exorcised.

When the strange behavior had begun more than a month earlier, the two women had tried remedies suggested by friends who belonged to a "church of deliverance" nearby—marking crosses in olive oil through-out the house, and burning a special incense. A clairvoyant from that church had told them their basement was "full of demons," so they had set up a table there with a candle and a Bible opened to Psalm 91: "No evil shall befall you, nor shall any plague come near your dwelling; for He shall give His angels charge over you, to keep you in all your ways." None of those measures helped, however, and the problems quickly began to spin out of control. Although Rosa and her daughter were Baptist, they sought assistance from other churches, though no one was interested in helping them. Above all, Latoya wanted her children back, but before that could happen, she needed to demonstrate she could keep them safe. Despite the accounts of the witnesses at the hospital, not everyone believed this was a problem that had a supernatural cause. One psychiatric report suggested that the children were performing to satisfy their mother's delusions, and that she had encouraged their behavior. At this point she felt she needed to rid herself of the evil that had taken such a hold over their lives, and saw exorcism as the only solution.

It took Father Maginot several weeks to prepare for their first formal rite. He reluctantly reported on the situation to his bishop, who suggested he talk to some exorcists in the region and get their advice. But he discovered that they had had little experience, and no one seemed to have a ritual, the book of exorcism prayers. There was a new rite and an older one, but because both were out of print they suggested that Maginot download the Latin and English versions from the Internet. One priest offered a clever tip: Maginot should take the Holy Eucharist along, hidden in his pocket, to see if Latoya would react to it.

Maginot decided to begin with a minor exorcism, which technically did not require the bishop's permission. He showed up at Latoya's house one afternoon in May with his assistant, a laywoman from his parish. Two policemen were on hand to act as restrainers (the priest asked them to leave their guns and any other weapons that could be taken from them in their squad car), along with members of child protection services. By now the story of the devil and the Ammons family had made the rounds of every law enforcement and social services worker in northern Indiana. The police wanted to film the proceedings, and Maginot had no objection.

He began the rite by sprinkling every room of the house with holy water and blessed salt. Following instructions from the Internet, he recited prayers in English over Latoya, who did not respond, but when he moved his crucifix near her, she convulsed, as she had earlier. Maginot then drew from his pocket a small pyx, a gold-plated receptacle containing the consecrated host of the Eucharist, and put it on Latoya's forehead. "Oh, that hurts!" she exclaimed. "That's burning! What is that?" He told her it was the Blessed Sacrament, but she had no idea what he meant.

Maginot called the bishop, and told him the minor exorcism had failed to resolve the problem, and that they would have to proceed to the full exorcism rite. The bishop gave him permission, though reluctantly.

Meanwhile Maginot went through Ammons's house a second time with police, who noticed that a section of the concrete floor had been cut out beneath the basement stairs. Maginot thought that if something had been buried there, such as an occult symbol, it could be a "portal" to the demonic world. They excavated the area and unearthed a number of strange objects, including a fingernail, a shoehorn, and a pair of boys' socks, but nothing that seemed particularly portentous.

On a Friday afternoon in early June, Latoya Ammons arrived at Father Maginot's Church of Saint Stephen Martyr, a modern structure at the end of a suburban cul-de-sac, for the exorcism rite. Near the entrance stood a tall white cross, decorated with a broken heart and a sign that reads: "In memory of aborted children." This neighborhood, like much of Merrillville, has undergone a racial transformation in recent years. The city had originally been populated during the "white flight" from Gary during the 1960s and 1970s, and Maginot's family had been part of that resettlement. But African Americans had gradually relocated in Merrillville as well, and now represented a majority of the population. What was once a fairly heavily Catholic area is today predominantly Baptist. At Saint Stephen's, Father Maginot is pastor to only 175 families—a tiny parish for an urban area.

Once again the police and social services showed up for this "major exorcism," bringing tripods and cameras. But if they were expecting a cinematic-style struggle with the devil, they were disappointed. Maginot prayed the exorcism rite over Latoya as she sat in a chair, and she showed no reaction, even when he placed his crucifix on her head. The priest gave her three plastic rosaries for her children and one large one, featuring Saint Benedict medals, for herself. Call if you need me, he told her, and she drove off.

A short while later, walking across the parking lot with his assistant, Maginot noticed a segment of the Saint Benedict rosary on the ground, then another, and another—the rosary had been torn to pieces. His assistant picked them all up and said she'd reassemble it. It was a strange ending to a strange day. "I don't think this is over," Maginot told her.

Latoya called the following day wondering what had happened to her rosary—it had disappeared from her purse. Maginot told her where they found it, and they agreed to do another exorcism. During the first rite, the priest told her, the devil had apparently been playing possum. Now they needed to up the ante. It was important that they determine the identity of the demon inside her, so that they could summon him and get him to speak. Latoya recalled that when all of this began she had gone to a computer and Googled "How to get rid of demons." On a spiritual "symptom checker" site she found a description of a possession that seemed to correspond to her family's afflictions. But when she tried to click to find the name of the demon responsible for it, her computer had crashed. Maginot managed to retrace her online steps, printed out the name of the demon, and placed it in an envelope; it was dangerous, he had been told, for others to see or speak such a name. He set it aside for their next exorcism, excited about the prospects of a more personalized combat with the devil. Then he went for a bike ride, one he took every Thursday, on a trail that wound through miles of suburban Indiana landscape.

As Maginot recalled later, the first odd sign along the bike trail was that every single family he passed greeted him warmly. Typically people never looked up from their yard work, but today they were unusually friendly. Then, where the trail exited onto a sleepy residential road, a speeding car slammed on its brakes and barely avoided hitting him. That had never happened before. On his way home every person or family he encountered along the trail would stare at him, as if they were trying to figure out who—or what—he was. At one point he was suddenly thrown from his bike, for no apparent reason, and suffered a small cut but no serious injuries. His heart was racing, and a single thought crossed his mind: *He had learned the name of the demon, and now it was coming after him.* He could have walked his bicycle home. But he told himself that would be letting the terrorists win, so he pressed on. Around the next curve he narrowly avoided a head-on collision with a racing bike, whose rider never looked up. More close calls followed in succession. By the time he made it back to the rectory, his head was spinning.

A week later, at the second exorcism, Maginot stood over Latoya and inveighed against the demon. He wore a surplice and a purple stole, reading the prayers in English from a printout: "I adjure you, Satan, enemy of human salvation, recognize the justice and goodness of God the Father, who has condemned your pride and envy with just judgment: Depart from this handmaid of God, Latoya." With two policemen at her side Latoya trembled in her chair, her face contorting as if she might speak, but no sounds came out. Maginot invoked the demon, using the name he had retrieved online, and Latoya's convulsions became stronger. He knew it was the responsibility of an exorcist to keep provoking the demon, so he repeated the name frequently. "I adjure you, Satan, deceiver of the human race, acknowledge the Spirit of truth and grace, Who repels your snares and confounds your lies: Go out of this created image of God, Latoya, whom He Himself signed with the heavenly seal; withdraw from this woman, whom God, with spiritual anointing, made a sacred temple." Maginot traced a sign of the cross on Latoya's brow as she grimaced and shook. "Withdraw, O Satan, in the name of the Father, and of the Son, and of the Holy Spirit."

Maginot went through the lengthy rite twice. When it came to an end, Latoya was falling asleep, which exorcists say is not uncommon. After she woke they recited prayers of thanksgiving for deliverance, with more hope than conviction: "Grant, O Lord, that the spirit of wickedness may no more have power over her."

Latoya called him a few days later. The demon was back; she was being tormented by nightmares. That morning, when she picked up her Saint Benedict rosary, she had found that the body of Christ had been pulled off its cross. She and Rosa had searched the house frantically without finding it. Maginot prepared for another exorcism, this one to be conducted in Latin, using the old rite. His lay assistant had to learn the Latin responses, which she practiced on a tape recorder, and was prepared by the time the third major exorcism was conducted two weeks later, at the end of June. Maginot asked his brother to serve as a restrainer, because this time neither social services nor the police chose to attend. The priest suspected they might be losing interest in what had been lengthy and fairly undramatic rituals. Truth be told, as Maginot himself remarked, Latoya's exorcisms were not up to Hollywood standards. There was no levitating, no rotating of the head, no foaming at the mouth or superhuman strength. Latoya's demon didn't even speak, at least so far. As Maginot went through the rite, he noticed that Latoya was calm when he read the prayers praising God, but trembled uncontrollably whenever he condemned the evil one. Because the prayers were in Latin, she could not possibly have been performing, as she didn't know a word of Latin.

"Exorcizo te, omnis immunde spiritus, omnis satanica potestas." Maginot liked the sound of the Latin, familiar from his days as a student. "I cast you out, unclean spirit, along with every Satanic power of the enemy, every specter from hell, and all your fell companions; in the name of our Lord Jesus Christ. Begone, and stay far from this creature of God." His words echoed off the walls of the church. "Exi ergo, transgressor. Exi, seductor, plene omni dolo et fallacia." "Depart, transgressor. Depart, seducer, full of lies and cunning, foe of virtue, persecutor of the innocent. Give place, abominable creature, give way, you monster, give way to Christ!"

After the rite was recited twice, Latoya fell asleep, and in fact was snoring. When she finally woke, she asked if she had "risen up," because she felt as if someone had been trying to lift her. No, they told her, none of them had witnessed anything like that. It occurred to Maginot that it might be easier for the devil to levitate a child than a full-grown woman.

The priest suggested they have another session, and Latoya said she'd call to schedule one. But weeks went by without a word from her; apparently the demon had departed. Latoya had moved to Indianapolis and was doing well, as were the children, who had been returned to their mother, as Rosa related to Maginot in a phone call months later. He never heard back from Latoya.

The whole episode seemed to have ended on that low-key note. Maginot went back to his normal duties, preparing Sunday homilies, meeting with the Bible study group, counting the collection money on Monday morning. But then, more than a year later, a reporter for the *Indianapolis Star* came to Maginot's residence and interviewed him for a story they were preparing about Latoya and her children. When the article finally appeared, early in 2014, it went viral. Latoya's house was described as the "portal to hell," and Maginot was cast as the priest who had dared to battle with the devil. TV reporters began showing up unannounced on his doorstep, and *The O'Reilly Factor* had him as a guest. Maginot was overwhelmed with media attention, and it wasn't long before movie offers appeared. He wondered what his bishop would think of all this, but the bishop simply wanted to be left out of it. Maginot had offered to prepare a report on the exorcisms, which would then have become diocesan property. But the bishop declined, telling Maginot to keep the report for himself. As far as Maginot was concerned, then, his story belonged to himself, and if it brought him a financial windfall, there were many good causes to fund. Eventually he made a feature-film deal with Tony DeRosa-Grund, whose paranormal horror movie, *The Conjuring*, had been a box-office hit the year before. Maginot also signed a separate contract for a documentary film with *Ghost Adventures* host Zak Bagans, who spent $35,000 to purchase the Gary house where Ammons had lived. Maginot said he was given assurances that the scripts would be true to life, and that the facts would not be dramatized out of all recognition. All he wanted, he explained, was for his story to serve as a lesson to people who think the devil is just fun and games, and a warning to those who dabble in the occult.

"I see God's hand in all this," he explained. "Exorcism is a mysterious thing to most people. There's a kind of mystique. And here's a chance to see it in all its realism. People need to know that evil is real, it works step-by-step, and slowly but surely it can take over your life. They need to know that demons are powerful creatures. But demons can only do what God allows them to do. Even if I were dealing with one of the top demons in hell, there's a limit to his power."

Father Francesco Bamonte sat at a desk in his office, a sparsely furnished room in the Church of Saint Anastasia in Rome. In a few moments someone would knock at the door, the first of a long string of appointments throughout the morning. He ran a hand through close-cropped silver hair and checked his agenda. The following week he would be on the road again, giving lectures outside of Italy, so he had to accommodate as many sessions as he could before his departure. Many of his visitors were regulars, and people who believed they were possessed worried when their exorcist was not on call.

The massive church, built in the fourth century beneath the imperial residences of Rome's Palatine Hill, today houses a well-publicized pro-life center that offers assistance to mothers facing unexpected pregnancies. Father Bamonte's ministry is not advertised, but is no less popular among Italians seeking spiritual liberation from demons. The priest spends several hours a day listening to their stories and either giving them a blessing or, in extreme cases, going through the exorcism rite. Some of the petitioners are well known to the priest, as they have been battling demons for years. Others turn up after hearing about Sant'Anastasia through the grapevine. Father Bamonte often tells people he's glad he actually lives elsewhere, as the demon-possessed would be "ringing the bell day and night—that's the way it is with exorcists."

The priest, who is president of the International Association of

Exorcists, has been conducting exorcisms in Rome since 2000, and he's convinced that cases of possession are increasing at an alarming rate. Modern society has become largely de-Christianized, he said, so instead of experiencing the transcendent in church, people find it in other places—in the occult, in spiritism, in New Age movements, in witchcraft, and even in Satanism. These esoteric practices have found their way into popular films, books, video games, and cartoons, and the Internet provides instructions on all manner of pagan practices, including how to sell your soul to the devil. People who consider themselves "spiritual seekers" often succumb to these temptations, and by the time they realize such practices lead to suffering, it's often too late for them to handle the problem on their own. They come to him, desperately hoping to be liberated. The devil, he said, is a very clever adversary.

While a successful exorcism can take years, Bamonte explained, typically there is also an immediate reaction. Anyone who doubts the existence of the devil should attend one of his sessions, he said, and hear the demon speaking through the individual possessed. "You sprinkle holy water on the person and you hear him cry out: 'It burns! It burns!' One time a demon told me, 'It's like having muriatic acid poured on top of you!' Another one said, 'I'd rather have dog piss thrown on me than holy water.'" Bamonte smiled, and added: "The devil can be a tragicomic figure, don't you think?"

In fact, after years of sparring with Satan and his minions, Bamonte believes he knows how to prevail over them. He sometimes makes ironic jokes at the devil's expense, in order to irritate him. The key factor is that the devil is not all-powerful and operates within certain limits, which is vital for a possessed person to understand. It's also imperative to make clear that the exorcist, with God on his side, is in charge. That's one reason why Bamonte, like other exorcists in Rome, uses the old rite. Unlike the new text, the older ritual highlights the dramatic confrontation between the exorcist and the devil, and encourages the exorcist to interrogate the possessing demon or demons with authority: What is your name? How many are you? When did you take possession of the victim?

Father Bamonte is one of a handful of younger exorcists in Italy who have been trained by a small group of veterans. Led by Father Gabriele Amorth, the ninety-year-old dean of the exorcism corps in Rome, these elders are looked upon as pioneers, having fought many battles with the hierarchy and the Vatican to restore exorcism as a legitimate ministry in the modern church. In recent years they have been called on to apprentice would-be exorcists from the United States and other countries, in connection with a training course offered by the Regina Apostolorum University, a Rome institute run by the Legionaries of Christ religious order. The Rome fieldwork experience of the novice exorcist Father Gary Thomas of California inspired Matt Baglio's 2009 book *The Rite*, which led to a movie of the same name. In the view of the old guard, this kind of popularization of exorcism runs the risk of sensationalism, but it's a risk worth taking. Beginning with William Peter Blatty's supernatural classic *The Exorcist* in the 1970s, a succession of books and films has led millions of people to rediscover the devil as a spiritual entity, and the exorcist as his chief foe.

With his kit full of crucifixes and his dire warnings against the "smoke of Satan," the imposing Father Amorth looks as if he walked out of central casting. Among reporters covering religious affairs he's known as a sound-bite machine, but many at the Vatican regard him as a loose cannon. Amorth says he has performed more than one hundred thousand exorcisms, a claim that some church experts find implausible. He uses restraining ropes to hold down the possessed during the ritual, which can become violent. During some sessions, he says, victims have vomited up pieces of metal or shards of glass, and others have coughed up rose petals. Amorth tends to see the devil at work almost everywhere: he believes that Hitler and Stalin were possessed, that yoga is Satanic, that Halloween is a devil's trick, and that Harry Potter books can open a dangerous door to the world of black magic. What alarms the hierarchy is when Father Amorth talks about the devil residing at the Vatican, as evidenced by "cardinals who don't believe in Jesus, bishops connected with demons." Even the clerical sex abuse scandal, in Amorth's view, reveals that "the devil is at work inside the Vatican."

Father Amorth has been billed as "the Vatican's chief exorcist," but that's not quite accurate. He works for the Diocese of Rome, not the Vatican, and on several occasions the Vatican has had to intervene to correct or clarify his statements. In 2007, for example, he was quoted as saying Pope Benedict had ordered bishops to establish exorcism squads to combat Satan around the world. The Vatican immediately dismissed the claim, stating that the pope "has no intention of ordering local bishops to bring in garrisons of exorcists to fight demonic possession."

On one spectacular claim, however, Amorth proved to be correct, despite Vatican denials. On a spring morning of 1982 a young woman named Francesca F., thrashing and cursing loudly, was placed in a car in a small town east of Rome by a bishop and her parish priest, who drove at full speed to the Vatican. Passing quickly through the Vatican checkpoints, the car pulled up in a courtyard beneath the Apostolic Palace, where Pope John Paul II resided. As papal advisers scurried to accommodate them, the woman's screams echoed down the Vatican's marble hallways. A few minutes after they arrived, John Paul himself walked into a dimly lit room and approached Francesca solemnly. He began pronouncing the formulas of exorcism in Latin. Held down by the prelates, she continued to writhe and moan as the pope prayed with increasing urgency. Finally he leaned over her and whispered, "Tomorrow I will say a Mass for you," and with those words she suddenly became calm. The demon appeared to have departed, and Francesca, looking confused and a bit embarrassed, apologized to the pope. Later, John Paul would tell a top aide that his duel with Satan felt like "a biblical scene."

According to Amorth, this was not the first time the Polish pope had performed an exorcism in the papal apartments. Vatican officials denied that, but a cardinal's memoirs later provided an eyewitness account of the pope's powerful encounter with Francesca F. It was an aspect of Pope John Paul's spiritual life that seemed to embarrass the Vatican.

Since the time of the Second Vatican Council in the 1960s, most theologians at the Vatican have preferred not to discuss demonic possession. The Catholic Church once had a special ministerial order of exorcists, but Pope Paul VI abolished it in 1972. By the 1980s exorcisms were very rarely performed, and only by specially delegated priests. In 1985 the Congregation for the Doctrine of the Faith, in a letter signed by its prefect, Cardinal Joseph Ratzinger, told bishops to enforce the limits on exorcism, making sure that unauthorized people did not lead prayer gatherings in which "demons are addressed directly." But a few months later, in 1986, Pope John Paul surprised his aides by launching a series of talks on the devil at his weekly general audiences, declaring that demonic influence can take the form of "diabolical possession," which could require an exorcism, and noting that Christ had given his disciples the power to cast out demons. Father Amorth realized he had a powerful ally in John Paul, who described the devil as "the father of lies" and a potent force in the world. In 1992, to the Vatican's irritation, Amorth founded the International Association of Exorcists.

In 1999, with Pope John Paul's blessing and over the objection of some doctrinal experts, the Vatican published a revised Rite of Exorcism, prompting press reports of a "renaissance" in exorcist ministry. In the years that followed, the Vatican offices dealing with clergy and worship cosponsored the Regina Apostolorum University study courses in Satanism and demonic possession, drawing dozens of exorcists or exorcists-in-training. In between the formal lectures on the theological, psychological, and sociological aspects of demonic cults, the priests shared stories about their own most difficult battles with Satan. For participants like Monsignor Marvin Mottet, an exorcist in Davenport, Iowa, these were much-needed strategy sessions against a forgotten enemy. As he told Catholic News Service: "This is warfare. We've gotten way behind. We've lost the concept of spiritual warfare."

As exorcism gradually regained a foothold in dioceses around the world, in Rome Father Amorth became a chief promoter of this movement, regaling journalists with dramatic tales of combat with Satan and writing books on the telltale signs of possession, the power of curses, and the inadequacies of the psychological sciences in defeating the devil. The inevitable headlines that followed discomfited many Vatican officials, who insisted that actual cases of Satanic possession were probably very rare, and that what exorcists were often dealing with were in fact psychological disorders.

Since 1985 the Vatican's doctrinal congregation had been warning against unauthorized exorcisms, and in 2004 it sent a letter to the world's bishops, asking each of them to designate and train a priest in their diocese who would handle cases of alleged possession. The intent was to give bishops more control, and make sure that most priests would not freelance as exorcists. But Father Amorth and others chose to interpret the letter differently, viewing it as a sign that the Vatican was encouraging a return to the ministry of exorcism in every diocese of every country.

A few bishops have taken up the call enthusiastically, and when that happens, it's always well publicized. In 2013 Cardinal Antonio María Rouco Varela of Madrid made news when he selected eight priests for exorcism training, to counter what he described as an unprecedented increase in cases of diabolical possession. In 2012 the Archdiocese of Milan doubled its number of exorcists, from six to twelve, and set up a phone bank to deal with what it said was an unusually high number of Catholics in search of liberation from demons. But across the broad spectrum of Catholicism, these initiatives remain exceptions to the rule.

Newspaper accounts sometimes give the impression that the modern Catholic Church, or at least its major archdioceses, are overflowing with exorcists. The view from within can be quite different, however. In the Diocese of Rome Father Bamonte said he's one of only three or four active exorcists, all of whom have other pastoral jobs: "In reality, there aren't very many of us. Often the bishop is reluctant to assign priests to this ministry, because they're concerned about the workload. A single case of possession can require repeat visits that last months or even years. As exorcists, we really should be full-time. But that's not happening."

What's worse, Bamonte said, is that many bishops are still not on board with exorcism at all. When it's time to pick a diocesan exorcist, they'll designate a priest who is actually hostile to the ministry, and "instead of doing exorcisms, he sends everyone to a psychologist or a psychiatrist." A less than enthusiastic bishop can also rein in an exorcist who has assumed too high a profile. In some cases, the bishop will withdraw the permission to conduct exorcisms and give the priest a new pastoral assignment, far from the limelight.

For Father Gabriele Nanni, a knock at the door used to signal the arrival of a person possessed, a man or a woman seeking help from the spiritual oppression of malevolent spirits. But Father Nanni has been removed from circulation as an exorcist. When a visitor arrived on a recent Saturday afternoon, it was just a parishioner dropping off colored paper for a catechism project. "We're making masks out of papier-mâché, for the three Magi," Nanni said with a smile. "This is my life now. Parish life."

The priest sat before a gas heater in a small stone house in Prata d'Ansidonia, a remote and ancient village in central Italy that was decimated by an earthquake in 2009. His mother, who lives with him, placed freshly brewed coffee on an embroidered tablecloth. Like all the homes in the area, this one suffered structural damage in the quake and, even after five years of repairs, is not very safe; a window recently fell out of the dining room. Most of the residents have left, and the streets of the old town center are deserted. Today the parish serves about 150 souls, and for a priest who was once one of the best-known exorcists in Italy, it has been a real comedown. Father Nanni calls it his exile.

"I don't do exorcisms anymore," Nanni explained. "At least not here. I don't have permission. I was put here three years ago. I've tried to talk to the bishop about it, but he won't even see me. I'm very angry."

Exorcists may receive a lot of media attention, Nanni said, but the higher you go in the Catholic hierarchy, the greater the resistance. "Many priests involved in exorcism suffer. They've been marginalized, denigrated, and given a tough life, and the worst part is that the blows come from inside the church. One Italian bishop said to me, 'Exorcism—that stuff? I don't want to hear about it. I don't believe it.' His vicar was supposed to be in charge of exorcisms, and he had nine cases pending. The vicar told me, 'I think they all need a psychiatrist.'"

Nanni sat beneath a portrait of Mary while his mother cleared the coffee cups. A handsome man with silver hair and a piercing gaze, he has been popular on the lecture circuit and in the Italian media as an articulate spokesman for a new generation of exorcists. For years he conducted exorcisms in the nearby Diocese of Teramo, an area of Italy where occult practices have long flourished. But when he left there, he lost his authorization to exorcise. He still travels in Italy and abroad, where he is sometimes granted permission by local bishops to deal with individual cases of possession. Ironically, he said, the only place he can't fight the devil directly is in his own parish.

Like other younger exorcists, Father Nanni tends to dismiss the "Hollywood image" of demonic possession, saying that the exaggerated and sensationalistic episodes give people a false impression. But when describing his own experiences, it's not long before Nanni begins to relate harrowing accounts of levitation, speaking in tongues, and walking up walls. A month earlier, he said, he witnessed a possessed woman suddenly arch rearward and, her body contorted in the form of a perfect bridge, walk quickly backward—just as in the famous "spider walk" scene in *The Exorcist*. Another woman he treated would run like a dog, prowl like a cat, and—as her jaw became elongated—howl like a wolf. One girl came to him with scratches on her shoulder that, on closer examination, turned out to be writing in Latin: *princeps mundi,* the "prince of the world" moniker often attributed to the devil. It disappeared when he daubed it with cotton balls soaked in holy water. After Father Nanni addressed a conference in Naples, a young man who asked the priest for a blessing went into a demonic trance and began speaking a strange language. The professors who were attending recognized it as ancient Aramaic, the dialect spoken in Jesus's time.

Nanni said spiritual crises are sometimes related to physical afflictions. He recalled a forty-year-old woman in southern Italy who, among other problems, hadn't menstruated in years. When he blessed her, he said, she vomited up "half a sack full" of a dark brown liquid that looked like old blood. That evening she got her period and her menstrual cycle has remained regular for years.

The skepticism frequently expressed regarding such cases is, to Father Nanni, the symptom of an overly rationalistic Western culture, a culture that has tried to banish the supernatural, to the great detriment of people's spiritual health. This culture sees "possession" as a psychological problem best treated with therapy or drugs, and considers the devil a folkloristic figure from a bygone era. But Nanni argued that the tendency to repress spiritual realities always backfires, and makes the devil's work easier. For example, he said, Satan has reemerged in the contemporary world in such forms as witchcraft and magic, which are seen by many as harmless pastimes. In Nanni's view, cultures that have a pre-Christian tradition of magic, like Italy or Mexico, are actually more open to the idea that the devil is a real being. Yet in the Catholic Church, priests keep their distance from exorcism precisely because they're afraid of fueling a revival of such superstitions.

That's one reason why seminary courses rarely touch on exorcism or Satanic influences, Nanni said. There is strong resistance in Catholic intellectual and academic circles to any discussion of the devil as an actual entity. Even the more general study of ascetical and mystical knowledge, sometimes called "spiritual theology," which treats the devil as an obstacle to Christian perfection, has pretty much been ignored in modern priestly formation programs. "Spiritual theology today is looked upon as an 'extra,' and this is a cultural impoverishment of the church," Nanni observed.

As a result, he said, most priests are unprepared to respond to the thousands of Catholics who need the help of an exorcist. "If you could see the suffering of these people, and what they endure for a church that is betraying them," Nanni said, as his eyes welled up. "Their suffering makes me cry. The church is the only institution that has the weapons to help them."

In recent years church officials in Rome have not been of much assistance in promoting greater awareness of exorcism, Father Nanni explained. "At the Vatican, this is a topic that puts you at risk, and that can get you removed."

If one searches the Vatican's extensive website, which includes thousands of documents, statements, and reports extending back decades, the ministry of exorcism appears only a few times—a telling sign of the low profile Vatican officials have imposed on exorcism, despite the well-publicized concessions made by Pope John Paul II in the 1990s. Their main fear is that by depicting the devil as an omnipresent and powerful threat, the church will eclipse a greater truth: that Christ, who redeemed human beings and defeated Satan, is by far the more powerful figure.

The revised Rite of Exorcism of 1999, portrayed in the media as the church's return to active combat with Satan, more accurately reflects the cautionary attitude of Vatican experts. When he introduced the new rite to reporters, Cardinal Jorge Medina Estévez, head of the Vatican's Congregation for Divine Worship and the Discipline of the Sacraments, emphasized that "cases of possession are not only uncommon but very rare." Before exorcizing anyone, the Vatican stated, priests must have the "moral certainty" that the person involved was not suffering from psychic illnesses or an overactive imagination. That meant referrals for psychological screening would now be part of an exorcist's responsibility.

The text of the new rite aimed at removing the melodrama from exorcism. It practically ignored the traditional authority of the priest to bless objects in his battle for dominion over the devil. It emphasized that the devil's power is limited, and featured a petitionary invocation written by Vatican liturgists. In essence, Vatican officials were suggesting that the modern exorcist's efforts should be directed toward praying to God, not issuing commands to Satan.

That immediately provoked the scorn of experienced exorcists, who believed cases of possession required direct engagement with the devil, not merely pious prayers. This watered-down version of the ritual that had worked well for hundreds of years lacked the force of the old rite and was far too passive in tone, introducing an option in which the exorcist *asks* the devil to depart, rather than commanding him to do so. Moreover, experience had shown that vernacular languages weren't as effective as Latin; for the devil, apparently, Latin carried the traditional ring of defeat. For all these reasons, most old-guard exorcists continued to use the earlier form, and although the Vatican was not happy about this, it turned a blind eye.

In 2001 Father Raniero Cantalamessa, a Franciscan Capuchin who served as the official preacher to the pope and Roman Curia officials, gave a Good Friday sermon in Saint Peter's Basilica that caught the attention of Pope John Paul and journalists covering the event. His theme was the devil, and when exorcists read the first part of his text, they were excited. Father Cantalamessa rejected the contemporary understanding of Satan as a merely symbolic personification of evil, and pointed to the popularity of fortune-telling, horoscopes, and even Satanic sects to demonstrate that the devil cannot be explained out of existence. "Thrown out through the door, Satan has come back in through the window. Thrown out of the faith, he has come back through superstition," Father Cantalamessa said. But then the papal preacher reminded his listeners that Satan is no match for Jesus Christ and that "seeing the devil everywhere is no less misleading than seeing him nowhere." Christ's sacrificial death on the cross, he said, tied Satan like a dog to a chain, and "Satan cannot bite anyone except the person who wants to be bitten."

That seemed to run counter to the experience of exorcists, who say many of the possessed genuinely want to break free from the devil's clutches but find it impossible to do so without their help. Cantalamessa also appeared to rule out curses and spells as a means of inflicting demonic possession on a person. Most exorcists believe that curses are real, and open a portal to possession. Father Amorth, for example, claims to have dealt personally with many such cases: a young man cursed by his father at birth, a woman cursed by her in-laws at her

wedding, and a man who suffered physical injuries after his grandmother cursed a photograph of him. Amorth and other exorcists say
that it is folly to deny the power of curses and spells, and note that the
Old Testament contains a number of references to families and individuals who were cursed.

Especially in recent years, though, the Catholic Church has emphasized that original sin is the only legitimate "generational" curse, and
that baptism frees the individual from such sin and its instigator, the
devil. To believe in ancestral curses is now considered a serious doctrinal
error. As for curses placed on individuals, the revised Rite of Exorcism
specifically prohibits priests from exorcising "overly credulous" faithful
who believe they've been placed under an evil spell. That led Father Amorth to denounce the new rite as "a farce" and an obstacle to those battling Satan: "Evil spells are by far the most frequent causes of possessions
and evil procured through the demon: at least ninety percent of cases. It
is as good as telling exorcists they can no longer perform exorcisms."

The tension between the Vatican and traditional exorcists is rooted
in a fundamental difference in understanding the personality and power
of the devil. The message emphasized by the hierarchy is that Satan is
merely a fallen angel, not a deity, and is therefore subject to God's providential design. Christ came to "destroy the works of the devil," and con-
sequently there's no cause for excessive alarm today. That approach is
reflected in the wording of the Catechism of the Catholic Church:

> The power of Satan is, nonetheless, not infinite. He is only a crea-
> ture, powerful from the fact that he is pure spirit, but still a crea-
> ture. He cannot prevent the building up of God's reign. Although
> Satan may act in the world out of hatred for God and his king-
> dom in Christ Jesus, and although his action may cause grave
> injuries—of a spiritual nature and, indirectly, even of a physical
> nature—to each man and to society, the action is permitted by
> divine providence which with strength and gentleness guides hu-
> man and cosmic history.

But many exorcists are convinced that this modern theological approach underestimates the influence and the resources of Satan. Far from a foregone conclusion, they argue, every battle with the devil goes down to the wire. And it's entirely possible for souls to be lost along the way.

Then war broke out in heaven; Michael and his angels battled against the dragon.

—THE BOOK OF REVELATION

Popularized as secret spiritual allies through the centuries, depicted in modern films—with or without wings—as ambassadors to God or celestial bearers of life's second chance, angels have always represented heaven's heroic warriors in the struggle against evil in general and Satan in particular. Frequent protagonists in both the Old and New Testaments, in the latter it was angels who announced Jesus's birth, ministered to him in the desert, and comforted him in his agony. Every pope, at one time or another, has endorsed the invisible activity of the angelic host. John Paul II gave a series of talks on angels, stating "they do exist" and have a "fundamental role to play in the unfolding of human events." Even the highly rationalist Pope Benedict XVI once said guardian angels were "ministers of divine care for every person," offering protection from birth to death.

In recent years, though, the Vatican has repeatedly intervened to curb what it considers extreme and unfounded beliefs about angels and their role in human affairs. Arguably church officials have given more attention to excessive angel worship than to Satanic cults. Whether its focus is on angels or demons, the Vatican's chief concern is that Catholics might believe that the world is caught up in a supernatural struggle between good and evil spirits over which human beings have no control.

In 2002, alarmed that the traditional role of angels was being contaminated by New Age movements and modern forms of superstition, the Vatican issued a document that warned against "deviations" in angelic veneration. Salvation is a progressive spiritual journey that requires effort by individuals, it stated, and it was "childish" to "ascribe all setbacks to the devil and all success to the guardian angels." In particular, it took aim at cults that featured a full roster of angels, each with their own names, personalities, and superpowers. The only angels that should be identified, the Vatican made clear, were those named in Scripture: Michael, Raphael, and Gabriel.

Most cases of exaggerated veneration of angels are handled quietly, before they can be publicized and promoted. But one angel cult that arose in Europe has proven especially problematic, requiring multiple warnings from the Vatican's doctrinal officials. Engelwerk, also known as Opus Angelorum (Work of the Holy Angels), was founded in the late 1940s by a Tyrolean housewife, Gabriele Bitterlich, who claimed she had experienced visions revealing the names, appearances, and job descriptions of hundreds of angels and demons engaged in an endless battle. She filled tens of thousands of pages with detailed accounts of angels' activities, which formed the basis of her movement. It turned out that many Catholics were eager not only to become acquainted with the angelic hierarchy but also to dedicate their lives to them. Some of the names of angels had a Kabbalistic ring, or seemed borrowed from other esoteric texts. A handbook published by Opus Angelorum described Astaroth, whose "attacking light is visible over Rome," and Gethuliel, whose laugh rings out "like a silver bell." The handbook also identified notable demonic figures, including Schebarschenoth, who sends rays from the planet Neptune and causes, among other things, improper bone development in children and circulation problems. Demons, the handbook said, had the power to radiate through certain people, including midwives and gypsies, and some animals, like black hens and short-haired dogs, were especially susceptible to these rays.

The movement devised unusual rituals and ceremonies of atonement and consecration to particular angels, and gradually grew to include tens of thousands of members in dioceses all over the world. Bitterlich died in 1978, but Opus Angelorum continued to attract new adherents, despite the warnings of some German bishops. Parents began complaining that their children had been psychologically damaged by the movement, or instructed to do only as their guardian angel "commanded" them. In 1983 the Vatican's Congregation for the Doctrine of the Faith ordered the group to end some of its practices and beliefs. This had little effect, however, and in 1992 the Vatican prohibited Opus Angelorum from venerating any of the hundreds of angels who had been identified in the visions of Gabriele Bitterlich, warning that such information was "foreign to Sacred Scripture." It ruled that Bitterlich's revelations could not be used in the organization's worship, prayers, or spiritual formation, and it banned consecration to individual angels. The decree was signed by Cardinal Joseph Ratzinger, who as head of the doctrinal congregation had been following the Engelwerk saga with increasing apprehension. In 2000 the Vatican tried to salvage Opus Angelorum by making it a fully approved Catholic organization, subject to changes in its operations. The move splintered the group, however, and in 2010 the Vatican once again warned that a remnant of Opus Angelorum hard-liners was trying to keep the old, forbidden practices alive.

The doctrinal crackdown on angelic lore reflected Vatican concern that angels were becoming the newfound darlings of pop culture, but with little theological substance. Throughout the 1990s angels seemed to be everywhere: in advertising campaigns, on greeting cards, in New Age books, and even as characters in video games. Websites offered to find your personal archangel based on your birth date. Peaceful "angelic harmony" CDs appeared in music stores. "Angel card readings" offered spiritual advice, similar to the tarot decks of old. According to traditional church teaching, angels are noncorporeal, yet many of these modern angels had attractive bodies—indeed, some looked like fashion models.

The superficiality of this new wave of devotion prompted the Jesuit journal *La Civiltà Cattolica*, whose articles receive prior review at the Vatican, to publish an unusually critical editorial. "It is dangerous to penetrate the angelic world with esoteric or magical intentions because this is idolatry in the worst case or stupidity in the case of superstitious naiveté," it said. Angels, it added, are not beings who perform magic on behalf of the people they protect.

It is true that the thirteenth-century theologian Saint Thomas Aquinas wrote extensively about angels in his *Summa Theologica*, a classic work of philosophy and theology. But Aquinas approached angels from a rational perspective, writing about their intellect, their will, and their capacity or incapacity for love in the order of natural law—not about their quirky personalities or their supposedly magical abilities. Aquinas believed that the power of angels lay in their influence on people toward good, not in performing wondrous deeds. He conceived similar limits on the powers of demons. As fallen angels, he wrote, they are "obstinate in evil" and incapable of repentance, having made an irreversible choice for sin. Demons that beset human beings employ real powers, he said, but their ability to tempt is offset by divine grace. In other words, God provides the means to repulse the assault of demons.

Like angels, Aquinas wrote, demons cannot perform real miracles. But they can do astonishing things, affecting people's imaginations and even their corporeal senses.

For centuries the Catholic Church has consciously kept angels and devils in the theological background. The chief reason is that excessive attention to these otherworldly beings is considered spiritually unhealthy for Christians, a distraction from their journey of salvation, which should be centered on Jesus Christ. At the Vatican, beyond the occasional papal tribute to angels, it is difficult to find anyone willing to seriously discuss such matters. And as is often the case at the Vatican, the exception to this rule is an American.

From his vantage point at Vatican liturgies, Monsignor John Cihak sees the church from a unique perspective. As an assistant master of ceremonies, he often gazes over the shoulder of the pope at the altar, toward the vast crowds in Saint Peter's Square, a global congregation embraced by the curving arms of Bernini's colonnade. It's a visually impressive scene, one that highlights the church's unity in worship. But over the years, Monsignor Cihak has grown increasingly attentive to things that are less visible and, at times, less benign. Away from the papal altar, in interactions with individuals seeking spiritual solace, he has encountered entities that are unseen but, in his judgment, very real: protective angels and destructive demons.

"I'm a big fan of knowing your guardian angel, knowing his name and invoking him. An angelic influence is helpful to us, absolutely, but it's very subtle. Demons are different. Demons are like bullies; they want to get in there and just have their way. An angel is much more gentle and respectful of our freedom, as is God. God is never going to 'possess' you in that way," Cihak said.

Now in his midforties, Cihak grew up in Corvallis, Oregon, where his father once assisted at two exorcisms—a fact that stayed in Cihak's mind as a young man. After studying medicine, he turned to the priesthood and spent several years pursuing degrees in Rome. Since 2009 he has worked at the Vatican, splitting his duties between papal Masses and behind a desk at the Congregation for Bishops. His other main interest, though, is healing, especially mental health. Cihak is convinced that many mental health problems are linked to spiritual issues—specifically, manifestations of evil in its natural and supernatural forms. In plain language, he believes some people are afflicted by demons. Cihak conceives of a "spectrum of demonic influence," capable of oppressing people and, in some cases, of possessing them.

Skeptics who would dismiss such speculation as a return to medieval superstition are not seeing the big picture, Cihak said in an interview: "What our faith tells us is that we're in a cosmic war since the fall of Lucifer, and personal evil is part and parcel of this. Evil in this case is a creature. It is located in a person, an angelic person who has a corrupted nature, a demonic nature. And he's out to wreck the sand castle, as it were."

This viewpoint makes sense, he said, because Catholics don't subscribe to a dualistic system, in which the material and the spiritual worlds are separate: "We're sacramental, so the spiritual and the material are intimately bound up. That leaves us open to good and bad influences. It means we're open to God and the saints and angels in heaven, but at the same time we should realize we have an enemy out there. And if we don't know our enemy, he's going to have a field day with us."

Cihak has never taken the exorcism course in Rome frequented by other American priests, but he has spent time watching an Italian exorcist at work. "He was fairly old-school, and he used the old rite, which is basically designed to beat the hell out of the demon until he leaves. The whole point is ordering the demon: tell me your name. And when the demon is finally forced to say the name, he loses power and has to go. So it's a woodshed approach, a struggle that typically provokes all kinds of violent reactions."

While he respects the Italian exorcism traditions, Cihak said he prefers a matter-of-fact approach to diagnosing and treating demonic possession. "It's better to keep the histrionics out of the conversation, because it's not really helpful," he said. Some people want the exorcist to simply wrestle the devil to the mat, and then figure the process is over. But while exorcism does break the devil's grip, Cihak believes that the work of spiritual healing remains. The goal of exorcism or any kind of deliverance ministry, he maintains, should be to get the individual back on track with the normal means of sanctification: attending Mass, practicing the sacraments, prayer, and virtuous living.

In Cihak's view, there's one other step that's usually helpful for those who want to put the devil behind them: psychotherapy. "Very often, under demonic influence, you'll have these thoughts of 'you're no good,' 'you belong to me,' 'you're only capable of evil,' 'you're really messed up.' So after an exorcism, the person really has to relearn how to think, and how to stop feeling bad about themselves." Unlike most Italians engaged in exorcism ministry, who tend to see in psychiatrists a rival priesthood, American exorcists are open to working with experts in psychiatry and psychology. In fact, Cihak said, there are signs of a growing collaboration. He believes the psychological sciences are breaking free of a traditional bias against religion. At the same time, a good exorcist today realizes that mental health issues and spiritual problems often coexist and feed upon each other. The modern exorcist usually benefits from calling in a therapist, both before and after the demons are confronted.

"In the old days, the exorcist was this kind of Lone Ranger priest, probably very old and super holy. He walks in and has his black cape on and hangs it on a hook. The new look of exorcism is not that. A priest has the permission of the bishop to perform the rite, always with a team. Catholic psychiatrists can be present to help with the discerning," Cihak explained. Some U.S. dioceses, in fact, have people sign consent forms before undergoing an exorcism, for liability protection.

In 2012 Father Cihak teamed up with Aaron Kheriaty, an associate professor of psychiatry at the University of California Irvine School of Medicine, to write *The Catholic Guide to Depression*. As the book's subtitle explained, the aim was to describe how "the saints, the sacraments, and psychiatry" can help people break free of depression, which affects both mind and soul. The book identifies "spiritual desolation" as a form of depression and, borrowing a concept from Saint Ignatius of Loyola, suggests that such desolation is instigated by a "bad spirit" that discourages individuals by inflicting them with sadness, self-hatred, and temptation. As Cihak put it, good psychotherapy—the kind that is not overly focused on mood-changing drugs—will always end up confronting the essential philosophical and theological questions about existence. And that means dealing with evil and its "bad spirit" advocates.

It's especially important for the church to build bridges to the psychological sciences, Cihak said, because it needs all the resources it can muster in the struggle against evil in contemporary society. People who are in the grip of the devil, he said, are typically afflicted by at least one of three forces: drugs, the occult, and pornography or disordered sex. But there are more subtle portals for the devil, some of which have become socially acceptable. Cihak believes that the New

Age movement, influenced by paganism as well as Eastern religions, has led people down the path to dangerous practices of all kinds.

"It's more prevalent than we would like to think. And the problem is that with the Internet, you can become a witch in the privacy of your own home. You can become a Satanist right there, and be connected with all sorts of really awful people," Cihak observed. Eventually, he said, those connections can lead to all kinds of moral mayhem: "I have known of people who have been in covens, and what they do is sickening. One woman my father helped was a 'breeder.' They would just get her pregnant and then sacrifice the children. It doesn't get much more evil than that."

Even in the Catholic Church, not everyone would blame the devil for such wickedness, and only a small minority would look for telltale signs of diabolical possession. Cihak sees the church at the very beginning of a revival of the ministry of exorcism. He acknowledges a lack of enthusiasm at the Vatican for such a development, and a general skepticism among the more theologically educated when it comes to devils and angels. But Cihak believes that high theology should not abandon the "commonsense" approach to good and evil. "Being sophisticated should not mean we don't take spiritual realities seriously," he said, and indeed, it would be a typical tactic of the devil to encourage Catholics to forget their traditional knowledge of demons and how to deal with them. "It's important that we not lose the collective wisdom of the church because, in a way, it's the only thing that competes with Satan."

The 2014 Grammy Awards featured Katy Perry performing "Dark Horse," a song about sexuality, magic, and, some would say, witchcraft. As Perry pole-danced around a broom, encircled by flames and demons, she intoned, "So you wanna play with magic? Boy, you should know what you're fallin' for. . . . Once you're mine, there's no going back." The lyrics exalted a woman who "eats your heart out, like Jeffrey Dahmer," a reference to the Milwaukee serial killer who ate his victims' corpses and who thought he may have been possessed by Satan.

The performance was too much for some people. One critic called the song a "love letter to Lucifer," while E! Online tweeted, "Um, did we just witness actual witchcraft during Katy Perry's #Grammys performance?"

In Cincinnati, Ohio, Father Earl Fernandes, dean of the Athenaeum of Ohio and Mount Saint Mary's Seminary, also took note. Perry's song and other parts of the Grammys seemed to confirm a worrisome embrace of Satanic elements by pop culture: "I try not to read too much into these things, but the performances were over the top, meant to incite and to attack Christianity."

Father Fernandes, one of a new breed of American exorcists, is particularly attentive to cultural signs of diabolical influence. The day the Grammys aired, he had already been concerned by a report from Rome a few hours before the broadcast. When Pope Francis, in an annual gesture of peace, released two doves from his apartment window, they were savagely attacked by a seagull and a large black crow, to the horror of thousands of pilgrims watching in Saint Peter's Square. Equally troubling to Fernandes, though perhaps coincidental, he said, was the theft the day before of a blood relic of Pope John Paul II from a church in Italy—a crime that occurred just as Satanists were marking the beginning of the reign of the demon Volac, a few days before the start of the Satanic new year.

While all this was unsettling, Fernandes said he took consolation in words of the Gospel of Saint John: "The light shines in the darkness, and the darkness has not overcome it." In the battle between good and evil, he said, good ultimately has the upper hand. But sometimes God needs a little help from his friends below, including priests willing to take on Satan directly.

Father Fernandes is not afraid to talk publicly about the devil and diabolical influence. Although he believes cases of demonic possession are fairly exceptional, he is prepared to deal with them. Fernandes apprenticed in Rome with the master exorcist Father Carmine De Filippis, witnessing shocking scenes that he can recount in detail.

One case in particular impressed him. A young Italian woman, a medical student, arrived in Father Carmine's office feeling that she was vexed by a vague sense of evil. Father Carmine decided to let a Jesuit exorcist-in-training handle the rite, as young Father Fernandes watched. When the priest started saying prayers over her, she began to writhe. That was an encouraging sign; the Jesuit was provoking the spirit. When he ordered the demon, "In the name of Jesus Christ, tell me your name!" Father Fernandes was astounded to hear a man's deep voice come out of the woman's body and reply, "I will never tell you my name!" The exorcist kept repeating the question, until finally the booming voice called out: "Rocco! Rocco!" The devil was certainly capable of lying about his identity, and "Rocco" was merely a generic Italian name, but *any* name gives the exorcist an entry point and makes the demon more responsive. The Jesuit asked more questions in rapid-fire succession: "How many are you?" "Just one." "How did you enter?" "The flesh, the flesh." "When will you leave?" "The third of January." The priest continued to pray over the woman for a while and then tapped her on her head. She came to and said she felt better.

As Father Fernandes watched her leave, he turned to the Jesuit and asked, "What in the world was that?" "I'm not altogether sure," the priest replied. He had only been doing exorcisms for three months, and this encounter was by far the most dramatic. The two men sat down and reviewed the facts. The demon said he was alone, but that answer could not be completely trusted. He would leave on the third of January—that was the feast of the Holy Name of Jesus, a significant detail. And he had entered through the flesh—*carne* in Italian. Perhaps that indicated some type of sexual sin, Fernandes suggested, but the Jesuit had a different theory: in all likelihood, he said, the woman had eaten some sort of meat that had been sacrificed to false gods or used in some ritual, a ritual performed by others and unknown to her. Fernandes just shook his head and wondered aloud whether exorcists ever became frightened by the world of evil they were uncovering. "Not really," the Jesuit responded. "Don't forget, you're the priest, the devil is afraid of you. You have the power of Jesus Christ to expel him."

Fernandes believes the United States is experiencing an increase in diabolical activity, and he pointed to two probable causes. Like others, he thinks many people in America's secularized society have drifted away from religious faith but are still looking for ways of encountering the supernatural. In doing so they risk exposing themselves to demonic manipulation. A second factor, he said, is that waves of immigrants from Latin America and the Caribbean have brought with them some strange religious practices. He offered two examples: Santería, a religion that blends aspects of Catholicism and traditional African spirituality, and the cult of the skeletal figure known as La Santa Muerte, Saint Death, which is especially popular among some Mexican groups. "There is a false worship going on here, and with it comes unhealthy, maybe diabolical, influences. In regions where you have large numbers of immigrants, in California and Miami, for example, you see this more and more," Fernandes said.

But in southern Ohio, where Father Fernandes is stationed, the immigrant community is small and the requests for exorcism are few and far between; those afflicted who do show up are usually satisfied with a blessing. For Father Fernandes, the Rome scenes of writhing, vomiting, and cursing in tongues seem very far away. "The calls we get here are typically people who say they hear noises in their house, or the electricity flashes on and off. It could be bad electrical wiring or an old house with creaky floorboards, those sorts of things. A house blessing usually resolves it. Sometimes people just want someone to pray with them," Fernandes explained.

When Fernandes is summoned, he takes a methodical approach that reflects his earlier studies in medicine. His father, who in 1970 moved to the United States from Mumbai, India, is a physician, as are three of his four brothers. Fernandes left a potential medical career for the priesthood, and today he sees doctors as important partners when treating cases of suspected possession. "We usually go as a team. I never go by myself, that's just part of the culture in which we live. But also because having two sets of ears, two sets of eyes, two noses for smells, that's all better for observation," he explained. Fernandes first asks the person in question to tell his story, including his spiritual history. "You listen for details. Then you look for things. There are certain diagnostic signs: Does a person have superhuman strength? Do they have knowledge of hidden things? Are they averse to sacred things, like holy water or the name of Jesus or the priest's purple stole? Is there the smell of sulfur or rotting flesh?"

A mental history is also important, Fernandes said, and before doing a major exorcism he'll ask the person to undergo a full psychological or psychiatric exam. It's important that the modern exorcist allow psychology to treat certain individuals, if possible, because "hyperspiritualizing" their problems can make them worse. On the other hand, he said, when true diabolical influence presents itself, priests need to be better prepared to recognize it. Despite the Catholic Church's centuries of experience in exorcism, Fernandes believes, priests today know very little about the devil: "There's such a knowledge gap. We're all trying to relearn this. It's not really covered in the seminary. Most priests don't get much training in demonology or in any spiritual phenomena." For that reason U.S. exorcists gather once a year for a workshop, learning from one another's experiences. And once every summer Father Fernandes organizes a spiritual retreat in Ohio for the same group, so exorcists can "get their spiritual batteries recharged."

While conducting a major exorcism is uncommon, Fernandes believes minor exorcism, a series of lesser rites and prayers against Satan's power, also has a place in the contemporary church. Increasingly these minor rites have surfaced in social and political battles. In 2012 Fernandes was quoted in a story that made headlines across the country. An Ohio pro-life group, led by a priest, received permission from the Archdiocese of Cincinnati to use the "exorcism of locality" in a public protest against an abortion clinic. "This prayer is said over a place that's infested with the evil spirit, to remove any evil that might happen to be there," Fernandes explained. He said the church recognizes that the devil works through institutions as well as individuals, and those involved in what he called the "abortion industry" might be acting out of personal sin or from "diabolical influence." On the edge of the clinic property in a suburb of Dayton, the group read a prayer composed by Pope Leo XIII in 1886, imploring Saint Michael the Archangel to "take hold of the dragon, the ancient serpent, which is the devil and Satan, bind him and cast him into the bottomless pit, so that he may no longer seduce the nations." The following year Bishop Thomas Paprocki of Illinois performed a similar exorcism as part of a reparation service for the "sin" of same-sex marriage. Father Fernandes promptly invited Paprocki to speak in Cincinnati, sparking public protests by the LGBT community outside Fernandes's seminary.

Exorcism as a weapon in the culture wars was a new twist, and it stirred debate even among Catholics, some of whom believed that use of the rite was a blatant attempt to "demonize" those on the other side of the abortion or gay marriage issues. "Only in America," one critic remarked, suggesting that U.S. Catholics were only too willing to politicize their religious beliefs. But then came a report from Rome, hinting that the exorcism revivalists in the United States may have found a new friend at the Vatican.

Well before he took his place before Pope Francis in Saint Peter's Square, Angel V. was well known to Rome's coterie of exorcists, including Father Gabriele Amorth. Angel had been spiritually tormented since 1999. In an interview with the Spanish newspaper *El Mundo* he described the day his ordeal began. He was taking a bus to his hometown in Michoacán, Mexico, when he felt a strange energy enter the vehicle. It came close and stopped in front of him, and then, Angel said, he suddenly felt as if "a stake pierced my chest." He thought he might be having a heart attack, and from that moment on his health deteriorated, he had nightmares about the devil, and he would sometimes fall into trances, blaspheming and speaking in unknown languages. He vomited frequently and had trouble walking and sleeping. Doctors could find no cause for his condition, which worsened to the point that he eventually was forced to use a wheelchair.

In 2009 he became convinced that he was possessed, and he began searching for an exorcist who could liberate him—in Mexico, in Spain, in

Italy. None of the exorcisms worked. Even Father Amorth hadn't been able to help him much, for after performing an exorcism, he concluded that Angel was possessed by multiple demons. It was an unusual case, Amorth contended, because in the mysterious design of providence, Angel had been chosen as a messenger: he would not be freed from possession until he had convinced Mexican church leaders to make an act of reparation for the law that had legalized abortion in Mexico in 2007. In effect, Angel V. was manifesting the evil that had infiltrated a solidly Catholic country and, as Mexican Father Juan Rivas put it, returned the country to "the pagan times of the Aztecs with their human sacrifices."

And then, in 2013, Angel had a dream about Pope Francis and decided to head back to Rome. Accompanying him was Father Rivas, a member of the Legionaries of Christ, who believed that Francis was prepared to meet this diabolical challenge. The pope, who at that point had been in office barely two months, had spoken candidly and frequently about the devil as a real force in the modern world, cautioning the faithful to be on guard against his provocations and to resist his tricks. Only a few weeks earlier he had startled many listeners by warning them of diabolical seduction. "One can't dialogue with Satan, because he is so cunning," the pope declared. The devil tries to "soften us" with flattery, but in reality he hates Christians and is always laying traps for them. In many respects Francis had quickly established a reputation as a radical innovator, but when it came to the devil, he was clearly a traditionalist.

Father Rivas had tried on several occasions to secure Angel a place among the group of the ill who received the pope's blessing after audiences and liturgies at the Vatican. Three times they had failed to get close enough for a papal encounter, but now, after the Pentecost Mass in Saint Peter's Square, the pope was only a few feet away.

What happened next was recounted in detail by Father Rivas. As Francis approached and greeted Angel, Rivas whispered in the pope's ear: "Holiness, this person needs a blessing. He has had more than thirty exorcisms, and the demons that live in him do not want to leave him." The pope responded by laying his hands on the head of Angel, who seemed to go into a trance. His body heaved, and his mouth opened wide. "At that moment a terrible sound came out of him, like the roar of a lion," Rivas recalled. "Everyone who was there heard it perfectly well. The pope certainly heard it, and his bodyguards heard it, as did a child who was at our side. But in spite of this horrific roar the pope did not let himself be moved; he continued with his prayer, as if he had faced similar situations before." Later Angel would say he felt much better, although he believed the demons were still inside him.

Vatican security guards quickly hustled the pontiff down the line, away from this embarrassing scene. They were used to dramatic episodes of emotion or excitement whenever a pope greeted the sick, but they recognized this one as potential trouble. In fact, it wasn't long before a video of the encounter appeared on YouTube with the caption, "Did Pope Francis perform an exorcism?" Newspaper headlines followed. The Italian church-run TV channel, TV2000, ran the footage and interviewed several exorcists who all agreed: this was a prayer of liberation from evil, a genuine exorcism. Among those appearing on the broadcast was Father Gabriele Nanni, who explained that, judging by Angel's reaction, the pope had clearly provoked the devil. Father Amorth weighed in, saying the pope had definitely pronounced a prayer of exorcism, even if he had not completed the formal rite. Amorth took the opportunity to complain that bishops around the world weren't appointing enough exorcists.

Within the Vatican the episode raised a public relations alarm. Officials in the Secretariat of State were irritated, and felt the pope had been manipulated. At their request the director of TV2000, Dino Boffo, issued a retraction and an apology to Pope Francis. (Several months later Boffo was dismissed from his job.) Father Federico Lombardi, the Vatican spokesman, released a statement: "The Holy Father had no intention of performing an exorcism but, as he often does with the sick and suffering people presented to him, he simply intended to pray for the suffering person before him." It was just a prayer, in other words—not an exorcism. Lombardi remarked privately that claims of exorcism risked generating "morbid curiosity" among the faithful. "We don't want everyone who thinks they're possessed to be coming into Saint Peter's Square," he said with a smile.

Despite the Vatican disclaimers, Father Amorth and his confreres were convinced that this pope from Latin America did understand the dangers of diabolical influence. Not only did he speak about Satan, but when confronted with a man possessed, he did what Jesus would have done—seized the devil by the horns and forced him to submit.

In the United States, meanwhile, the devil was running amok on the cultural landscape. The staging of a Satanic "black Mass" at Harvard University in 2014, proposed as a learning experience in cultural diversity, was canceled at the last minute after Catholic leaders expressed outrage and sixty thousand people signed a petition to stop the event. A spokesperson for the Harvard Extension Cultural Studies Club, which was sponsoring the event, defended Satanists as a misjudged minority, arguing that many of them were artists and animal rights activists with a strong sense of community.

A few months later devil worshippers prepared to hold a similar ceremony at the Oklahoma City Civic Center, despite protestations by local Christian leaders. Traditionally a black Mass involves taking the Eucharist from a Catholic Church, ritually desecrating it through sexual acts, and offering it to the devil. In this case Satanists said the rite would be toned down to comply with Oklahoma laws banning public nudity and sexual acts. The sponsor of the event, the New York–based Satanic Temple, was the same group that had designed a Satanic statue to be placed on the grounds of the state capitol in Oklahoma City. The sculpture depicted Baphomet, a winged and horned pagan idol once worshipped in the Middle Ages, seated on a throne with two adoring children at his side. Billed as an exercise in free speech, the Baphomet figure was intended to contrast with a monument to the Ten Commandments erected at the capitol a few years earlier. The Satanic Temple, however, was careful to portray its devilish idol not as a symbol of evil but as an image of tolerance and benevolence, one that would "serve as a beacon calling for compassion and empathy among all living creatures."

For the Catholic Church, this effort to neutralize Satan's evil nature marked a new challenge, one that reflected an ongoing transformation of the devil in popular culture: recast as a complex psychological figure, Satan was now being depicted as a creature who was misunderstood by organized religion and who, in the modern age, might actually help people find their own way to the divine. To exorcists like Father Fernandes in Ohio, this cultural makeover of the devil has been aided and abetted by some Catholic theologians who, he argued, have depersonalized and psychologized the devil out of all recognition, and made the truly diabolical seem like something "only the superstitious and primitive people believed in anymore."

One person who wasn't buying the kinder, gentler version of the devil was Pope Francis, who despite murmured criticism within the Vatican refused to back away from the topic. Throughout the second year of his papacy, he continued to warn of the vitality and power of the devil, using language that brought consolation to exorcists around the world: "Some people might say: 'But Father, how old-fashioned you are to speak about the devil in the twenty-first century!' But look out, because the devil is present! The devil is here . . . even in the twenty-first century! And we mustn't be naïve, right? We must learn from the Gospel how to fight against Satan."

Whether such sentiments translated into his believing in demonic possession was another thing, however. The pope spoke of the danger of giving in to small temptations and allowing this to become habitual behavior, describing it as the insidious nature of the devil's path, but he did not refer to curses and diabolical portals and elaborate rituals to cast out Satan.

In the summer of 2014, with no warning, the Vatican announced it was giving formal approval to the International Association of Exorcists. To the casual observer this appeared to be another gesture to boost the lost art of exorcism. But a closer look at the statutes of the association, authorized by the Vatican's Congregation for Clergy, revealed that official recognition came at a price. Among other conditions, the Vatican was insisting that membership be limited to those priests specifically licensed as exorcists by their bishops. It required association members to respond to the needs of the local bishop and diocesan officials, and to work closely with other pastoral agencies. Most surprising was the stipulation that the association was to "promote cooperation with medical and psychiatric experts who are also competent in spiritual affairs." In effect, by recognizing the exorcists, the Vatican was bringing them under closer supervision, imposing a more psychological approach to their ministry, and neutralizing their more flamboyant exponents. One Vatican official chuckled after hearing the news: "They approved them so they could control them."

CHAPTER FIVE

The Miracle Trail

In 1936 Audrey Toguchi was an eight-year-old Catholic school-girl. She remembered the principal, Sister Callista, shepherding all the students down to Bishop Street in Honolulu. It was like watching a parade: the sunny streets lined with men and women in their fine clothes and straw hats, marching bands as far as the eye could see, and, finally, an open car bearing Father Damien's coffin. At the harbor they swung it on ropes onto a big ship headed for San Francisco and then to Belgium. Audrey had waved good-bye that day to Father Damien, but he always had a place in her heart.

More than seventy years later, in October 2009, she found herself walking up the main aisle of Saint Peter's Basilica, carrying a lock of the priest's hair encased in an acrylic reliquary, to an altar where Pope Benedict XVI would proclaim Damien a saint. At eighty-one, Audrey did not move all that quickly, and her doctor, Walter Chang, held her arm as she navigated the steps to the papal platform. She wore a white muumuu and, around her neck, a golden lei. The Hawaiian pilgrims seated to one side craned for a better look, as a papal usher opened the reliquary and displayed it on a small stand near the pope. All eyes were on the wiry, white-haired Audrey, whose wrinkled face radiated happiness as she took her seat of honor. In the spillover crowd that watched the event on video screens in Saint Peter's Square, Italians murmured to each other: "La miracolata!"

The spotlight was not a comfortable place for Audrey. The previous year the Vatican had declared her cure from cancer a miracle, attributed to the intercession of Father Damien. The media attention was overwhelming, and it only increased as the canonization date drew near. Documentary film crews, newspapers, and TV stations all wanted interviews. The sick sought her out, including people with cancer who wanted advice, comfort, and, perhaps, a miracle like her own. Arriving in Rome for the canonization Mass, Audrey checked into her hotel under another name, but she soon realized there was no escape from reporters, and all week long she had been meeting the press and telling her story.

Audrey had spent much of her life as a social studies teacher. She had a master's degree in educational psychology and was firmly convinced that school-age children needed, above all, "a lot of loving care." Her nurturing approach to students earned her the nickname "Ma," and she was greatly missed when she retired in 1995. She turned her attention to gardening and other at-home activities, but in 1996 she fell, and her husband noticed a lump on her left hip. It wasn't until 1997 that she saw a doctor. It initially appeared to be a hematoma, a blood-filled swelling, but when it wouldn't heal, a family physician thought surgery might be needed. The prospect filled Audrey with dread, mainly because she'd had some bad previous experiences with doctors. Instead, she turned to a familiar figure, one whose memory was still very much alive among Hawaiians.

Damien de Veuster, a Belgian missionary, traveled to Hawaii in 1864, at a time when the native population of the islands was being decimated by diseases brought by sailors and merchants of the Pacific. Among them was leprosy, now known as Hansen's disease, which was wrongly believed at the time to be highly contagious and sexually transmitted. (Some doctors thought leprosy was a final stage of syphilis.) In 1865 Hawaiian authorities decided to quarantine lepers in two colonies on the Kalaupapa peninsula, on the island of Molokai. For those who were relocated there, few health services were offered, and life became a form of exile that ended only in death. In 1873 the local bishop decided to send missionaries to offer spiritual care to the Molokai residents. Father Damien, at the time only thirty-three years old, was the first to volunteer.

Damien arrived at the Kalawao colony with little more than a breviary. No house had been provided for the priest, so he camped under a sprawling pandanus tree, using an adjacent rock for a table. He quickly got to know each of the several hundred lepers of Kalawao. Their suffering was horrific, and Damien soon recognized that much of it was unnecessary, the result of abandonment and neglect. With a cheerful demeanor he provided minimal health care to the lepers, washing their bodies and dressing their wounds. He engaged the residents in projects that gave them a sense of pride, helping them to build roads, houses, gardens, and a boat landing. He taught them to play musical instruments and organized a brass band—not an easy task, because many of the lepers were missing fingers. Gradually he helped restore their dignity. Visitors to Kalawao came away shocked, not at the affliction endured by lepers, but by their sense of joy and purpose. A persistent critic of the Hawaiian government's treatment of lepers, Father Damien gained a reputation in bureaucratic circles as a bothersome and headstrong nuisance. He was just as tough as a pastor, demanding an end to immoral behavior among his flock. His Masses at Kalawao attracted overflow crowds, and the church had to be enlarged.

As the years passed and Kalawao's fame grew, Damien successfully raised money from international donors, a development that irritated Hawaiian authorities because it made them look negligent. He built a hospital and orphanage and helped the village get running water. Damien's notoriety also fueled jealousy among other Christian missionaries, who considered leprosy a divine punishment for the "licentiousness" of the native population.

Although he lived in fear of contracting leprosy, Damien took few precautions against contagion. He touched the lepers, fed them, bandaged them, and considered himself one of them. As he famously wrote to a fellow priest in Belgium, "I make myself a leper with the lepers to gain all to Jesus Christ." One day, while soaking his feet in a bucket of hot water, Damien realized that he felt no sensation of heat and knew immediately that he had contracted leprosy. He refused to leave Molokai for treatment, however, remaining with his colony for five more years until his death in 1889, at the age of forty-nine. His legacy endured, and in 1995 Pope John Paul II presided over Father Damien's beatification, a major step toward sainthood.

Like many in Hawaii, Audrey Toguchi had a personal connection to Damien, as her aunt and uncle had been exiled to Kalaupapa and were buried there. Her grandmother had suffered greatly when her two children were sent away. As Audrey once remarked, "Honolulu is not that far from Molokai, and yet what a heartbreak because you would never see your children again." The children's fate had long been a family secret, because of the stigma attached to leprosy. As a child Audrey had heard many stories from relatives about the good work Damien accomplished among the sick. So when her hip failed to heal, she and her two sisters decided to make a pilgrimage to Molokai and pay a visit to Father Damien's original grave at Kalawao. His body was no longer interred there, but the tomb, decorated with leis of flowers, contained a relic—bones from Damien's right hand, sent back to the island by the Belgian government after his beatification. Audrey prayed to him as if she were having a conversation: "Father Damien, I fell down, and I didn't realize as a result of it that there would be this lump. And so right now they think that lump could be a hematoma according to the sonogram reports, so please help me because I don't want to go through surgery. Please take that away from me." If she couldn't be healed, she added, perhaps Damien could at least make sure she found a competent doctor.

Audrey did find a good doctor, Walter Chang, a Honolulu surgeon who in January 1998 removed the fist-size lump from her hip. Then came bad news: tests determined that the lump was a liposarcoma, an aggressive form of cancer that attacked the fat tissues. More tissue was removed, and Audrey underwent radiation treatment. Several months later Chang ordered follow-up X-rays and was alarmed at the results. When Audrey came to his office in September 1998, Chang told her the cancer had spread, and the scans had revealed three new tumors on her lungs. Audrey later recalled that Dr. Chang was very direct: "He told me that cancer robs, but this cancer is going to rob and kill you." If the cancer had spread to only one lung, he could remove it. "But in two lungs," he said, "I am so sorry."

Audrey had been praying to Father Damien for months, and now she turned to him again. "I really need your help because I'm being pressed against the wall. Father Damien, please rescue me."

Dr. Chang suggested chemotherapy but did not hold out false hope. After considering the prospects, and despite pressure from her husband and son, Audrey decided against treatment. She would simply live whatever life she had left. "I'm going to pray to Father Damien," she told the doctor. "Mrs. Toguchi, prayers are nice, but you still need chemotherapy," Chang insisted, but she declined and soon began planning another trip to Damien's tomb on Molokai.

One month later Audrey had another visit with Dr. Chang. When he examined her new X-rays, he was startled to see that the tumors had shrunk in size. "What did you do?" he asked. Had she seen another doctor or received some form of treatment, perhaps herbs or acupuncture? No, nothing, Audrey replied. The change was remarkable, but Chang waited to see if it was just a temporary improvement. To his amazement the tumors continued to get smaller, and by May 1999 they were completely gone. When he saw the clean scans, the doctor was practically jumping up and down in the office, Audrey recalled later. The cancer—this deadly form of cancer—had spontaneously regressed. Chang, who was not a religious man, told Audrey, "This is incredible. I won't call this a miracle, but you'd better tell Rome about it."

Audrey did inform Rome, via a letter to Pope John Paul II, telling him of her prayers to Damien and her sudden healing. This appeared to be what the supporters of Damien's sainthood cause had been waiting for: the miracle that would lead to his canonization.

The church's bureaucratic wheels moved slowly, however, partly out of prudence—a possible recurrence of the malignancy could not be ruled out. Follow-up tests, however, confirmed that Audrey remained cancerfree. In 2003 the Diocese of Honolulu convened a tribunal to investigate Audrey's healing. The process took six months, and included interviews with Audrey and her relatives, two priests who had counseled her, and six medical doctors. One important consideration was whether the radiation treatment of Audrey's original hip tumor might have somehow affected the subsequent lung metastases, but doctors dismissed that possibility, all of them testifying to the extraordinary nature of the cure. A key witness, of course, was Dr. Chang, who had already documented his patient's "complete spontaneous regression of cancer" in an article published in 2000 by the *Hawaii Medical Journal*. The diocesan tribunal forwarded its conclusions to Rome, where the evidence was examined by the Vatican's Congregation for Saints' Causes. In 2005 the congregation asked for clarifications. As months passed, church leaders in Hawaii began wondering what was causing the delay and were told to be patient.

Finally, in October 2007, the congregation's seven-person panel of medical experts, the Consulta Medica, ruled that Audrey's healing was "unexplainable according to available medical knowledge." That still left one major hurdle before a miracle could be declared: a panel of theologians had to verify that the alleged miracle was realized through the intercession of Father Damien. They needed to establish a causal link between prayer and cure.

The Consulta Teologica studied the documentation assembled in Hawaii, in particular the statements of priests and other witnesses who had testified to Audrey's deep devotion to Father Damien. When they looked carefully at the timeline of prayers and healing, however, what had appeared to be a foregone conclusion began to unravel. Some of the theologians found the testimony on Audrey's prayers and her trip to Damien's tomb confusing. In the end the panel sent Father Damien's file back to the congregation, saying there were too many doubts and unanswered questions. There was only one way this cause would move forward: someone would have to fly to Honolulu and cross-examine Audrey Toguchi directly.

Monsignor Robert Sarno's third-floor office window at the Vatican afforded an impressive view of Saint Peter's Square. Visitors presumed it was one of the perks of having toiled at the Congregation for Saints' Causes for more than twenty-five years. But Sarno, a native of Brooklyn, was not one to stand at the window and admire the vista. Hardnosed and efficient, he spent his days at his desk, where documentation for pending cases was deposited in tall stacks or, more and more frequently, digitally delivered to his computer. The office appeared small for someone who dealt with virtually all the English-language business of the congregation. The monsignor had decorated the walls with religious imagery, mostly pictures of the Virgin Mary. Behind him, a well-worn breviary lay within reach.

Sarno was an important source for English-speaking journalists, and his brusque manner sometimes intimidated them. He did not suffer foolish questions gladly, but because he did recognize the importance of the media, he always tried to set reporters on the right path. There were so many misconceptions about sainthood and miracles—even among Catholics—that Sarno inevitably began with explaining the fundamentals.

The congregation's first step is to evaluate evidence that the sainthood candidate lived a life of holiness, a life worthy of imitation by all Christians. Once that is confirmed, it looks for evidence of intercession: that prayers to the candidate resulted in a miracle or favor granted by God. For the congregation, a miracle is divine confirmation of its judgment on the holiness of the person, a sign that this would-be saint is truly in heaven. "The whole idea is based upon the fact that there is a God, that he can act and he does act in the world," Sarno explained. That doesn't mean the sainthood congregation hunts for all manner of supernatural signs, as it generally doesn't deal with phenomena like apparitions, stigmata, or other mystical gifts—in fact, those elements might complicate the investigation of a sainthood cause. The miracles examined by the Vatican are more objective occurrences, events that can be investigated in a systematic fashion. The congregation works patiently, and although no statistics are kept, experts have estimated that at least half the miracles proposed for sainthood causes have been rejected. Whenever a miracle is approved, there is joy among the promoters of the cause. The Vatican bureaucrats, too, feel a sense of satisfaction, but their reaction is surprisingly low-key, consisting of terse statements issued two or three times a year, duly noting new batches of confirmed miracles, as if this were routine.

Unfortunately, Sarno said, many people today, including Catholics, are interested in miracles for the wrong reason—namely, to prove that God exists. That is not the Vatican's goal. In canonizing individuals, Sarno explained, the church is not exalting their ability to produce miracles but rather offering them as exemplars of how to live the Christian life. In this sense, miracles are simply "signposts toward holiness."

Likewise, Sarno said, the congregation is not in the business of proving miracles in a scientific manner: "A miracle is a theological term, not a medical term. It comes from the Latin term *miraculum*, which refers to something that is wonderful to behold. In this case, the wonder is that God has intervened in human reality."

In modern times 99 percent of the miracles reviewed by the congregation are medical miracles, Sarno explained. There are several reasons for this. For one thing, many dramatic events or moments in life occur so quickly that one simply doesn't have time to pray. "But with an illness, there is usually plenty of time to pray and think, 'Oh, my God, I'm going to die.' And so you either pray for your health, or for strength, or for whatever you might need to deal with that threat to your life," he said. And in order to be corroborated, the miracle must be something verifiable—another reason why medical conditions, which are typically well documented by unbiased professionals, are ideal. Any healing that is presented as a possible miracle must be sudden, complete, permanent, and unexplained by any medical therapy employed. The Consulta Medica examines the prognosis, the diagnosis, and the treatment. "If there's any hint that the therapy may have caused the person's healing, it's thrown out," Sarno said.

The Consulta Medica does not, however, pronounce on whether an inexplicable healing is actually a miracle. If its judgment is positive, the medical experts simply state that there is no scientific explanation for what occurred. That opens the door for the Consulta Teologica, the theologians who must determine a connection between prayers and divine intervention. This is a trickier assessment, because it involves personal recollections and spiritual realities, not the empirical data provided by medical records. The judgment made by the Consulta

Teologica is always one of "moral certitude," not absolute scientific certainty, and moral certitude inevitably implies a margin of error. That does not mean, however, that the theologians are any less rigorous in their approach, for they, too, study the evidence and the testimony of witnesses carefully, confirming that credit for a miracle is correctly assigned, and that prayers for healing were specifically addressed to the candidate in question.

That was one of the problems with Audrey Toguchi's miracle, as Monsignor Sarno soon discovered. The medical world clearly had no explanation for her cure, which at nine years and counting appeared to be lasting. No treatment could account for her healing. But as Monsignor Sarno liked to say, "Just because there was no human intervention doesn't mean there was divine intervention." The issue was whether Audrey had prayed to the right person at the right time. There had to be a very clear invocation of Father Damien, followed by sudden recovery. And here, the record was muddled, at best. All along, it seemed, Audrey had been praying to several other saints as well.

Sarno had long been a devotee of Father Damien and believed that he should have been declared a martyr of the faith, as someone who deliberately risked his life to bring spiritual aid to outcasts, eventually succumbing to a disease for which there was no cure. Sarno recalled that in the 1980s, Mother Teresa had once come knocking on his office door. She wanted Damien to be declared a saint, and the two of them drafted a letter to Pope John Paul II to help the cause along. On that occasion Sarno had taken Mother Teresa to the congregation archives to show her the file on Father Damien. Mother Teresa took out a religious medal and asked Sarno to tape it inside the file folder. Both of them had signed it, in an unusual act of solidarity. In 2007, when he reopened Father Damien's file, he saw the medal and remembered their effort. Sarno was therefore hardly an impartial observer, yet it was he whom the Vatican was sending to Hawaii to conduct a one-man tribunal on Father Damien's alleged miracle. He would have to set aside his personal biases.

"I didn't go there with the idea that I'm here to prove the miracle,"

Sarno later explained. "I went to find out what happened. I wanted to come back to Rome with either a yes or a no. But it had to be accurate."

In effect Sarno played devil's advocate, a role he knew well. For centuries an official of the congregation had been formally appointed as devil's advocate, whose task was to take a contrarian view and challenge the arguments for sainthood and miracles. When Pope John Paul II eliminated the devil's advocate office in 1983, the media saw it as a move to make canonization easier. That's another misconception, Sarno said: "It hasn't been abolished; in fact it's been amplified, because everyone's supposed to be a devil's advocate. We're not to accept anything at face value here in this office; we're supposed to be professional and critical."

When Sarno arrived in Hawaii, he was prepared to be the bad guy. First he questioned other witnesses, including Audrey Toguchi's sister Velma, and then summoned Audrey herself. Interrogating her with the thoroughness of a prosecuting attorney, he took nothing for granted. He asked about the nature of her prayers following her diagnosis of liposarcoma.

Q: The day after you got this news, did you think of praying to Father Damien for help?

A: Oh, yes! Right along.

Q: What did you pray? Did you say a novena or a rosary?

A: A novena, but mostly when I talk to him, it is like when I am talking to you.

Q: So it is like a constant conversation?

A: Right.

Sarno then asked whether Damien was the privileged intercessor or one of many.

Q: Did you pray to Padre Pio?

A: Velma told me, think about Padre Pio because Padre Pio is very helpful to me. I asked him to please help me find a doctor.

Velma is so into Padre Pio, so I asked him to please find me a doctor.

Q: After you found out that it was liposarcoma, did you continue praying to Padre Pio?

A: No, I kept asking Father Damien for help.

Q: Did you ever pray to Mother Teresa?

A: Mother Teresa, again, I read about her. So when it came time to look for a competent doctor, I asked Mother Teresa to help me find one.

Q: Did you pray to anyone else?

A: I also asked Blessed Mother. But the main person I kept talking to was Father Damien.

Sarno next turned to Audrey's trip to Father Damien's tomb, which had figured so prominently in the sainthood narrative provided by the promoters of the cause. Audrey's first visit to the site was in 1997, with her sisters Velma and Beverly.

Q: Was it your idea to go to Molokai or Velma's idea?

A: It was both of our ideas to go to Molokai, because Velma said that's what we should do.

Q: Your sister Velma in her testimony today said that you offered to take her anywhere for her birthday. And then *she* said, let's go to Molokai.

A: That's right.

Q: But you said that *you* said, let's go to Molokai.

A: She suggested, but I said yes, let's go.

Sarno's goal was to clarify the timeline. One problem with it was that Audrey had first gone to Damien's tomb a year before she learned her liposarcoma had spread, and returned there again in 1999, well after her cancer had regressed. But if the miracle occurred in late 1998, a month after her lung tumors were discovered, where was the connection with Damien during that crucial period?

He read to Audrey a statement she had made to local church officials, stating that after she learned that her cancer had spread to her
lungs and that the situation was hopeless, she decided to go back to
Damien's grave to pray for help.

> Q: I have a problem. You say you "decided to go." Do you mean you
>   decided to go to Kalaupapa, to Molokai? Did you want to go to
>   the tomb of Father Damien?
> A: Yes.

But as Sarno pointed out, Audrey had waited more than a year to
make that trip, well after her cure had begun. Why?

> A: I cannot tell why I didn't go right away.

As Sarno pressed for an explanation, Audrey protested that she
was "confused with all these dates."

"This is our problem," Sarno told her. "We are confused, too."

"I went to Father Damien," Audrey insisted.

That was a strange phrase, Sarno thought. Perhaps she intended
something else.

> Q: And what does "I went to Father Damien" mean to you?
> A: It means that I went on a pilgrimage to Father Damien . . .
> Q: No, no. You didn't until May 1, 1999.

Audrey, exasperated, tried to make this monsignor understand. "I
said I went to Father Damien, and that does not mean physically, and
I went to him and I said to him, please help me."

Monsignor Sarno reflected for a moment. It was now clear that the
entire story of Audrey's pilgrimage to Damien's tomb had no bearing
on the miracle. But it wasn't necessary, he realized; Audrey had immediately prayed to Damien for help, and that was the key factor.

"My problem is I cannot remember the dates," Audrey added. "All

I can tell you is that when you are so tied up in all this, all your mind is 'Please help me.' So all these dates, I can't even explain it. So when I say I went to Father Damien, it doesn't mean that I flew back and forth to Kalaupapa."

"Excellent," Sarno said. He quickly concluded his questioning and boarded a plane for Rome, leaving church officials in Hawaii wondering what the outcome would be. They found out seven months later, when the Vatican announced that Pope Benedict, following the recommendation of the sainthood congregation, had approved the miracle attributed to Father Damien. He would be canonized a saint.

"I knew that the world was watching this case, and I knew that God would be watching my conscience," Sarno said later, explaining why he had taken such an uncompromising approach to his assignment. "There was a lot riding on this—the integrity of the congregation, the integrity of truth. I wanted to be precise about the information. The only way I could do this was by being a bastard. If people say I was tough, I certainly stand happily accused."

The call came out of the blue. Jacalyn Duffin, a twenty-eight-year-old Canadian who in 1986 was doing a fellowship in history at the University of Ottawa, listened carefully as the doctor at the other end of the line explained the unusual proposal. Duffin was also a hematologist, a specialist in blood diseases, and the caller asked if she would look at a set of blood and bone marrow slides that had been taken from a patient several years earlier. Duffin would conduct a blind study, meaning she would be told nothing about the patient, the treatment, or the outcome. Based on her findings, she would then write a report on the diagnosis and the course of the disease. For Duffin it would mean extra money, and she did love hematology, so she agreed to the proposal.

Weeks later Duffin sat in a lab room of the Ottawa General Hospital and began her examination of a cardboard container containing about thirty slides, the first of eighteen trays that would occupy her for days. Each tray held dated blood samples and bone marrow smears, material that had been removed from the patient with a syringe. Duffin began to place the series of slides under a microscope and to count blood cells by hand. She used a machine that looked like an old-fashioned cash register, with a key for each type of cell; when one hundred white blood cells were recorded, a little bell rang. It was an enormously laborious and time-consuming task, one she couldn't do for more than a few hours each day.

The slides in each tray had been taken at one-month intervals beginning in 1978, and Duffin soon had a clear picture of the clinical history of the case. The patient, a female (that much she could tell from the blood), had presented with acute myeloblastic leukemia, the most aggressive kind. The second set of slides showed the typical toxic effects of chemotherapy treatment. After three or four months, the patient had gone into remission, but four or five months later the leukemia had returned. More treatment followed, and then a second remission. Duffin knew that these were all clear signs that the patient had eventually succumbed to the disease. The pattern for leukemia remissions was that they became shorter and shorter, and the disease was ultimately incurable after a relapse—at least at that time, before bone marrow transplants became practicable. Oddly, however, in this case the second remission lasted a long time, and for the next ten months or so, the slides were consistent in that regard. In fact, the final bone marrow slide was normal, too. At this point Duffin had formed a hypothesis about the patient: the woman had enjoyed an unusually good run, a second remission that lasted far longer than normal, but had no doubt died suddenly from some kind of infection, perhaps pneumonia or sepsis, which sometimes afflicts patients on maintenance therapy. By now Duffin had come to assume that her blind study would be used in a lawsuit, perhaps to defend a doctor who had treated the woman. She wrote up her report, a very long one, and submitted it.

Several days later she ran into Jeanne Drouin, the physician who had commissioned the study, and the two decided to go out for coffee. On the way, bursting with curiosity, Duffin asked Drouin: "OK, can you tell me anything about this case at all? Is it a lawsuit?" and then added in jest, "Or is it a miracle?" Drouin calmly looked her in the eye and said, "It's a miracle. You'd better sit down."

Drouin, as it happened, had been the treating physician for the patient, twenty-nine-year-old Lise Normand, a woman from the nearby city of Gatineau. Drouin, like Duffin, had expected the second remission of her patient's leukemia to be short-lived. But as the months went by, there was no sign of relapse. Drouin smiled and added, "She's still alive. And doing fine."

After several years of remission, in fact, Lise Normand had come to Dr. Drouin and declared herself cured and in need of no further treatment. When Drouin expressed her concern, Normand explained, "I now have to tell you. I prayed to Marguerite d'Youville, and I believe I've been healed by her." Normand thanked the doctor for acting as "the hand of God," but believed it was her prayers, not any medical treatment, that had saved her.

Marguerite d'Youville founded the Sisters of Charity, better known as the Grey Nuns, in Quebec in 1737. But she was better known locally for her pioneering efforts in social justice. Married to a bootlegger who traded illegally with Indians and made home life miserable, she experienced a religious awakening and, after her husband's early death, joined a small group of women to perform acts of charity. They were the nucleus of a religious order that would eventually build a hospital, take in prostitutes, open shelters for battered women, and fight for the rights of the poor on four continents. In 1959 Pope John XXIII beatified Marguerite d'Youville, calling her the "Mother of Universal Charity." But her sainthood cause had stalled there, and she was still awaiting another miracle before canonization. When the Grey Nuns in Quebec heard about Lise Normand, they were convinced they had found it, and that Blessed Marguerite would be named a saint.

Normand's cure was documented in the early 1980s, and Quebec church officials sent the material to Rome. They waited patiently until the Vatican finally notified them that its panel of medical experts was not convinced. Specifically, they determined that Normand had experienced only one remission, not two, a disease course that would have made her survival unusual but not miraculous. The Canadian doctors were offended at the suggestion that they didn't know how to recognize a leukemia remission. The Grey Nuns, meanwhile, did not give up in their efforts and kept pestering officials at the Congregation for Saints' Causes, who agreed to reopen the case if the nuns could find a "blind witness" to read the bone marrow results and settle the question of relapse and remission.

Jacalyn Duffin had never heard of Marguerite d'Youville, had no knowledge of this particular clinical case, and was not a Catholic, or even a believer—all of which made her a perfect choice for the task. She was the objective observer par excellence, someone whose opinion Rome would have to take seriously. And now she was agreeing with what Marguerite d'Youville's promoters had been maintaining all along: there was no medical explanation for the survival of Lise Normand.

Duffin agreed to testify at a formal session of a tribunal of the Quebec archdiocese, whose findings would be forwarded to Rome. Although a little nervous, she was by now enjoying this foray into the medical side of sainthood. Duffin brought along articles on leukemia survival rates, with key passages highlighted. The questions she was asked were technical and pointed, and Duffin was surprised at the degree of detail she was required to provide. Several hours after the tribunal hearing, a group of Grey Nuns appeared at her house with the transcripts of her testimony so she could correct any typos. They gave her two small children a coloring book on the life of their foundress. Before leaving, one of the nuns took Duffin aside to make an important point. "You know, it's not about the sensation of the miracle that we're doing this. Yes, we need to get a miracle so that she'll be a saint. But we need her to become a saint so she'll inspire others to live the good life that she lived herself." Duffin, touched, was even more impressed with their cause when she read a biography of Marguerite d'Youville. In many ways, Duffin thought, this eighteenth-century nun who ran a soup kitchen and looked after the sick was a key part of Canadian history, and a saint for the modern age.

As always the Vatican took its time evaluating this new evidence.

They had more questions, and at one point required Duffin to personally meet Lise Normand and examine fresh blood samples, which again confirmed her cure. In 1990 Duffin received another call from the Grey Nuns. Would she like to go to Rome to attend Marguerite d'Youville's canonization? Duffin eventually found herself in Saint Peter's Basilica with Dr. Drouin, Lise Normand, and about three thousand other Canadians who had made the trip to honor the country's first native-born saint. She met Pope John Paul II and before leaving the Vatican was given a gift: a copy of the *positio super miraculo*, a bound volume of the documentation used to authenticate Marguerite d'Youville's miracle. As she leafed through the book, Duffin was stunned at the wealth of medical information it contained—hospital records, comprehensive reports from doctors, and, of course, her own testimony. They even had included her highlighted articles on leukemia from medical journals.

That gave Duffin an idea. Several hundred saints had been proclaimed since the Vatican established formal vetting procedures in 1588, which meant there was a *positio* on at least one miracle for each of them. It seemed impossible, but if she could obtain these documents, she'd have not only a history of modern miracles but also a record of medical treatments over the last four centuries. For a medical historian like herself, this would be a gold mine. Duffin returned to Rome some time later during a sabbatical year, armed with a letter establishing her as a bona fide scholar. She went to the Vatican Secret Archives and to her utter amazement within an hour she was reading the miracle files. They had all been preserved, neatly bound and undisturbed, on the archives' shelves. As she had suspected, the files contained detailed accounts of the medical science of every era, including sworn testimony from doctors about diagnoses, treatments, and cures. After researching for ten years, in 2008 Duffin published a book titled *Medical Miracles: Doctors, Saints, and Healing in the Modern World*. What impressed her most in her research was the Vatican's insistence on consulting topnotch medical experts when it came to verifying miracles. The Catholic Church, she realized, did not want people to stop going to doctors so they could be healed by prayer. On the contrary Vatican officials wanted to confirm that a patient had received the best possible medical attention and that in spite of such care the individual's condition was deemed hopeless from a scientific point of view. They were looking for hard evidence of diagnosis, dire prognosis, and unexplained cure.

"The Vatican takes all this very seriously. It was always insisting on up-to-date medicine, it was always insisting on medical corroboration. And it didn't much care if the doctor was a believer or not," Duffin said. "They don't want to go around declaring miracles when there is a scientific explanation for what happened. They don't want to be duped by wishful thinking. In the face of a medical situation, they are attempting to diagnose transcendence."

While Duffin still considers herself a nonbeliever, in her own way she has come to believe in miracles and in the power of faith: "A miracle is literally a thing of wonder. It's a good event that I can't explain scientifically. I also believe faith is a miracle, and it's one that hasn't happened to me."

Declaring a miracle is risky business, and no one is more aware of that fact than Dr. Patrizio Polisca, president of the Consulta Medica at the Congregation for Saints' Causes. Polisca, a specialist in cardiology, anesthesiology, and reanimation, served as Pope Benedict's personal physician and has been director of the Vatican health services since 2010. Behind the scenes he has also worked for decades on assessing the alleged miracles submitted for sainthood causes. He is a well-known figure to most of the clerics who work in Vatican City, but unlike the monsignors who populate the Roman Curia offices, Polisca was hired for his lay expertise in medicine, not for theological training or ecclesial connections. When it comes to judging miracles, he takes a professional approach. As head of the Consulta Medica, he reviews from thirty-five to forty cases each year, guiding the members of the panel to judgment. About half are rejected, he said.

In his office at the health services, a building lodged between the Vatican Post Office and the city-state's discount supermarket, Polisca, a tall man with graying hair and a winning smile, and elegantly dressed in a dark blue suit, spoke about the miracle vetting process. "We look for the best medical advice," he said. "The goal is to research every aspect, until—and if—it emerges that the healing was unexplained by medical science." The Consulta Medica does not ask from science an absolute judgment on a miracle—that's not the role of medical experts, Polisca explained. In fact, it does not insist on a unanimous decision by its seven members; a majority of five positive votes is enough to move a miracle forward. The Consulta changes its roster frequently, and not all its members are Catholic.

The possibilities for false steps are numerous. To ensure authenticity of medical miracles, the Consulta still follows the criteria established in 1734 by Cardinal Prospero Lambertini, the man who set down the foundational principles for judging modern sainthood causes. To begin with, the disease must be a serious one, considered difficult or impossible to cure. It must not be at a stage where it has run its course and spontaneous regression is possible. Pharmaceutical treatment should not have been used; if it has been, the medicine must be shown to have had no curative effect. The healing must be sudden and instantaneous. It must be complete, and not simply an improvement. It must not follow a physical crisis that could have precipitated a natural cure. Finally, there must be no relapse of the disease or associated infirmity.

The Lambertini criteria have served the church well for nearly three centuries. But as Polisca and his confreres have discovered, they are not always a perfect fit with contemporary medical science. For example, diagnosis today is not so straightforward: a battery of complementary tests may be used on a patient, requiring careful analysis of false positives or false negatives. What constitutes a "serious" disease is ambiguous, too, and the Vatican has taken an increasingly flexible view on that topic; among the miracles under study in 2014, for example, was the healing of a boy born cross-eyed. Treatment options today are much broader than in the eighteenth century, especially with medicines, and it is unlikely that any modern patient had gone completely untreated. The stipulation of an "instantaneous" cure is also subject to interpretation.

The Consulta now recognizes that a healing that occurs over a period of months can be just as miraculous as one that happens overnight.

But the most precarious aspect of affirming a miracle is the final proviso—the disease cannot recur. Nor can the eventual death of the person be linked to the disease for which the miraculous healing occurred. Satisfying those conditions requires the Consulta to delay its final decision, sometimes for many years. "If we're talking about a cancerous tumor, for example," Polisca explained, "you need ten or fifteen years to say it's a lasting cure."

The issue of possible recurrence arose in dramatic fashion in 2006, when church officials were trying to choose from among more than two hundred submissions the miracle that would lead to the beatification of Pope John Paul II. After much debate the promoters of the cause chose the inexplicable healing of a French nun, Sister Marie-Simon-Pierre, who claimed to have been cured of Parkinson's disease after praying to John Paul exactly two months after the pontiff's death in 2005. The healing had several convincing elements. The nun, who had been crippled by the incurable disease, said a prayer to John Paul one night and awoke the next morning able to move and walk normally—the kind of instantaneous healing considered ideal by Vatican saint makers. "I was sick and now I am cured," she announced to reporters, and indeed a year later, back at work in a maternity hospital, appeared to be in perfect health. There seemed to be a providential symmetry involved, too: as Pope John Paul II himself suffered from Parkinson's for several years before his death, he would have been the perfect intercessor.

Yet Polisca and the other members of the medical board immediately saw potential difficulties. Diagnosis of Parkinson's disease is notoriously difficult, and even experts have trouble distinguishing it from other parkinsonian syndromes, some of which may spontaneously go into regression. To definitively exclude the possibility of a relapse, the Vatican would have to wait until Sister Marie-Simon-Pierre died—which was clearly not an option. "I don't think the Consulta had a unanimous judgment on this miracle," Polisca said. "Because some thought, if this woman experiences a strong emotional moment in the future, what will be her somatic response? What's going to happen in the future? We consulted the best Parkinson's experts in the field, and they gave their best judgment. But it can never be an absolute judgment, because medicine is always evolving."

In 2010, as the Consulta waited and debated, a Polish newspaper reported that the nun had suffered a relapse. That provoked apprehension at the Vatican, but it turned out to be a false rumor. Finally, at the end of 2010, five of the seven members of the Consulta Medica voted to approve the healing as inexplicable by medical science, and John Paul was beatified the following year. In 2014, after yet another miracle was attributed to the intercession of the Polish pope, Sister Marie-Simon-Pierre returned to the Vatican for John Paul's canonization, and everyone's eyes were on her as she took her place near the altar in Saint Peter's Square. "Thank God so far she's fine," Polisca said. "Otherwise it would provoke laughter—if not tears."

Polisca teaches classes on miracle investigation at an annual Vatican-sponsored course for the promoters of sainthood causes. He emphasizes prudence, patience, and careful preliminary study of any supposed miracle, because a falsely attributed miracle would not only set back the progress of a cause but also create embarrassment for the church. Despite the risk of recurrence and the potential for errors in judgment, though, the Vatican's track record on confirming miracles has been amazingly consistent. Scholars have reviewed the congregation's files, Polisca said, and as far as he knows, no one has found any cure accepted long ago as a miracle that now has a medical explanation. There have been contested miracles, however, and one of the most controversial was a miraculous cure attributed to the intercession of Mother Teresa of Calcutta. The case still causes heartburn at the Vatican.

In 1997, two months after Mother Teresa's death, a twenty-nine-year-old Indian woman, Monika Besra, became ill with fever, headaches, and vomiting. After being diagnosed with tuberculosis and tubercular meningitis, she was admitted to a home that was run by Mother Teresa's

Missionaries of Charity in West Bengal. Although she received antitubercular drugs, her symptoms continued, and her abdomen began to swell. An ultrasound in 1998 revealed what appeared to be a large ovarian cyst. Doctors wanted to do exploratory surgery, but only if the sisters' care could strengthen the woman's weak health. On September 5, 1998, the first anniversary of Mother Teresa's death, the sisters prayed to her for Besra's healing. They also placed on Besra's stomach what they called a "miraculous medal," which had been touched by Mother Teresa. Besra fell asleep but awoke in the middle of the night, shocked and elated to discover that her tumor was gone and her abdomen had contracted to its normal size. The sisters proclaimed it as a miracle.

In 1999 church officials in Calcutta began a yearlong inquiry into the case, interviewing all the doctors involved in treating Besra. Their consensus was that the sudden disappearance of this type of cyst, with no signs of rupture or ill effects, was inexplicable. The case was forwarded to the Vatican, where it was selected from some eight hundred potential miracles to support Mother Teresa's beatification. The Consulta Medica conducted its own study and gave its approval in 2002. In 2003, nearly five years after Monika Besra's healing, she came to Rome for the beatification Mass. Dressed in a pink sari, the slender woman spoke softly through an interpreter, explaining how she had converted to Christianity from Hinduism after her cure. "I was so sick and I was healed. That is why I became a Christian," she said in an interview with Catholic News Service. "Those who believe in God and in Mother believe it is a miracle. Those who love God, they believe in miracles; Hindus, too, if they have a pure mind." Besra told how her remarkable recovery had an effect on her entire family, including her husband, who had previously often come home drunk. "After my cure, my husband stopped drinking," she said with a laugh. "There is so much joy in my house now. We laugh all the time. That is another miracle."

As miracles go, though, this one was almost too perfect. In fact, the story had already begun to fray at the edges. Besra's husband, who refused to come to Rome for the beatification, told *Time* magazine that the supposed miracle was "much ado about nothing," declaring: "My wife was cured by the doctors and not by any miracle." A similar note was struck by the leaders of the Science and Rationalists' Association of India and by a former state health minister, all of whom claimed the healing was the result of medical treatment, not of prayers to Mother Teresa. Some Indian doctors questioned the original diagnosis of a cyst; it may simply have been abdominal swelling, they argued, that could have been resolved by the antitubercular drugs. Two of the doctors who cared for Besra testified that her recovery had come gradually, in response to their treatment.

Reacting to these challenges, the promoter of Mother Teresa's sainthood cause, Father Brian Kolodiejchuk, pointed out that all the doctors, including those skeptical of a miracle, had testified in the inquiry, and that their opinions had been taken into account. The Vatican likewise held to its position. "This woman had a tumefaction the size of a soccer ball. She couldn't go to the bathroom alone, couldn't get out of bed. Then after the prayers, at one o'clock in the morning the sisters saw her walking around, her stomach was flat! Our doctors here said there was no possible way this tumor could have gone anywhere. If it had exploded, it would have killed her," said one Vatican official. But the controversy cast a shadow over the beatification ceremony and seemed to give ammunition to critics and skeptics of the miraculous.

Monika Besra never had any doubts that she had been healed by a miracle. But in 2007, as the Catholic Church prepared to mark the tenth anniversary of Mother Teresa's death, Besra shocked the Vatican when she sharply criticized the Missionaries of Charity. She told the British newspaper the *Telegraph* that after the beatification, Mother Teresa's nuns had abandoned her to a life of poverty. "They made a lot of promises to me and assured me of financial help for my livelihood and my children's education," Besra said. "After that, they forgot me. I am living in penury. My husband is sick. My children have stopped going to school as I have no money. I have to work in the fields to feed my husband and five children."

That, too, is a lesson Vatican officials have learned: that miracles do not always bring fairy-tale endings.

In the Judeo-Christian tradition miracles have marked key moments in salvation history, dating back as far as the Book of Genesis. The Bible recounts that the Israelites were recipients of many miraculous favors during their journey from slavery in Egypt to the Promised Land, and the parting of the Red Sea and the raining down of manna from heaven are still evoked today as classic deeds of an interventionist God. In the New Testament, the miracles of Jesus—including healings, casting out of demons, raising of the dead, and wondrous acts like calming a storm or changing water into wine—were considered signs of his divine powers and acts of love and compassion. The early Christian evangelizers also had reputations as miracle workers. As the church has developed, however, the emphasis on miracles has lessened, and a debate has arisen over whether the miracles of the Bible should be taken literally.

A crucial consideration in the discussion of miracles is whether they violate the natural order. The eighteenth-century philosopher David Hume, who considered a miracle to be a superstitious delusion, defined the term in this way: "a transgression of a law of nature by a particular volition of the Deity, or by the interposition of some invisible agent." But the church has always taken a wider view. As Saint Augustine said famously in the fifth century, "Miracles are not contrary to nature but only contrary to what we know about nature." Saint Thomas Aquinas later refined that concept, arguing that miracles were events that may or may not occur within the laws of nature. Because God is at home in the natural order, miracles should not be seen as an intrusion into that order.

While a miracle may be difficult to define, most Catholics today would probably agree that they would know one when they saw one. That judgment usually hinges on personal experience or subjective beliefs rather than philosophical reasoning or the findings of forensic study conducted by panels of experts.

"This is an expression of a natural religious need," said Jesuit Father

Mihály Szentmártoni of Croatia, a professor at the Institute of Spirituality at Rome's Pontifical Gregorian University. Miracles have value, Szentmártoni said, because they offer spiritual enlightenment and grace to an individual, who may or may not be seeking such a sign.

"A principle of spirituality is that God doesn't perform miracles where human beings can do their part," he explained. "But every now and then an encouragement is needed, a sign. This needs to be better understood: a miracle, even a healing, is not a miracle because it's inexplicable by science, but because it offers a sign that someone needs to interpret."

Belief in miracles can never be imposed, Szentmártoni said, and it's pointless to try to convince nonbelievers of their validity. That was well illustrated by a visit to Lourdes by the French novelist Émile Zola in the late nineteenth century. Like many of his time, Zola believed that science had effectively debunked all religious mysteries. In 1892 he traveled to Lourdes, the site of France's most famous Marian apparitions, with the intention of discrediting the supposed miraculous healings that were occurring there. On the train he met an eighteen-year-old girl, Marie Lemarchand, on her way to the shrine to pray for healing from an advanced stage of lupus, pulmonary tuberculosis, and skin ulcerations. Zola described her face as "a frightful distorted mass of matter and oozing blood." The girl went into the waters at Lourdes, and when she reemerged, her lesions had disappeared and her skin was restored. Examinations revealed that her lungs were now healthy, too. Zola, who had witnessed the entire sequence of events, was unimpressed. "I don't want to look at her," he said. "To me she is still ugly." Sixteen years later, Marie Lemarchand remained healthy, and her healing was certified as miraculous by the Lourdes medical board. Zola went on to write a skeptical book about Lourdes, taking a rationalist approach to claims of wondrous cures.

A healing at Lourdes was the occasion of a very different experience by another doubter, Alexis Carrel, a French surgeon and future Nobel laureate in medicine. Raised in a Catholic family and educated by Jesuits, Carrel had stopped practicing the faith and considered himself a rationalist. In 1902, as a favor to a doctor friend, he agreed to do medical duty on a train carrying pilgrims to Lourdes in southern France. The sickest person on the train was Marie Bailly, a young woman suffering from tubercular peritonitis, a diagnosis confirmed by Carrel himself when he was called to the woman's side during the trip. Bailly could not keep food down and had a terribly swollen stomach, and Carrel doubted she would make it to Lourdes alive.

Bailly did reach Lourdes, however, and Carrel accompanied her when she was carried on a stretcher to the shrine's grotto. Because of her condition, immersion was ruled out, so Bailly asked that pitchers of Lourdes water be poured over her distended abdomen. Carrel stood by and took notes while the procedure was carried out, and to his amazement, after several minutes the woman's stomach had completely flattened. The swollen masses that the doctor had felt with his own hands only a few days earlier had vanished before his eyes. That evening Bailly began eating regularly again, and the next day dressed herself and felt fine. After returning to Paris, she joined a religious order, dedicating her life to acts of charity. She died thirty-five years later without ever suffering a relapse of tuberculosis.

Carrel was intrigued by what he had witnessed but said nothing publicly about it, fearing that if his name was linked to a Lourdes miracle it could damage his medical career. But the news of the cure—and of Carrel's presence at it—was published by a newspaper, and Carrel felt compelled to write about the case. He didn't call it a miracle, but he believed that some mysterious, perhaps natural, process was at work at Lourdes, and he argued that the medical profession should have a more open mind when it came to reports of miracles. Though very carefully worded, his account was sufficient to provoke hostility in the medical community. His reputation tarnished, Carrel had to leave his position at the University of Lyons, eventually immigrating to Canada and then the United States, where he worked for much of his life.

Carrel's story has several odd postscripts. For one thing, Marie Bailly's cure was never accepted as an authentic miracle by the International Medical Committee of Lourdes. When it finally examined the healing in 1964, the committee objected that the woman's doctors had not considered the possibility of pseudocyesis, or psychologically induced false pregnancy. The rejection surprised those familiar with the case, who knew that the diagnosis of tubercular peritonitis had been well documented. But it underscored the rigorous vetting of miracles at Lourdes, where to date only sixty-nine cures have been classified as miraculous, out of thousands of candidates.

As for Carrel, he remained fascinated by Lourdes, continuing to make frequent pilgrimages there, but did not return to the faith—at least, not immediately. In 1941 he came back to live in France, where his support for eugenics and euthanasia and his acceptance of support from the Vichy government during Nazi occupation led to accusations of collaborationism and the threat of arrest. Before dying of heart failure in 1944, he received the last rites from a Catholic priest. Four years after his death, his book *The Voyage to Lourdes* was published, a novelistic treatment of his experience with Marie Bailly, offering a minute-by-minute account of the encounter between a skeptical scientist and a woman seized by the power of faith.

Father Szentmártoni, who is a consultant to the Congregation for Saints' Causes, observed that most miracles neither make headlines nor inspire books, nor should they. Miracles, he said, are typically very private experiences that may have deep meaning for the people involved, but do not necessarily have the same significance to the wider world or even the universal church. While the Vatican congregation does verify particular miracles as evidence of saints' holiness and their powers of intercession, it does not encourage miracles as an ideal experience for Catholics. In other words, the church is not promoting the miraculous as a way of spiritual life.

When evaluating sainthood causes, the Vatican's experts have to be convinced that a specific event is truly supernatural, and not merely a subjective epiphany or a coincidental cure. Proving this to their satisfaction requires more than simply an amazed doctor and a recovered patient. The process also requires an advocate, someone with the experience to navigate the Vatican's bureaucratic maze and the marketing skills to sell a miracle.

The legal studio of Avvocato Andrea Ambrosi is hidden inside a medieval tower a few steps from Piazza Navona, across from a *gelateria* frequented by hordes of tourists. In early evening savory aromas waft into the second-floor office from the tables of a pizzeria directly below. Ambrosi, a genial man with an oval face and an easy smile, works in a room that is lined floor to ceiling with old law books, many of them dating to the 1960s, a time when Ambrosi studied for multiple degrees in church and civil law. Most of these volumes became useless in 1983, the year the Vatican adopted a new code of canon law and a simplified process for declaring saints. Preparing sainthood causes was Ambrosi's specialty, and he was forced to change with the times. Today, seated at his desk, he works on an iPad mini.

In an interview Ambrosi explained that when Pope John Paul II streamlined the rules and accelerated beatifications and canonizations, he saw it as a sound and prophetic idea. "These saints were useful to people. They're good examples," he observed. At the same time, he said, the traditional severity in judging causes was abandoned, and the value of sainthood has suffered from a type of inflation. "It's like they say in economics, a simple matter of greater supply," Ambrosi remarked with a smile.

The proliferation in the number of new saints, however, has been a boon to Ambrosi's business. His training at the Congregation for Saints' Causes gave him inside knowledge about how the Vatican assessed the candidates' "heroic virtues" and miracles. He began to specialize as a postulator—a role that was opened to laypeople with the 1983 changes—and spent his days documenting causes and shepherding them through the Vatican's vetting process. With Pope John Paul encouraging new sainthood applicants from every continent, Ambrosi gradually expanded his staff and added services in several languages, advertising them on a website. Over the years he has written the *positio* for some five hundred would-be blesseds (those proposed for beatification) or saints. Among them were several causes with U.S. connections. One of his best-known assignments was Mother Théodore Guérin, a French-born nun who in the mid-1800s opened a convent in Indiana. Her cause had been lingering in the congregation's files for decades, and Ambrosi read through the documentation carefully. He reproposed a 1908 healing that had been attributed to Mother Guérin's intercession and this time won Vatican approval, opening the way to her beatification in 1998. Her canonization came several years later, and it hinged on a new miracle in Indiana, the restoration of sight to a legally blind man. That cure was described in detail in *The Third Miracle* by Bill Briggs, a book that helped make Ambrosi a household name among U.S. Catholic experts.

Cardinal John Henry Newman, the influential nineteenth-century English theologian and writer, was beatified after Ambrosi won Vatican approval for the miraculous healing of a Massachusetts deacon's spinal disorder in 2001. Soon others were knocking on Ambrosi's door. He became the chief advocate for American and Canadian sainthood causes, including many that had been stalled for years in the Vatican pipeline. Among the candidates on his working roster were Archbishop Fulton Sheen, the celebrated television and radio preacher; Cardinal Terence Cooke, the much-loved archbishop of New York; Mother Henriette Delille, a freeborn woman of African descent who founded a religious order of black sisters in New Orleans; Bishop Simon Bruté de Rémur, an early evangelizer in the United States; Father Michael J. McGivney, founder of the Knights of Columbus; Father Patrick Peyton, who launched the Family Rosary Crusade in the 1940s; Father Edward Flanagan, founder of the orphanage known as Boys Town; and Brother André Bessette, the saintly doorman of a church-run college in Montreal.

Ambrosi is known for his blunt appraisal of a sainthood candidate's virtues and an unerring eye for identifying credible miracles. He is above all a canny strategist, knowing what kind of evidence will sway the Consulta Medica and which arguments will carry weight with the

Consulta Teologica. Typically Ambrosi pays an initial visit to the promoters of a cause to evaluate the chances of success. The process is easier if there are living witnesses, people who knew the candidate personally and can describe how he or she lived the Christian virtues heroically. Finding a miracle comes later, and is more challenging. Often local church officials will have assembled documentation of several potential miracles, and Ambrosi is called in to select the strongest case. If a miraculous cure is involved, he examines first the diagnosis, to verify that there were never any medical doubts or second opinions. Often he will deal directly with the doctors involved in treatment, and this is where problems can arise.

"Some are not very willing," said Ambrosi, who speaks an accented English. "It doesn't depend on their religion. I've dealt with Jewish doctors, Hindu doctors, and they can be more open than Christians. Today, the problem is insurance and liability—especially when I call and they're told someone is on the phone from a legal studio. *Mamma mia*, they're afraid!" For that reason, when introducing himself, Ambrosi sometimes prefers to call himself "doctor," an honorific title commonly used in Italy by anyone with a college degree.

Ambrosi must ascertain that any potential miracle cannot be linked to treatment, and he has found that U.S. doctors generally keep impeccable records and are very clear when they find no medical explanation for their patient's healing. Still, Ambrosi hunts for personal stories that can bolster the case, aware that sometimes the most convincing piece of evidence can be anecdotal, not scientific. He recalled one episode involving an Italian man dying of stomach problems who suddenly got out of bed and asked for a prosciutto sandwich, and then ate it with gusto. Medical tests confirmed that the man had completely recovered—but it was the prosciutto sandwich that impressed the Vatican experts.

The miracle does not always have to be a cure from a deadly disease, and Ambrosi is a champion of what he calls "wondrous deeds" that are just as authentically miraculous. He recounted what happened in 1974 to an Italian nun, Sister Matilde, who was holding a two-inch-long pin between her lips as she adjusted her veil. Amused by another sister's joke, she laughed abruptly and accidentally inhaled the pin. X-rays revealed that it was lodged deep in her left lung. For three days doctors monitored the situation, but the pin did not move. Thoracic surgery was scheduled to prevent the possibility of inflammation. Sister Matilde prayed to the founder of her order, Father Agostino Roscelli, who had died some seventy years earlier, for a good outcome.

The next morning, before she was wheeled in for the operation, incredulous doctors gathered around a final X-ray. The pin was gone; there was no trace of it in her lung. Additional scans revealed that it had traveled, inexplicably, to her colon, where it was making its way out of her body. "They told me, well, it wasn't exactly a healing," Ambrosi recalled. "I said, maybe not, but it's an extraordinary occurrence. There was no way a pin like this jumped from the lungs to the digestive system!" Although the episode was twenty years old when he took on the cause, Ambrosi retrieved the medical documentation and presented it successfully to the Vatican. It was declared a miracle, and Roscelli was beatified in 1995.

In addition to doctors, Ambrosi always likes to interview the subjects of the miracles in question, but their testimony is less important than people imagine. In fact, he explained, there are times when *miracolati* are totally uncooperative, and unwilling participants in their own miracles. He related the account of a thirteen-year-old German girl, Margit Heim, who was swimming with a friend in an irrigation reservoir in 1986 when the two were sucked down by an eddy. They disappeared underwater for twenty-two minutes. Friends finally dragged her friend's corpse out, and then the body of Margit, which appeared to be lifeless, too. Remarkably, however, her heart began to beat after resuscitation efforts. Margit was taken to a hospital in a coma, and doctors diagnosed severe brain damage. Her friends opened a prayer chain, invoking the intercession of Maria Crescentia Höss, an eighteenth-century nun who had lived in the area. To the astonishment of doctors Margit made a full recovery and returned to a normal life. Reading the medical reports several years later, Ambrosi knew he had found a miracle.

"Someone underwater for twenty-two minutes—that doesn't happen! They die!" Ambrosi said. But when he sought to gather evidence to submit to the Vatican, Margit, now a young woman, refused to testify. "She didn't give the minimal cooperation. She didn't want to hear talk of a miracle," Ambrosi recalled. The Vatican ultimately did give its approval to Höss's canonization, but the miracle woman did not attend the 2001 ceremony.

There is one other issue Ambrosi always raises with prospective clients: money. Documenting a sainthood cause can take years of sleuthing, interviewing, traveling, and politicking, and Ambrosi has to confirm that the cause's sponsors aren't going to run out of funds in midstream. Ambrosi does not publish his rates, but he estimated that most causes today end up costing between $200,000 and $300,000. That sum can provoke sticker shock, especially because there's no guarantee of beatification or canonization at the end of the process. Nevertheless Catholic groups in the United States continue to line up for his services. As Ambrosi pointed out, his clients are getting decades of expertise: "I know how to operate in this environment."

Despite his relatively high success rate, a proposed miracle sometimes falls short, and when that happens, Ambrosi takes its failure almost personally. In 2013 the Consulta Medica rejected a healing for the sainthood cause of Mother Delille, a descendant of slaves, who in the 1800s founded a congregation of black sisters that cared for the poor and disadvantaged of New Orleans. The city's church leaders wanted her beatified and spent years documenting her life and virtues. They discovered that Delille had challenged the *plaçage* system of women of color living as concubines with wealthy white men, saying it violated the teaching of the Catholic Church. Researchers also uncovered evidence suggesting that as a teenager Delille herself may have given birth out of wedlock to two sons, who died at a young age. In her twenties she underwent a deep religious experience and, after selling her property, assembled a small group of women to assist poor black children. Her religious order, the Sisters of the Holy Family, has flourished for more than 150 years, and today continues to run schools and nursing homes.

Under Ambrosi's guidance, the file arguing the case for sainthood for Mother Delille was sent to Rome in 2005. Five years later Pope Benedict declared her "venerable," which meant that to qualify for beatification she needed only a miracle, and Ambrosi was convinced that he had already identified one. Marilyn Groves was four years old when she was hospitalized in Houston in 1998 with double pneumonia and a bacterial infection. Her condition worsened, and doctors diagnosed septicemia. Her small body was shutting down, and she was placed on an ECMO machine, which provides oxygen to patients whose lungs and heart are severely damaged. Meanwhile Marilyn's mother, who knew of Henriette Delille through family connections, prayed to her for the healing of her daughter. Prayer cards were distributed to friends and relatives, asking for Mother Delille's intercession.

Marilyn Groves stayed on the ECMO machine for more than twenty days—well past the time most children survived such treatment—and had been effectively given up for lost when she suddenly made a remarkable recovery, one that took her doctors by complete surprise. She returned to good health and a normal life.

Marilyn was a junior in high school when Ambrosi presented the evidence for her miraculous healing to the Vatican in 2010. The cause had a lot in its favor. The doctors supported the inexplicable nature of the cure, and the Vatican seemed receptive. Even President Obama, through his ambassador to the Vatican, had expressed his interest in sainthood for Mother Delille (though Ambrosi wasn't certain that Obama's endorsement was necessarily a benefit). But three years later the Consulta Medica was still studying Marilyn's healing, and a positive judgment was looking more and more doubtful. The problem was that the Italian doctors on the Consulta were unfamiliar with the limitations of the ECMO treatment: for them, the machine was a form of therapy, so the patient's improvement could not be considered a miracle. "The American doctors were all convinced that the girl could not be saved because they were beyond the time limit consented for the machine's use, and that if she did live, she'd have brain damage. Instead, she's fine, doing great in school. I understand why the Consulta is strict, but they really shouldn't doubt the judgment of the doctors involved—especially the Americans, who are very avant-garde," Ambrosi said. Disappointed, he began hunting for another miracle that would take Mother Delille to beatification.

In 2013 Avvocato Ambrosi focused his attention on another U.S. sainthood cause, one he'd been working on for several years. Father Emil Kapaun, a Kansas-born priest and Army chaplain, died in a North Korean prisoner of war camp in 1951, and his heroism and faith were renowned among those who served with him. In 1993 the U.S. military archdiocese began the process of declaring him a saint, but the cause had stalled. When the Diocese of Wichita decided to promote his canonization in 2004, they contacted Ambrosi, who advised them on how to prepare their case. In 2011 Ambrosi flew to Wichita to tie a red ribbon on the collection of documentation (amounting to more than eight thousand pages), which was airfreighted to the Congregation for Saints' Causes. Now, two years later, he returned to Wichita on a reconnaissance mission, trying to decide which of several potential miracles to submit to the Vatican's experts. Ambrosi also had to decide on a strategy for Father Kapaun's cause. If the Vatican formally recognized the priest's "heroic virtues" and approved one miracle, he could be beatified; another miracle would then be needed for canonization. But Ambrosi could take a different route, that of martyrdom: if the Vatican deemed Father Kapaun to have been a martyr, no miracle would be needed for beatification, speeding up the process considerably. As Ambrosi reread the files and weighed the evidence, the notion that Kapaun had died for the faith seemed more and more credible.

The son of Czech immigrants, Emil Kapaun grew up on a farm near the tiny community of Pilsen in eastern Kansas. He entered the seminary as a young man but worried whether he was up to the spiritual demands of the priesthood. Shortly before ending his studies in 1940, he wrote in a letter to friends: "I am far, far from being a saint." After his ordination, he joined the Army as a chaplain during World War II but saw no combat. He returned to work as a local pastor in rural Kansas, but, finding the work uninspiring, signed up again with the U.S. Army Chaplain Corps. Kapaun was stationed in Japan when North Korea invaded South Korea in 1950, and his division of the Eighth Cavalry Regiment was among the first sent to the battle zone. He became a familiar figure to the soldiers, often celebrating Mass on the hood of his jeep. A few months later, on the march past the thirty-eighth parallel into North Korea, his unit was overrun by thousands of Chinese Communist troops. During the battle Kapaun risked his life to rescue several wounded soldiers. Shunning opportunities to escape, he stayed with his men until they were pinned down in a dugout and taken captive. At one point, as astounded Chinese soldiers stood and watched, Kapaun saved an American sergeant from execution by boldly pushing away an enemy combatant's rifle. The sergeant, Herb Miller, had had an ankle shattered by a grenade, so Kapaun hoisted him over his shoulder and carried him.

The prisoners were marched sixty miles to a North Korean prison camp, where Kapaun threw himself into action. He nursed the sick and wounded, fashioned iron vessels to store clean drinking water, and, defying camp guards, led spiritual services for fellow captives. He washed the inmates' soiled garments and picked lice from their bodies. At night he would artfully slip into unguarded areas to steal extra food. His courage and compassion became legendary among the POWs, as did his sense of humor. Love your enemies, he would tell his companions, but then add the Latin joke phrase, "Ne illegitimi carbo-rundum esse" (Don't let the bastards grind you down). His Chinese captors viewed Kapaun as an agitator, one who openly resisted the Communist indoctrination programs. When the guards mocked him for his faith, he would preach to them, saying that his God was as real as the air they breathed but could not see.

After seven months of captivity and a brutal winter, hundreds of prisoners had died, and Kapaun himself was weakened by pneumonia and malnourishment. Over the strong protests of other prisoners, Chinese guards arrived one day to move him to a nearby "hospital"— in reality, a place where the sick prisoners were left to perish. Kapaun died there at the age of thirty-five, and his body was buried in an unmarked grave.

The stories about Father Emil Kapaun endured, however, and were told and retold by the returning POWs long after the end of the Korean War in 1953. Fellow prisoners of every faith testified to his heroism and his kindness. He was posthumously awarded the Purple Heart and the Distinguished Service Cross for valor in combat. His fame grew, and in 1955 he was played by James Whitmore in a TV episode about his service in Korea.

One of the few artifacts to have survived from the camp was a crucifix carved by a Jewish prisoner, Major Gerald Fink, as a tribute to Father Kapaun's memory. Assembled from scrap wood, with twisted radio wire representing Christ's crown of thorns, the four-foot-long crucifix was carried out of the camp by surviving prisoners at the end of the war. It eventually made its way back to Kansas, where it was put on display at Saint John Nepomucene Church in Pilsen, and later at a Wichita Catholic school. Kansas Catholics began praying to Father Kapaun, and his prayer cards were distributed to local families, who placed them on mirrors and on top of dressers. They were certain he was a saint.

The deeper Andrea Ambrosi dug into the files on Emil Kapaun, especially the testimony of fellow POWs, the more he believed that the priest had suffered a martyr's death. But the Vatican might not agree, so to prepare for that eventuality Ambrosi did want to have at least one documented miracle, one that could take Kapaun to beatification. He flew back and forth to Wichita, conducting interviews and sifting for evidence to prove to the Vatican that someone had prayed to Father Kapaun for a specific cure, and that Father Kapaun had listened. Ambrosi had begun his investigation of the healings in 2009, questioning the individuals involved, their doctors, and other witnesses, and at first glance appeared to face what Italians call *l'imbarazzo della scelta*, an embarrassing wealth of choices. At least three remarkable healings had been documented by local church authorities in Kansas, all of them involving young people. More strangely, all involved athletes who were struck down during competition: a college pole-vaulter who landed on his head, a marathon runner who collapsed at the finish line, and a soccer player who began spitting up blood after scoring a goal for her junior high team.

In his hometown of Colwich, Kansas, population 1,327, Chase Kear is known as the Miracle Man, yet he does not strike most people as someone who owes his life to heavenly intercession. He chews tobacco, gets into fights, chases girls, and hangs out at the local tavern. When they turn the music up, he sometimes dances and does karaoke to country western songs. "You should hear me wail 'Copperhead Road'!" he said without a trace of false modesty.

Kear sat in a booth of the Keg, the local watering hole in Colwich, after his evening shift at a nearby Walmart, where he sold guns in the sporting goods department. It was the summer of 2014, and the bar was filling up after local softball games. Kear wore a black T-shirt and a baseball cap. Around his neck hung a chain made of used fishing swivels. Everyone in the Keg knew Chase Kear, including a number of young women who greeted him or gave him a hug. Occasionally he doffed his hat, revealing a head that looks completely normal. People in Colwich are aware, of course, that Kear's hair covers a grid of scars and that a ceramic plate holds his brain in place. They also know that, according to doctors, he shouldn't even be alive today.

Kear had been a pole-vaulter, and while warming up for a community college track meet in 2008 catapulted himself well beyond the landing mat and crashed directly onto hard pavement. His head was whiplashed into the concrete, and although his skin wasn't even broken, his skull split from ear to ear. Medics airlifted him to a Wichita hospital, where doctors held out little hope for recovery. By the time Kear's parents arrived, a priest had already given him the last rites. Lying in bed unconscious, his head shaved and a probe protruding from his skull to measure pressure, he was bleeding from his ears.

The Kear family decided to put Chase on their church's "prayer line," invoking the help of Father Emil Kapaun. The village of Pilsen,

Kapaun's hometown, wasn't far from Colwich, and even fifty-five years after his death the priest was a well-known and much-revered figure among local Catholics. Chase's father placed a Father Kapaun prayer card at the foot of his son's hospital bed and distributed other cards to visitors and hospital workers.

The following day Chase took a turn for the worse, and doctors induced a coma to allow the pressure in his brain to stabilize. A few hours later his brain began swelling so rapidly that surgeons had to remove the right portion of his skull, along with sections of his frontal lobe. When his mother, Paula Kear, asked what would happen to the skull fragment, a doctor told her not to worry—Chase wouldn't be needing it. The Kears were given a grim prognosis: in the unlikely event that their son survived surgery and possible infection, his brain damage would be severe. "They thought he was not going to make it, and if he did, he was going to be a living body with nobody home. Institutions, diapers, a vegetable. That's basically what the doctors told us," Paula recalled.

The prayer line quickly grew to include area parishes. The Kears' two other sons, meanwhile, posted the Father Kapaun prayer on a Facebook page dedicated to their brother's recovery.

Defying expectations, Chase hung on, and it looked as if he might survive after all. But he continued to be unresponsive to stimuli, and his family began planning for long-term institutionalized care. Every now and then his parents thought they saw a finger move, but the medical staff warned them not to get their hopes up, as it was probably just a reflex reaction. Then, ten days after the accident, a nurse asked Kear to squeeze her hand if he understood what she was telling him. To her surprise he did so, and his parents knew that his brain was still working. He eventually regained consciousness and before long could move his limbs and wiggle his toes. Then he began speaking. With physical therapy he was able to walk, a few steps at first and gradually with greater confidence. The doctors were stunned. Seven weeks after he cracked his skull open, Chase Kear walked out of a rehabilitation hospital and returned to Colwich, where townspeople cheered his recovery.

Kear resumed his life with the energy of a Kansas good ole boy. He was confident that divine intervention had given him a second chance in life, but he was determined to live it on his terms, not as an altar boy. He did not consider himself a saint in this story, and in fact hadn't even prayed for his own healing. He was just the happy recipient of a miracle, which offered him something doctors said he would never have: a normal life.

Looking back on the event six years later, he is lenient with himself. "I wanted to be me again, and that was the me I knew. I was wild," he said, placing a bit of chewing tobacco inside his lower lip. He partied like he had in the old days, let people buy him drinks, and enjoyed the celebrity. "Women came up and wanted to give me a hug, men came up to shake my hand. That's kind of cool." He was featured on a segment of ABC's 20/20 in 2010, and his fame outgrew Colwich. News media reported his fun-loving ways, in profiles that made him look a little like a Catholic antihero. One article described him as a "beer-swilling poon hound." It was around then that Kear began to tone down his behavior.

"I realized that I couldn't be crazy all the time. People were watching me," he said. He looked around the Keg, twisting his bottle of O'Doul's. "I also started to understand what the miracle was all about. Me walking out of the hospital was nothing. But being able to sit here and talk about this now—that's the miracle. I don't even have a full brain!" At the age of twenty-five, an older, wiser Chase Kear had just earned an associate degree in general education and was headed to Fort Hays State University to study public relations and coach sports. He had also begun speaking to church and school groups about his experience. Although reluctant to put too spiritual a spin on things, he is certain he was saved through Father Kapaun's intercession. It certainly wasn't through his own merit, he says, so it must have been the power of prayer.

In May 2011 Nick Dellasega, a twenty-six-year-old former athlete, still in great condition, drove from Wichita to Pittsburg, Kansas, where he had grown up, to run in the 5K "Get Busy Livin'" charity marathon with more than six hundred other racers. He was nearing the finish line when a younger cousin, Caleb, tried to pass him in the final stretch, and Dellasega decided to turn it on. Then, in an instant, he was on the ground, his limbs flailing uncontrollably. Dellasega's uncle, a doctor, happened to be nearby and quickly ran to his nephew's aid. By then Dellasega showed no signs of life. His face was turning gray, a symptom of cardiac arrest, and the doctor pumped his chest to keep the blood flowing as they waited for an ambulance. Someone found a defibrillator in a nearby school, but it produced no pulse. When the ambulance took him away, eight minutes after his collapse, Dellasega was still not breathing, and his relatives were already preparing to call his parents and give them the terrible news that their son had died.

One of the relatives at the scene was Jonah Dellasega, a fourteen-year-old cousin, Caleb's younger brother, who was running a few minutes behind Nick. When he arrived, the doctor was already administering CPR, and spectators were being kept away. Jonah wanted to help, and he had an immediate thought. He stepped a few feet from the road, dropped to his knees, and began praying to Father Emil Kapaun. He kept praying throughout the day.

When the ambulance arrived, the two emergency medical technicians saw the victim and were shocked to recognize an old friend. They had grown up with Nick Dellasega and now, gazing into his ashen face, they feared the worst, as they were both familiar with the symptoms of a fatal cardiac arrest. Still, they kept feeling for a pulse and then unexpectedly got one—a weak pulse, but strong enough to keep hope alive. A few minutes later, just before the ambulance arrived at the hospital, Dellasega opened his eyes and recognized one of his old friends. "What's going on?" he asked.

In the opinion of doctors, Dellasega should have been dead or at least brain-damaged. His hospital stay was brief, and he was sent home after a small defibrillator was implanted in his chest. His heart, it turned out, had an electrical problem, but he was going to be fine.

Three years later, over a calzone at Old Chicago in Wichita, Dellasega showed no trace of his brush with death. Energetic and fit, he still runs races, even in the Kansas summer heat. A recent visit to the Mayo Clinic confirmed his excellent health. Reflecting on what happened that day in 2011, Dellasega said it changed his outlook on life. He had vaguely believed in divine intervention before, but now it had become tangible. He said his inexplicable recovery appeared to depend on a series of coincidences—the doctor who happened to be at the finish line, the defibrillator found almost by accident, and, most of all, the presence of a young cousin who was devoted to Father Kapaun. "But 'coincidence' has been redefined for me. I don't know if there's a real coincidence out there," Dellasega said. "I believe I was saved by a miracle. I was saved by Father Kapaun."

The first sign that something was wrong with Avery Gerleman came during a soccer game in October 2006. Twelve years old at the time, she scored a goal, walked to the sidelines, and began vomiting blood. She wanted to get back on the field, but her coach sat her on the bench. It was an away game in Arkansas, and afterward she was taken to a local hospital, where doctors thought she might have pneumonia. But the amount of blood she was spitting up increased to alarming levels. Back in Wichita, she was immediately admitted to Wesley Medical Center and, as doctors and her parents watched in horror, her condition grew worse. In rapid succession her lungs and kidneys shut down. She was put on a ventilator, and her heart nearly stopped beating from the pressure of fluids that had accumulated in her chest cavity. To buy time doctors induced a coma. They had no idea what was ravaging the young girl's body, but they knew she would die if they didn't find out quickly.

Shawn and Melissa Gerleman, Avery's parents, kept a vigil in their daughter's hospital room. The girl's two doctors, who had children of their own, were sympathetic, but as the days turned into weeks, they had nothing but bad news. Avery's blood vessels were disintegrating, and her other organs were weakening under the assault of a disease they still were unable to identify. Shawn, meanwhile, had begun to pray. A lifelong Catholic, he had heard about the power of intercession, and he directed his prayers to a figure that had always inspired him, Father Emil Kapaun. He was keeping a diary of Avery's ordeal, and on October 28 he wrote: "Father Kapaun, take all the prayers said for Avery this week & lay them at the feet of the Lord. Intercede & obtain a miracle for Avery, full & immediate recovery for the Greater Glory of God." The prayers to Father Kapaun soon spread among the Gerlemans' friends and beyond.

Avery was now on dialysis, and the swelling around her heart required surgery, which the surgeon thought was pointless, because the girl would not survive over the long term, and in fact was unlikely to live through the operation. But Avery did make it through the surgery, and by now doctors believed they had identified her disease: pulmonary renal syndrome, a term that refers to a group of rare and often fatal autoimmune disorders. Avery was given plasma exchange treatments, in the hope that they would slow the self-destructive process. Shawn and Melissa continued to hope, and to storm heaven with the "Father Kapaun prayer." But privately Avery's doctors believed that any recovery now would be short-lived, because the damage to her organs was probably irreversible. They tried to prepare her parents for the inevitable loss of their child.

But in November came a few signs of improvement. Her condition stabilized to the point that her breathing tube could be removed. Then, more than a month after Avery's kidneys had shut down, they began to function again. The doctors were amazed; earlier testing had shown the organs had been severely damaged, and should not be working. According to Shawn, Michelle Stuart Hilgenfeld, the pediatric kidney specialist who had been treating Avery, remarked at the time: "If there is a person that does not believe in God, introduce them to Avery Gerleman." Against all odds Avery continued to make progress. Once out of the induced coma, she began to eat and drink. She slowly gained back most of the thirty pounds she had lost. The medical tubes were removed, and the medication reduced. In early December she stood up, the beginning of a physical therapy program. The medical staff was astonished, no more so than when they scanned Avery's lungs and kidneys and found practically no permanent damage. This was a girl who, doctors believed in the best-case scenario, would be on oxygen and dialysis for the rest of her life. Instead, she walked out of the Wesley Medical Center a week after Christmas. Six months later she was playing soccer again.

Watching his daughter race down the field, Shawn Gerleman had no doubt: Father Kapaun had answered their prayers with a miracle.

In a series of three visits between 2009 and 2013, Andrea Ambrosi got to know Wichita fairly well. He liked the friendliness of the people he met, he liked the vibrant parish life he encountered, and he liked the big rib-eye steaks served at the local restaurants. But most of all he was pleased to discover a widespread practice of praying to Father Emil Kapaun, a devotion that made life easier for a miracle hunter like himself. He came neither as a devil's advocate nor as a cheerleader, but as something in between. In questioning witnesses about supposed miracles, his tone was noncommittal. If there were discrepancies in their accounts, he wanted to discover them now, before everyone's time was wasted.

Ambrosi drove to Colwich and visited Chase Kear at his parents' home. He brought along his interpreter and assistant, Madelaine Kuns, an Ohio native who worked in Ambrosi's office in Rome. Sitting on their living room couch, Ambrosi asked question after question: How high was the fall? Who saw it happen? How fast was the recovery? When did the prayers begin? He got the answers he needed. The Kears' story was compelling, especially when Paula Kear described in detail how the family had organized the prayer chain to Father Kapaun. Chase Kear found Ambrosi good-natured and affable. "What makes you a miracle?" Ambrosi asked him. Chase had an answer, but it was something of a "smart-ass" response, as he acknowledged later. Ambrosi had turned serious, however, and asked, "How has it changed your life?" He left Chase with questions he would ponder for several years.

When Ambrosi interviewed Kear's doctors, he was surprised at their decisiveness: there was simply no medical explanation for the rapid and complete healing of a young man who should never have come out of the hospital. "It was miraculous," Raymond Grundmeyer, Kear's neurosurgeon, stated bluntly. "Don't say it's a miracle," Ambrosi quickly responded. He wanted the doctors to weigh in with medical facts, free of any religious convictions that could color their testimony. Ambrosi asked whether Kear's treatment might have brought about his recovery. No, the doctor said, the only thing he tried to do was relieve Kear's brain swelling so that the young man could die a more peaceful death.

Avery Gerleman posed a different kind of challenge for Ambrosi. Her parents, for one thing, were anxious to protect the girl from publicity, and he was not even certain they would meet with him. But they did cooperate, and Ambrosi was astounded at their story. Well before her illness, it turned out, Avery had learned about Father Kapaun from her grandfather, and had written a school report on his heroic life and death, concluding with the words, "Chaplain Kapaun, pray for us!" Remarkably her parents had saved the eleven-page report and gave it to Ambrosi. Then Shawn Gerleman told Ambrosi about his prayer diary, in which he had registered every single invocation of Father Kapaun's intercession, along with the prayers offered in his parish. To Ambrosi this was gold. Most sainthood causes rely on the prayers of a single person, are rarely documented, and often are directed toward more than one intercessor. In Avery's case, the prayer history was all on the record and all directed toward Father Kapaun. "Do you believe Father Kapaun is a saint in heaven?" Ambrosi asked Avery's parents. "Yes," they answered, "we do."

There were only a few potential problems with this miracle. One was the girl's medical treatment. Avery Gerleman, as her own parents acknowledged, had received the "best medical care in the world" and had remained in the hospital for eighty-seven days. Did her treatment account for the disappearance of her illness? And given such a lengthy recovery period, could her cure possibly be characterized as sudden or "instantaneous," as required by the Vatican? Ambrosi posed these questions to Avery's doctors, who assured him that nothing they had done, including plasma exchange, could explain her survival. Even if such a patient survived, he or she would experience chronic kidney failure and lung scarring, they said. Avery showed no signs of either.

Ambrosi then pressed them about the timing. Was there a single moment that could be described as representing the onset of healing? Perhaps a day when Avery had suddenly opened her eyes and showed interest in her surroundings? To prove that a miracle occurred, Ambrosi knew he needed to narrow the time frame and, if possible, identify a turning point in her recovery. Here, the doctors were more ambiguous. Avery had recovered in small steps that seemed miraculous when viewed in their entirety. Ambrosi posed the same question to Avery's parents. Shawn Gerleman recalled the day Avery's kidneys unexpectedly began to work. That was a critical moment, and it came after the Gerlemans had asked members of their parish to recite the Father Kapaun prayer at the end of Sunday Mass. Ambrosi could work with that.

Nick Dellasega's cure was added to the Father Kapaun file in 2011, and his story seemed no less persuasive. Ambrosi would question Dellasega in 2013, and he came away convinced that this, too, might well be accepted by Rome as a miraculous intercession. He now had an incredible trifecta of potential miracles. *These Kansas Catholics don't do things halfway*, Ambrosi thought to himself as he boarded a plane for Rome. Choosing the best case for submission to the Vatican would not be easy. And, ironically, it might not be necessary. If the Congregation for Saints' Causes accepted the argument for Father Kapaun's martyrdom, these miracles would end up as minor chapters in Kapaun's legacy.

Each of Ambrosi's visits to Wichita provoked more media attention and raised hopes among the Catholic community. Roy Wenzl of the *Wichita Eagle* wrote a series of articles that brought Father Kapaun back onto the front pages and tried to explain the Vatican's complex sainthood procedures for the average reader. Every now and then Ambrosi would try to lower expectations. Despite the overwhelming evidence in favor of Father Kapaun, he wanted Kansans to be prepared for the possibility of disappointment from the Vatican. Over the course of his career, Ambrosi told reporters, he had investigated some five hundred sainthood causes. One hundred had resulted in beatification, and of those, only fifteen were canonized.

"The bar is high," he said.

In April 2013 President Barack Obama awarded the Medal of Honor, the nation's highest military honor, to Father Emil J. Kapaun for gallantry beyond the call of duty during combat. The award gave deep gratification to the Kansas activists and former POWs who had lobbied for years on his behalf. The Medal of Honor was not normally given to chaplains, and it took special legislation from Congress to grant the citation more than sixty years after the priest's death. On hand for the ceremony in the East Room of the White House were nine men who had been prisoners with Kapaun in the North Korean camp and who personally witnessed his acts of heroism and charity. In a speech Obama described how Kapaun had boldly saved Sergeant First Class Herbert A. Miller from execution and then carried the wounded man on his back for miles. Miller, now eighty-six, was seated in the audience. As the president spoke, he recalled kneeling before the North Korean soldier and watching, incredulous, as another captured American with a cross on his helmet walked up and simply pushed the soldier's rifle to one side. "Why he never shot him, I'll never know," Miller said afterward. "I think the Lord was there directing him what to do."

Obama described Father Kapaun as "an American soldier who didn't fire a gun, but who wielded the mightiest weapon of all, a love for his brothers so pure that he was willing to die so that they might live." Kapaun, the president said, gave his fellow POWs the gift of faith and hope, and the ability to see "a touch of the divine" even in the hellish conditions of their prison camp. "His fellow soldiers who felt his grace and his mercy called him a saint, a blessing from God," the president said, and then presented the medal, a five-pointed star on a blue sash, to Ray Kapaun, Father Kapaun's nephew.

The president's words moved everyone in the room, even nonsupporters of Obama like Chase Kear (who, for political reasons, later declined to shake the president's hand). Bishop Michael Jackels of Wichita told reporters the ceremony felt almost like a "secular canonization." He wanted to send a copy of Obama's speech to the Vatican, to help advance the sainthood cause.

"It's about time," one of the POWs had remarked about the Medal of Honor. The Kansas Catholics who headed back to Wichita had similar sentiments about the sainthood process, which seemed to be moving at an impossibly slow pace. Three miracles had occurred, and they were still working on the documentation. Some grumbled that by the time the Vatican got around to canonizing him, no one who actually knew Father Kapaun during his lifetime would be alive.

One person who was not worrying too much about the timeline was Avery Gerleman. Now nineteen, Avery played soccer at college, where she was studying to become a pediatric nurse. As for her cure, she realized the Vatican might not accept it as a miracle for Father Kapaun. "They don't need me, really. I mean, it'd be cool, but I wouldn't be bummed out about it," she said. "As long as Father Kapaun is a saint, I'll be happy." In 2014 Avery got a tattoo and posted a photo of it on Facebook. It was the handwritten phrase *"talitha koum,"* from the Gospel of Saint Mark. The words, in Aramaic, mean "little girl, arise," and they were spoken by Jesus when he restored good health to an apparently dead twelve-year-old child. Shawn Gerleman had pronounced the words repeatedly at his daughter's bedside while she was in a coma. Now Avery had them inscribed below her ribs on her right side, close to her surgery scar, as a permanent reminder of her own miracle.

When Pope Francis was elected in 2013, Vatican officials had no reason to believe the new pontiff would change the procedures for handling sainthood causes. They were in for some surprises.

As part of his review of Vatican finances, Francis wanted to know how much was typically spent on the sainthood process. He suspected that documenting the virtues and miracles of candidates was costing so much that the "poor" among them—those with no religious order or major organization to finance their cause—were effectively being sidelined. He knew that the Congregation for Saints' Causes had established a fund for these impoverished candidates, but he had also heard that the fund was lying dormant. So he requested a detailed report on the finances of saint making, including the Vatican bank records of postulators, the ones who managed the causes and decided where to spend the money. The sainthood experts considered this an affront; they were being treated as if they were running a racket. Nevertheless Pope Francis insisted that the "poor saints" fund be revitalized and financed with contributions from wealthier sainthood causes.

That attempt at resource redistribution didn't go over especially well. Andrea Ambrosi, whose livelihood depended on the willingness of sainthood backers to invest in his services, put it this way: "The pope is talking about poverty, about not spending too much money. Yes, there is a value in poverty. But first there is a need for justice." He knew that documenting a miracle sometimes required years of research, interviews, travel, and printing costs, all of which had to be repeated if that particular miracle was rejected.

There was more shocking news to come from Pope Francis. To the surprise of just about everyone, the Vatican announced that Pope John XXIII would be canonized—but without a new, officially accepted miracle credited to his intercession. Pope Francis had decided to pair him with John Paul II, and proclaim the two men saints in a single ceremony in 2014. The Polish pope had his miracle papers in order, in the case of a well-documented healing of a Costa Rican woman of a brain aneurysm. But officials were still vetting miracles for John XXIII, trying to choose from several possibilities. Pope Francis decided there was no need to wait, saying John XXIII's "fame of holiness" was sufficient to name him a saint. In a single stroke Francis had effectively made miracles an optional element for sainthood.

Officials at the saints' congregation insisted that miracles were still part of the beatification and canonization process—the pope's decision regarding his predecessors was the rare exception to the rule. Yet

Francis seemed to be moving in a different direction. In his first fourteen months in office, he created five other new saints using a formula known as "equivalent canonization," skipping the requirement for the formal documentation of miracles because the candidates already had a universal reputation of intercessory power. In other words, Catholics—or at least, certain groups of Catholics—had long since decided that these individuals were saints in heaven. In the pope's view, there was no need for Vatican bureaucrats to rubber-stamp what was firmly believed by the people of God.

The reaction to this new approach was a mixture of apprehension and applause. Ambrosi spoke for many postulators when he called it "a dangerous precedent." The impression left with the faithful, he said, was that for John XXIII, the price of sainthood had come with a discount. At the Congregation for Saints' Causes, Monsignor Robert Sarno was more philosophical. On one hand, he had spent years poring over evidence on the authenticity of miracles, and he firmly believed these divine favors were valid and important signs for the entire Catholic Church. But he was also concerned that Catholics and non-Catholics alike understand the true significance of miracles. "Let's be clear about one thing," Sarno explained. "The requirement of a miracle is ecclesiastical law, not divine law. Which means the Holy Father can wake up tomorrow morning and say we don't need miracles anymore for canonization—if you can prove holiness, I'll canonize them. A miracle is not divinely required; what is divinely required is holiness of life. That's the epitome. We've gotten too hung up on this idea of miracles and intercession." Others weighed in, including Father Marc Lindeijer, a Dutch assistant postulator for the Jesuit order in Rome, who said that widespread popular devotion was a more reliable indicator of sainthood than miracles, and had a longer tradition in the church's history.

Was the Catholic Church moving away from adjudicating miracles as supernatural signs? History certainly seemed to be trending in that direction, as Monsignor Sarno knew from personal experience. When he first arrived at the Vatican, the road to canonization required at least four and as many as eight miracles, which Sarno considered absurd.

John Paul II reduced the number to two (or one, in the case of individuals who had suffered martyrdom), but some believed the time had come to get the Vatican out of the miracle business altogether.

Other experts thought the Vatican was too focused on medical miracles, and needed to expand its vision to include different kinds of supernatural events. In the 1980s Jesuit Father Paolo Molinari, probably the most experienced postulator in Vatican history, was working on a miracle that didn't fall into the usual medical categories. It was credited to Victoire Rasoamanarivo, a nineteenth-century laywoman in Madagascar who helped keep Catholicism alive in the African country after the expulsion of French missionaries. Forty years after her death, a brush fire broke out in a Madagascar grassland and, whipped by high winds, quickly threatened to wipe out a nearby village. As the blaze drew closer to huts built of wood and dried branches, a catechist brought a picture of Victoire Rasoamanarivo to the edge of the village, knelt, and held the image toward the flames, saying, "If you are truly the Servant of God, stop this fire." In that instant the wind shifted and the village was saved. Local Christians had long considered it a miracle, but before the Vatican would accept it, Molinari had to send two experts to conduct studies in Madagascar: a French specialist in wind patterns, and the head of the Vatican's fire department. In other words, the Vatican was still insisting that all miracles, even nonmedical ones, needed to be backed by scientific evidence.

For years Father Molinari and others had maintained that prayers to intercessors had brought about spiritual conversions, sudden reconciliations, and even unexpected acts of charity. These "moral miracles" were no less wondrous than unexplained medical cures, they argued, yet the Vatican would not accept them as proof of sainthood.

Shortly before his death in 2014, Father Molinari recounted how he had once tried to convince Pope John Paul II to take a wider view of miracles. In a private conversation Molinari told the pope that the focus on miraculous medical cures, which often relied on advanced technology for diagnosis and testing, risked discriminating against poor countries, where health care resources were lacking. "I told him, in the

United States we deal with respected hospitals that document everything. But that's not going to happen in the forests of the Congo," Molinari said. Pope John Paul was intrigued by the priest's argument, because he was interested in finding saints—and miracles—from developing nations. Molinari suggested that the Vatican consider other kinds of "miraculous" changes in people's lives, and he offered examples: a husband and wife who were about to separate, but resolved their differences after their children prayed to a would-be saint; a young man addicted to drugs who turned his life around following prayers by his parents; a family struggling for survival prayed for help, and a job offer arrived the next day. "I told the pope, can't the church look into these cases and take them seriously? And he told me, you're right," Father Molinari recalled. But faced with much internal opposition, Pope John Paul never relaxed the rules on moral miracles.

Vatican officials argued that this type of miracle was simply too ambiguous and ephemeral, and as a result postulators were discouraged from submitting them in support of their sainthood candidates. The issue arose in the cause of Matt Talbot, an Irish laborer and recovered alcoholic. Talbot drank excessively for sixteen years, but through prayer and self-sacrifice managed to take the pledge and stay sober for the last forty years of his life. Daily Mass, penitential practices, and long hours of Eucharistic adoration were key elements of his recovery program. In the years following his death in 1925, he became known as the "holy man of Dublin," and his story encouraged families that were dealing with alcoholism in Ireland and abroad. They began to pray to him, and many were convinced their prayers had been answered—that Matt Talbot was in heaven, interceding on behalf of alcoholics and drug addicts everywhere. Talbot became an inspirational figure in several countries, including the United States, and his beatification cause was launched at the Vatican in the 1970s. But a miracle has yet to be approved. The problem in this case was that the wondrous favors granted through Talbot's intercession typically involved recovering alcoholics. As Vatican officials would point out, the "cure" for alcoholism only lasts until the next drink, and the relapse rate is very high. Moreover, most recovering alcoholics or addicts have been through some form of treatment. Discerning precisely what prompted an alcoholic to abandon the bottle was simply beyond the competence of the Vatican's experts.

In effect, the Vatican had ceded control over miracles to the scientific community. In the view of its saint-making officials, spiritual or moral conversions were too difficult to document, relied on subjective testimony rather than objective evidence, and brought a high risk of embarrassment if the recipient of such a "miracle" reverted to his unholy habits.

With the arrival of Pope Francis, however, there have been calls for a broader recognition of miracles, an approach that is less concerned with medical charts and more focused on extraordinary acts of faith and charity.

Father Giulio Maspero, an Opus Dei priest and theologian at Rome's Pontifical University of the Holy Cross, believes the Catholic Church is experiencing an evolution in its understanding of miracles. In biblical times and in the early centuries of Christianity, he explained, the abundance of "extraordinary signs" responded to a need by believers to witness God's intervention in human affairs. But in the modern age, these kinds of miracles risk being seen as objects of curiosity rather than invitations to faith. Instead, Maspero said, the church is increasingly open to what he calls "miracles of communion," those wondrous and heroic demonstrations of love and faith that are capable of changing lives: "It's not that we were wrong before. But the Holy Spirit is letting us see that we need to demonstrate mercy, and attract people more to the real meaning of miracles."

That may not align perfectly with the requirements of the current canonization process, Maspero acknowledged. But it reflects the original idea of miracles as an encouragement to enter into a relationship with God. As an example, he pointed to a figure some people consider the first saint, the "good thief" who was crucified next to Jesus, and whom Jesus himself declared to be in heaven. "The good thief didn't have miracles or healings, he didn't need to go through some process. The essential thing is that he believed in the mercy and love of Christ," Maspero observed.

Those in search of a miraculous sign or healing sometimes find that the "miracle" arrives in a more subtle form. Father Szentmártoni, the Gregorian University professor, described a trip he made to Lourdes, where he saw many elderly people seeking cures for their ailments, from backaches to migraines. As a psychologist Szentmártoni had always been deeply moved by the suffering of children with brain disabilities, and at Lourdes he found himself wondering why God couldn't cure these children, too. "They say no one leaves Lourdes without an answer, so this was my question," he said. The priest was standing in front of the Lourdes grotto, where the older pilgrims lined up to immerse themselves in the waters, when he was distracted by the sound of a girl, about eight years old, who stood off to the side. She was seriously disabled, foaming at the mouth and thrashing her arms in uncontrolled movements. As Szentmártoni recalled, "I said to the Virgin Mary: 'Look at her! How can this be? Why can't you help *her* with a miracle?'" At that moment the girl's mother came up to her and, after hugging her with great tenderness, calmly carried her away. Watching the scene Szentmártoni began to weep. "I had my answer. There are miracles, and there are miracles. I couldn't stand to see this child even for one minute, but this woman would love her all her life."

CHAPTER SIX

Prophecies, End Times, and Alien Saviors

The motivation behind Pope Benedict's resignation in 2013 was analyzed at length by church historians, journalists, and pundits, most of whom pointed to a decline in the German pontiff's health and his frustrations in governance. One observer, however, viewed Benedict's decision from a much different angle, offering an interpretation based on Scripture, medieval prophecies, and the "secrets" of recent apparitions. Expounded in 180 pages, *Il libro segreto di papa Ratzinger* (The secret book of Pope Ratzinger) was published in Italy shortly before the conclave to elect Benedict's successor and became one of the biggest sellers in the bookstores around the Vatican. The book argued that Benedict's resignation was best understood not simply as a move to modernize the papacy but as an apocalyptic event, one that made sense only when viewed in the context of a divine plan, whose design was evident to those who made the effort to sift through the tantalizing clues.

And the clues were everywhere, it seemed—for example, in Revelation, the enthralling final book of the New Testament, which sketched out a period of persecution for the church and a prophetic role for two witnesses, a role that could be discerned in the frequent criticism of the prevailing secular culture by Popes John Paul II and Benedict XVI. Or they could be found in the prognostications contained in *Vaticinia de summis pontificibus*, a mystical medieval manuscript that foresaw the arrival of a *pastor angelicus*, an "angelic shepherd," who would reform the Vatican and return the church to the simplicity and splendor of the Gospel era. Clearly the cardinals arriving for the conclave of 2013 were looking for such a pope. Likewise, the "Prophecy of the Popes," a litany of enigmatic phrases attributed to the twelfth-century Saint Malachy of Armagh, although considered a fraud by many church historians, could not be completely set aside as a source of clues. It foresaw a series of 112 popes, a tally that appeared to end with whoever would be Benedict XVI's successor, the "final pope" before the arrival of the End Times. Most important, Pope Benedict himself, although considered by many a supreme rationalist, had been describing his decision to resign in surprisingly mystical terms. When Benedict told the faithful that he was being called by God to "scale the mountain," was this not an echo of the third secret of the Marian apparitions of Fatima, which envisioned a pope climbing a mountain before sacrificing himself for the faith? Indeed, *Il libro segreto di papa Ratzinger* suggested, Benedict seemed to hint that he was part of a great prophetic project, in which his resignation opened a new era of suffering and penitence for the Catholic Church.

Il libro segreto di papa Ratzinger barely stopped for breath as it rolled out one supernatural scenario after another. It all might have been dismissed as baseless speculation unworthy of serious attention, except for the fact that its author, Simone Venturini, is a leading researcher at the Vatican Secret Archives, the primary depository for Vatican historical documents and a center for their study. A biblicist by training and a lay professor at the Opus Dei–run Pontifical University of the Holy Cross in Rome, Venturini stands out like a swatch of bright color on the Vatican's gray clerical landscape, and his writings, which view historical and contemporary church developments through a mystical lens, have landed him in trouble with higher-ups. As a scholar in his late forties, Venturini is not eager to sacrifice his career, but he does believe he has a responsibility to speak out against what he calls a "dictatorship" of Catholic academics who would exclude any supernatural influence in contemporary events.

In an interview at his tiny archives office, Venturini argued that while the language of Scripture and prophecy does not provide precise formulas—like the dates for the second coming of Christ or the end of the world—it does offer a framework for interpretation, one that views God in communication with human history. The Book of Revelation is perhaps the best and most controversial example. Often known simply as the Apocalypse, the twenty-two-chapter biblical text presents a symbolic storyboard for salvation, in which the fall of "Babylon the Great" is preceded by a great spiritual struggle and an attempt to establish the kingdom of Satan in this world. Venturini sees in this account a possible correspondence in the rise of Nazism and Communism, ideologies that he believes aimed to "exalt man in all his terrible omnipotence, his delirium of omnipotence." Matching historical episodes to biblical passages is a secondary consideration, however. What's more important, he maintained, is the conviction that the Kingdom of God preached by Jesus is something that has an impact on human events, and is not simply an abstract ideal.

The problem, as Venturini sees it, is that the dominant school of modern Scripture scholarship rejects any effort to link biblical texts to mankind's unfolding history. Known as the historical-critical method of biblical interpretation, it has focused instead on the historical and human context of scriptural writings, and tends to demystify the texts, at times even downplaying Jesus's own divinity, he said. It's an approach that is inclined to understand Scripture in strictly human terms, and to view accounts of miracles as literary devices or instructive legends. In Venturini's view this approach has impoverished the faith and left Catholics detached from the supernatural.

"This kind of thinking was born of an intellectual elite that holds power in theological and biblical studies," Venturini argued. "Their ideas have passed into the minds of priests, through seminaries and universities, and filtered down to the people through Sunday sermons and in other ways. They look on scriptural texts as if they were a wonderful literary narrative, but when you ask them if they think these accounts are real, they say, 'I don't know.' And this is the great problem. When Scripture speaks of miracles, devils, and angels, for example, do they really exist or not? The historical-critical method tends to say no. And thus the relationship between the believer and Scripture has changed. Before, the Bible helped people understand their relationship to the cosmos, to creation. Today, this cosmic awareness has been 'demythologized,' virtually eliminated. People are spiritually disoriented because the coordinates that connected human beings to the supernatural have been dismantled—and unfortunately it's been theologians, biblicists, and philosophers who, unwittingly or not, have brought us to this point."

In his previous books Venturini sympathetically explored other manifestations of the supernatural, including Marian apparitions, miraculous
signs, and the casting out of demons. He acknowledged that his writings
have provoked "open hostility" among some Vatican officials, who view him
as a reactionary voice undermining the cause of rational interpretation.

"It's true that there are people who search for supernatural signs
everywhere, which is not healthy," Venturini acknowledged. "But on
the other hand, many Catholics are suffering from the separation
that's been imposed between their own lives and the supernatural.
Can God act in our physical world, in our lives? Obviously as believers
we should say yes, but at some very high levels of the church and the
academic world, the answer is not so clear."

When it comes to the End Times, the Vatican walks a careful path that
steers clear of specific dates and circumstances. In its interpretation of
the Book of Revelation, the Catechism of the Catholic Church states
that before Christ's second coming, the church will pass through "a final trial that will shake the faith of many believers." It will be a time of
persecution and religious deception, culminating in efforts by the Antichrist to glorify the human being in place of God. God's triumph over
the revolt of evil will take the form of the Last Judgment, which Catholics profess every Sunday at Mass when they pray, "He will come again
in glory to judge the living and the dead."

All that may seem dramatic enough. But the Vatican's vision lacks
the specific details that have made the End Times so fascinating in the
popular imagination. Most notably missing from the official Catholic
version of the apocalypse are three relatively modern elaborations: the
Rapture, the first stage of the second coming, in which true Christians
are instantly taken up to heaven; the seven-year Tribulation, a period of
great suffering and destruction on earth; and the Millennium, the
thousand-year reign of Christ on earth. These beliefs were developed in
the 1800s by a fundamentalist movement called dispensationalism,
which used the Bible to divide salvation history into a series of historical

periods or "dispensations." They have become the basis for many of the books, movies, videos, and other merchandise that have turned the End Times into a growth industry over the last forty years.

Given the widespread popularity of such doomsday narratives, especially in the United States, the Vatican has occasionally warned the faithful against putting any stock in them. Vatican agencies and theologians have declared there is only one second coming, not a series of theatrical chapters. They have described the Antichrist as a composite of forces working against the church, not a specific individual whose identity can be guessed through clues. They have repeatedly condemned "millenarianism," the idea that Christ will rule on earth for a thousand years. More generally, they have argued that the time is not yet right for the Last Judgment. As apocalyptic fever spread with the approach of the year 2000, Pope John Paul II pointed out that it made little sense to talk about Christ's second coming as long as his command to preach the Gospel to all nations went unfulfilled. "History advances towards its goal, but Christ has not specified any chronological date. Attempts to predict the end of the world are therefore deceptive and misleading," the pontiff announced, a message that was reiterated by his successor, Pope Benedict XVI.

There is another reason the Vatican downplays a timeline for Armageddon. In the view of many church officials, people who focus on the apocalypse countdown tend to turn their attention away from genuine problems in the contemporary world—problems that require a Christian response. For example, if the earth really is doomed to imminent destruction, why should anyone care about environmental damage, or any number of other long-term political and social issues? The Vatican, therefore, describes the present moment as a time for waiting and watching, but also for acting and doing good works. Christians today should be transforming the world, not simply waiting for the End Times show to begin.

In essence, the church has prescribed a balanced approach designed to defuse fanaticism: Christians should not obsess about the end of the world, but they should nevertheless always be prepared for the coming of the Kingdom of God, which may not be far off. Still, anytime a pope talks about the second coming, it grabs people's attention, and there's plenty of apocalyptic material in papal speeches and sermons to occupy End Times analysts. In his 2013 book *Heralds of the Second Coming*, Stephen Walford argued that recent popes have been particularly cognizant of an approaching apocalypse. Walford combed through papal statements over the last century and connected them with Scripture passages and the messages of approved Marian apparitions, concluding that signs of the end were clearly and urgently sensed at the highest levels of the Catholic hierarchy. In particular he interpreted Pope John Paul II's criticism in 2003 of Europe's "silent apostasy," or a great falling away from faith, as a deliberate reference to Saint Paul's warning of an apostasy that would precede the second coming of the Lord.

What gave Walford's book an unusually high profile was the fact that it carried a bishop's imprimatur and endorsements from several church officials, including Cardinal Ivan Dias of India, who until 2011 served as the top Vatican evangelization official. In a foreword to the book, Cardinal Dias wrote that the high number of Marian apparitions and messages—including those not yet approved by the church—shed a new light on the Book of Revelation and signaled an impending showdown with the devil: "The Blessed Virgin is weaving an enormous network, building up a large army of her devoted children in order to launch a frontal and final assault against Satan."

Yet while popes and cardinals have sometimes borrowed the prophetic language of the Book of Revelation, they have done so with the primary aim of raising awareness of ultimate judgment, not of warning the world of imminent doom. Pope Benedict XVI, for example, continually rejected the idea of an angry God coming to destroy a disobedient world; instead, he argued that the coming of the Kingdom would occur through a "series of transformations" that began with the crucifixion and would end with the triumph of the civilization of love.

End Times devotees often cite a statement made by Pope Paul VI, who reportedly told the French theologian Jean Guitton in a private conversation: "I sometimes read the Gospel passage of the End Times and I attest that, at this time, some signs of this end are emerging." Quoted less often, however, are the words that followed: "Are we close to the end? This we will never know. We must always hold ourselves in readiness, but everything could last a very long time yet."

If the Vatican has avoided speculating on specific end-of-the-world scenarios, Catholic prophecy trackers around the world have filled the gap, citing a crescendo of dark warnings delivered by visionaries over the last two hundred years. Doomsday seers have appeared on every continent, and several have even been recognized as authentic by local bishops. In 1973 Sister Agnes Sasagawa was told by Mary in Akita, Japan, that "fire will fall from the sky and will wipe out a great part of humanity" as part of a divine punishment, and that "the work of the devil will infiltrate even into the church in such a way that one will see cardinals opposing cardinals, bishops against bishops." In Kibeho, Rwanda, in the 1980s, schoolchildren said the Virgin Mary told them they would know the second coming was at hand when religious wars broke out. The messages also forecast a prelude of terrible violence—a "river of blood"—for Rwanda, which some later saw as a prophecy of the country's genocidal civil war in 1994. Beginning in 1983 a housewife in Argentina, Gladys Herminia Quiroga de Motta, reported a series of messages from Mary and Jesus warning of the imminent coming of the Lord and the destruction of "half the world."

The child seers of La Salette, France, who claimed to have witnessed the Blessed Virgin in 1846, wrote down Mary's secret messages and sent them to Pope Pius IX. The original texts were hidden away and kept from the public until their discovery in the Vatican Secret Archives in 1999. The messages predicted that a series of disasters would be visited upon humanity by an angry God, a God disturbed by failures and sins even within the ranks of priests: "[Among] God's ministers, and the Spouses of Jesus-Christ, there will be some who will go astray, and that will be the most terrible." The notion that sexual abuse by clergy could be a warning sign of the apocalypse is not unusual among Catholic End Times enthusiasts. The La Salette visionaries also foresaw that the faith would decline in France to the point that three-quarters of the population would no longer practice religion—a prophecy that supporters say would have been inconceivable in the mid-1800s, but which seems quite possible in today's secularized French culture. Although the La Salette apparitions are considered authentic by the church, the Vatican has never pronounced on the content of the messages.

The nineteenth-century Italian visionary Anna Maria Taigi is among several Catholic seers who have predicted "three days of darkness" over the earth, a time of divine punishment in which, she said, the air will be "infected by demons" and the enemies of the church will perish. The Vatican beatified her in 1920, but again has not pronounced on her private revelations.

In some cases church authorities have distanced themselves from seers they believed to be fraudulent. In Ireland self-proclaimed prophet Christina Gallagher amassed a fortune in donations while proclaiming apocalyptic visions, including civil war in the United States, "storms such as the world has not seen," and other calamities sent by God to "purify the stench of sin and evil from the world." After the hierarchy issued cautionary statements in 2008, she claimed that many in the Catholic hierarchy would "go willingly in union with the Antichrist because of the control he wields."

One of the few visionaries who have drawn a direct Vatican intervention is Vassula Rydén, an Egyptian-born former model and tennis player who was said to have received thousands of prophetic messages. The messages began one day in 1985, when Rydén was writing out her grocery list. She said her hand was suddenly guided by a supernatural force and transcribed the words: "I am your guardian angel and my name is Daniel." Additional messages soon came from Jesus and Mary and took on an apocalyptic tone, warning of the annihilation of entire nations, as well as earthquakes and floods. The Vatican did not typically pay attention to predictions, failed or not, about the weather and natural calamities, but it did take exception when Rydén began confusing the persons of the Holy Trinity and predicting an imminent period when the Antichrist would prevail in the church. A notification from the Congregation for the Doctrine of the Faith in 1995 cited doctrinal errors and warned Catholics not to disseminate Rydén's messages. Rydén, who was then living in Switzerland, tried to make peace with the Vatican's doctrinal officials, saying she considered her messages private meditations and not supernatural communications. But in 2007 the Vatican reiterated its warning and said Catholics should not participate in prayer groups organized by the popular seer.

The figure of the Antichrist is something Vatican officials prefer to speak of in strictly generic terms. But in 2007, in a series of Lenten sermons delivered to Pope Benedict XVI and Roman Curia heads, Italian Cardinal Giacomo Biffi suggested that the Antichrist may already be among us—and may look a lot like liberal Catholics. Citing the work of Vladimir Soloviev, a nineteenth-century Russian philosopher, Biffi told the pope that "the Antichrist presents himself as a pacifist, ecologist, and ecumenist. He convokes an ecumenical council and seeks the consensus of all the Christian confessions, conceding something to each one. . . . The crowds follow him, except for tiny groups of Catholics, Orthodox and Protestants. Chased by the Antichrist, they tell him, 'You have given us everything except for the one thing that interests us, Jesus Christ.'" Cardinal Biffi implied that the modern Catholic Church risked supplanting doctrine with dialogue, and might already be putting itself "on the side of the Antichrist." At the end of the weeklong retreat, all eyes turned to Pope Benedict, as Curia cardinals wondered how the pontiff would respond to Biffi's provocation. But Benedict, in his summation, chose not to address End Times or Antichrist speculation, and simply thanked the cardinal for his "somewhat audacious theology."

Even before Pope Francis was elected the 266th pontiff, a media and Internet meme had begun characterizing Pope Benedict's successor as "the last pope." Citing the prophecies of Malachy, these reports fed an age-old interest in discovering a secret key to historical events, a fascination with the possibility that God might be using a coded language to offer humankind clues about the future. Vatican officials considered such conjecture worthless fluff, and some theologians suspected it was a way to reduce religion to superstition in the minds of the media-consuming public. But if the hierarchy viewed pope prophecies as marginal and ephemeral, many rank-and-file Catholics found them either entertaining or intriguing.

With every papal election in modern times, Malachy's "Prophecy of the Popes" has been given another spin on the circuit. The origins of this work are shrouded in ambiguity. The manuscript was said to have been discovered in the Vatican Secret Archives in 1590 by a Benedictine historian, Arnold Wion. The text presented 112 cryptic phrases in Latin that supposedly reference the complete line of future popes, beginning with Pope Celestine II in 1143. Wion attributed the work to Ireland's Saint Malachy, who according to tradition came to Rome in 1139 and had a vision of all the pontiffs to come, which he duly recorded and left with the Vatican. The fact that contemporaries of Saint Malachy made no mention of such a manuscript is one reason why many historians consider the "Prophecy of the Popes" to be a forgery, one that was probably contrived to influence the conclave of 1590.

Such doubts have done nothing to undermine the prophecy's perennial popularity, however. Nor have the labored interpretations of its Latin phrases, in an attempt to match them with the identity of popes of recent times. The description of Pope John XXIII as "pastor and sailor," for example, was explained by his role as patriarch of Venice—though Pope John was himself certainly no sailor. "Flower of flowers" for Pope Paul VI was said to refer to his papal crest, which bore three fleurs-de-lis—flowers that are in fact also found on the crests of many other popes. The phrase "of the half moon" for Pope John Paul I was thought to allude to his birthplace, Belluno—a name, however, that refers to a hill and not to the moon. For Pope John Paul II, "from the labor of the sun" was construed as a connection to eclipses of the sun that occurred, somewhere in the world, on the day of his birth. With the election of Pope Benedict XVI, "glory of the olive" was read as a reference to the Olivetan monastic order, which is one branch of the Benedictines, the order founded by Saint Benedict, whose name was chosen by the new pope. Or perhaps "the olive" simply referred to Pope Benedict's efforts in favor of peace. Whatever the phrase drawn from Malachy, modern "symbologists" working Dan Brown–style were able to find some convenient interpretation by hunting through papal names, insignia, places of origin, or career histories.

The last of the 112 popes named in the prophecy was given the tag "Petrus Romanus," and the descriptive text was longer and more ominous: "In the final persecution of the Holy Roman Church there will reign Peter the Roman, who will feed his flock amid many tribulations, after which the seven-hilled city will be destroyed and the dreadful Judge will judge the people. Amen." With Pope Benedict's resignation in February 2013 the speculation intensified, as did the portents and precursors: seven hours after Benedict announced he would be leaving office, the dome of Saint Peter's Basilica was struck by a tremendous bolt of lightning during a violent evening thunderstorm. The image was captured by an Agence France-Presse photographer and published around the world under the caption: "A sign from God?" It seemed the perfect visual accompaniment to the final chapter of Malachy's dire predictions. If the literal interpretations could be believed, the church was now counting down to the apocalypse.

When Cardinal Jorge Mario Bergoglio was elected pope and took the name Francis, it wasn't long before websites proclaimed him "the doomsday pope." But it soon became apparent that finding a concordance between Pope Francis and Petrus Romanus would require some effort. The new pope was certainly not Roman. His given name was not Peter, nor did he take the name Peter as pope. Could it be a reference to the father of Saint Francis of Assisi, whose name was Peter? That seemed a stretch. Some noted that Pope Francis immediately described himself as the "bishop of Rome." Indeed, in a generic sense, every pope could be considered to be Petrus Romanus, the successor of Saint Peter in Rome.

To most people, though, no matter how tortuously "Peter the Roman" was deciphered, an apocalyptic showdown did not appear to be looming on the horizon. Perhaps the end was not so near, after all; perhaps an adjustment in chronology would have to be considered. Before too long the Internet's "pope and End Times" buffs were explaining that Malachy's text might leave room for one or several pontiffs between Benedict XVI and Petrus Romanus. As exegetes of the supernatural, they had learned that when it comes to prophecies, the ability to call an audible is a very valuable skill.

What bothered Vatican officials even more than the media's preoccupation with "last pope" theories was their accompanying subtext of internal church conflict. In this view the "tribulations" over which the final pontiff would preside were centered in the Vatican. As the popular Italian journalists Giacomo Galeazzi and Ferruccio Pinotti expressed it: "A type of gang warfare is shaking the church, which appears to be in deep crisis. The election of Pope Francis is only the first chapter of an internal war that will be long and difficult." In their view the Vatican increasingly resembled a passage from Saint Malachy's prophecy: "a church divided by groups fighting against each other, far removed from sacred Scripture, consumed by power games."

The Vatican viewed all this as fantasy, and it learned long ago that the best response is silence. It would be pointless to attempt to "deny" a prophecy, and official reaction would only add fuel to the fire. But it does concern church officials when Catholics pay too much attention to this kind of interpretive code breaking. "It borders on the occult," one Vatican expert said. "People have forgotten what Jesus told his disciples about the demand for 'signs'—that it was evil and showed a lack of faith."

Eight months after his election Pope Francis surprised listeners in Saint Peter's Square when he began speaking about the dangers of false prophets. As always the pope took his cue from Scripture—in this case the Gospel account of Jesus's description of the second coming and the trials that would precede the Last Judgment. But on this occasion Francis did not dwell on the tribulations that Christians might face as the End Times drew near. Instead, he warned them not to be taken in by doomsayers and "false apocalyptic visions." The twenty-first century, the pope declared, is full of supposed seers and gurus and holy people who attract a following, often by preaching an imminent end to the world. Looking over one's shoulder for an impending Armageddon is no way to live, he said: "Don't let yourselves be fooled by false messiahs and don't be paralyzed by fear."

The pope's words echoed a sermon he had delivered a few days earlier, in which he cautioned against a "spirit of curiosity" with respect to things like supernatural clues or communications from the Virgin Mary. Becoming too preoccupied with the search for signs and divine messages actually distances people from God, he added.

To reporters covering Pope Francis, his comments seemed to come out of left field. But the Vatican is keenly aware of the proliferation of visionaries and cultish movements that have attracted millions of Catholics, precisely by appealing to the thirst for hidden knowledge of God's plan. Such figures and groups, who at one time might have generated only local interest, today can become global spiritual celebrities by using websites and social media. The pope may also have had a more personal reason for speaking out on this subject: whether motivated by mysterious visions or ecclesial politics, several of the more popular websites had determined that Pope Francis himself was the most notable sign of approaching doom. "The Biblical False Prophet Has Arrived" proclaimed one site, which called Francis the "anti-pope" and an impostor to the papacy who would lead the world to embrace a pagan religion. The anonymity afforded by the Internet enabled some of the most popular cult leaders to operate under strange aliases without ever disclosing their real identities. "Maria Divine Mercy" was a case in point.

In November 2010 an Irish Catholic woman who, as she put it, had been "drifting toward agnosticism" began having visions of the Virgin Mary and other Christian figures. She claimed that Mary, Jesus, and God the Father were giving her messages and ordering her to deliver them to "a disbelieving world." These were not the brief phrases of Saint Malachy but full-fledged lectures, alternating between expressions of compassion and dire threats, according to the shifting mood of the heavenly speaker—"my mercy knows no bounds" would segue to warnings of everlasting punishment for "the most hardened of sinners." The sins of abortion and "immorality of the flesh" received particular attention. The seer gave herself the name Maria Divine Mercy and launched a Facebook page and a website. She warned that after a period of "cleansing" was offered to sinners—the "divine mercy" aspect of the prophecies—then chastisement and divine retribution would begin, because God was "very angry," and his patience was wearing thin. A cross would appear in the sky one day, along with comets, and the suffering would begin. All this dragged on a bit longer than foreseen, however; although she had warned in early 2011 that only "a few months" remained for conversion, by 2012 she had adopted a more ambiguous timetable for the great reckoning. Meanwhile, some of her specific predictions failed to materialize, notably when she foretold that there would be "three world leaders assassinated shortly one by one." Maria Divine Mercy offered, in effect, a garden variety of apocalyptic prophecy. The difference was that it was circulated online and without disclosing the visionary's real identity—a necessary precaution, she explained, in order to protect her family and avoid "distraction from the messages." As time passed, attention waned and her web traffic became more modest. And then events in Rome gave this seer, and the prophecy industry in general, a big boost.

For several months in 2012 Maria Divine Mercy had been predicting that Pope Benedict would be "forced out" of office and exiled from Rome. After Benedict resigned in February 2013, the visionary claimed to have accurately foreseen this historic move (even though the German pope had not been ousted but left office willingly, and was never cast out of Rome but moved to a residence in the Vatican Gardens). For Maria Divine Mercy, it was all part of a dark plan that could easily be deciphered through signs. That lightning bolt that struck Saint Peter's, for example, was foretold by a passage in the Gospel of Saint Luke: "Jesus said, 'I have observed Satan fall like lightning from the sky.'" She began to speak of Pope Benedict as the last legitimate pope, one who would be followed by a false prophet on the throne of Saint Peter. Shortly before the conclave to choose Benedict's successor, she published a new message from Jesus, warning of the "cunning imposter" who would soon be elected pope. "He has carefully manipulated his position and soon his pompous demeanor will be seen amidst his splendid court. His pride, arrogance and self-obsession will be carefully hidden from the world in the beginning. . . . He has been sent to dismantle My Church and tear it up into little pieces before he will spit it out from his vile mouth."

The election of Pope Francis, who could hardly be accused of living in the "pompous splendor" of a papal court, did nothing to soften the rhetoric of Maria Divine Mercy. Pope Francis, she said, would "be applauded by the secular world because he will condone sin," and would soon undertake a heretical project to "unite all churches as one." The timeline now was clear, she warned: the false prophet would join forces with the Antichrist to establish a "New World Religion," prompting God to give "the Warning." Billions would convert, the second coming would follow, and a thousand-year era of peace would be established on earth.

With her provocative verbal bite and a new audience of traditionalist Catholics who distrusted the liberal Pope Francis, Maria Divine Mercy suddenly gained tens of thousands of adherents—"fans" would seem to be a more accurate term than "devotees." People pored over her supposedly divine messages, which had been translated into thirty-eight languages and now numbered more than eight hundred, along with more than one hundred supernaturally dictated "crusade prayers," five litanies, and twenty other invocations. By late 2013 her "Jesus to Mankind" Facebook page had more than fifty thousand "likes." Unauthorized satellite websites had sprung up, relaying her messages and promoting her notion that God was preparing an "Intervention of Great Mercy" that would separate the spiritually weak from the strong: "Some will not survive My Intervention, because it will shock them beyond their endurance."

As her popularity spread into local parishes, bishops around the world began speaking out against Maria Divine Mercy. Archbishop Denis Hart of Melbourne, Australia, for example, sent a letter to every parish in his archdiocese, urging priests to warn their faithful and to destroy any messages or leaflets that were being circulated. Similar admonitions came from church leaders in Europe and the United States, who understood that her "prophecies," taken to their logical conclusion, would lead followers to a schismatic break with the Catholic Church. Meanwhile her website, www.thewarningsecondcoming.com, continued to assert vaguely that Catholics were free to believe or not in her messages: "Unlike public revelation i.e. Sacred Scripture the Church herself has no providential protection in the realm of private revelations." That was not exactly true, for although the Vatican would much rather ignore dubious prophets, it has on occasion pronounced against them when their messages or revelations clearly contradicted Catholic doctrine. Maria Divine Mercy had now crossed that line, but her anonymity offered her a degree of protection from direct ecclesial penalty. That, however, was about to change.

In late 2013 an article titled "Maria Divine Mercy: The Woman Behind the Curtain" appeared on a blog called *Midway Street*. It reported that research into the identity of Maria Divine Mercy had led to the doorstep of Mary Carberry, a fifty-eight-year-old public relations executive in Dublin who did business under her maiden name of Mary McGovern. A somewhat dated LinkedIn profile photo revealed an attractive blue-eyed blonde with an intense gaze. Mary McGovern-Carberry had worked as a promoter for the Irish visionary and medium Joe Coleman, and after witnessing his popularity she apparently decided to go independent in 2010. The *Midway Street* blogger, who wrote under the pseudonym "Mark Saseen," became suspicious of Maria Divine Mercy not only because of her doctrinal contradictions and harsh language but also because of the sometimes sloppy presentation of supposedly divine messages. "[There are] even problems with sentence structure and punctuation! (Is no one checking these for grammar?)," Saseen wrote. The blogger discovered that McGovern-Carberry had a network of business connections, including a publishing company that handled her merchandise. In 2009 her marketing skills had been praised by the Irish magazine *Business and Leadership*, which explained how she helped websites generate online publicity and social media campaigns. Her recipe for success, the magazine reported, was to attract repeat visitors and promote "stickiness" by "engaging readers on issues they care about as opposed to a hard sell advertising message." In the eyes of her critics, McGovern-Carberry had simply applied her marketing savvy to a field that was the ultimate in "stickiness" as far as some Catholics were concerned: the second coming and the apocalypse.

The Archdiocese of Dublin began receiving letters and e-mails of complaint, requesting that the hierarchy take steps to rein in Maria Divine Mercy, now that her identity had been revealed. In cases like this, the last thing church authorities desire is to create a martyr by acting in a public and punitive manner. According to *Midway Street*, Archbishop Diarmuid Martin of Dublin had already tried a discreet approach: in 2010 he had assigned a priest, reportedly an exorcist, to meet with the seer and explain that her messages were false. That, however, did nothing to dissuade her, and the visionary continued for years to issue her warnings that Christ's enemies were seizing control of his church. She also launched a potentially lucrative sales campaign for a newly minted "Medal of Salvation," whose unique design included a crown of thorns on Mary's head and two crossed swords—"one which slays the beast and the other which pierces the hearts of the most hardened sinners," in the words of the online promotion. In April 2014 Archbishop Martin formally denounced the messages of Maria Divine Mercy, stating that they were contrary to Catholic theology and should not be promoted or used by church organizations. By now, however, the effort was like trying to stop a runaway train. The prophecies continued unabated, and a few months later her Facebook "likes" had increased to 350,000.

In February 2015 the *Irish Mail* published a major story linking McGovern-Carberry to Maria Divine Mercy and citing the business partnerships associated with the movement. Soon after, the seer published a purported message from Jesus that proclaimed, "My Mission to save humanity is almost complete." A few weeks later, the official Maria Divine Mercy website and Facebook pages were shut down, though a new website offered archives of the prophetic messages and "crusade prayers."

If church authorities showed patience with Maria Divine Mercy, convinced that any intervention would only spur greater interest in her, other Catholic groups around the world were more proactive, setting up websites and Facebook pages that critiqued her messages and contrasted her behavior with that of the great mystical figures of the church. One blog called *Maria Divine Mercy—True or False?* used the Irish visionary as the model for a tongue-in-cheek online course called "Deception 101: The Art of Marketing Prophetic Garbage." To launch a lucrative business in false prophecy, it said, you had to know your market, establish anonymity, ignore church authorities, and say whatever your audience wanted to hear. In branding yourself, it helped to find an established religious movement and make it your own. Maria Divine Mercy, for example, borrowed words, prayers, and images used by the church-approved Divine Mercy movement founded by Saint Faustina Kowalska, a Polish mystic whose followers included Pope John Paul II. Today, Maria Divine Mercy's bastardized version of Saint Faustina's devotion is often confused with the original, and in some places has become more popular. As "Deception 101" saw it, the lesson was clear: "That's the way to make an easy name for yourself. Steal it. Every identity thief out there knows this."

On a warm spring morning in May 2015, the eighty-eight-year-old retired pope Benedict XVI finished praying the rosary in a secluded corner of the Vatican Gardens and walked toward a waiting guest. Although he had removed himself from public life, the German pope emeritus continued to meet privately with occasional visitors who wrote and requested an audience, including some who were not personally known to the ex-pope or to his private secretary, Archbishop Georg Gänswein. The pope noticed that today's guest, a well-dressed Italian named Mimmo Rocco, held in his hands a big red box. Inside the box was an unusual gift for the retired pope: a book containing prophetic messages that denounced his successor, Pope Francis, as an impostor.

Franca Miscio, an Italian visionary known to her followers as Conchiglia, in 2001 formed an international movement inspired by the sixteenth-century Marian apparitions in Guadalupe, Mexico. For years, she had claimed to receive divine messages with assertions ranging from the dire to the bizarre: a Masonic plot to take over the Catholic Church, the divinity of the Virgin Mary as co-redeemer of the world, the modification of human DNA by alien races, and a global conspiracy operating out of the basement of Saint Peter's Basilica. Conchiglia was pretty much ignored by church authorities until her messages took aim at Pope Francis, whom she described as "the iniquitous man seated on the throne of Peter." Like other seers, Conchiglia considered Pope Benedict the true pope and his successor a heretic placed in power by enemies of the church. That prompted one Italian bishop to publicly condemn her messages as contrary to church teaching.

Pope Benedict was unaware of all this as he opened the oversize book, exclaiming at the beauty of the wax seal on its cover and turning the illustrated pages in polite appreciation. Archbishop Gänswein held the heavy tome for Benedict and saw that there was an inscription from Conchiglia herself. The courtesy visit was soon over, and the guest departed, leaving the volume behind.

It wasn't long, however, before Conchiglia's website posted several photos of the encounter, which was itself described as a fulfillment of her prophecies. The implication was that the German pope was somehow endorsing her "revelations." Too late, Gänswein recognized the ploy and was forced to make a public statement. He told the online news outlet *Vatican Insider* that neither he nor the former pope had known Mimmo Rocco or were aware of the contents of the book. When they went home and took a closer look, they were shocked at its "strange and incredible" claims and prophecies. Benedict's reaction was predictable: he sent the gift to the Congregation for the Doctrine of the Faith for doctrinal examination.

Gänswein, who prided himself on protecting the privacy of the retired pope, seemed to express a degree of exasperation when he remarked, "There are a lot of people who go around calling themselves 'seers.'"

For centuries, the Catholic Church has not only accepted mystical experiences but also viewed them as particular signs of holiness, frequently elevating mystics to sainthood. At the same time, the church has developed criteria for distinguishing genuine visionaries from those who are deceiving others or themselves about supernatural contact. Private prophecy, in particular, requires careful discernment, because by its very nature it has great potential to attract the curiosity of believers and influence their spiritual health. Especially in modern times church leaders have come to view self-proclaimed prophets with suspicion. Many have been revealed to be spiritual charlatans in search of attention or financial gain. Even "authentic" seers can represent a challenge to authority, especially when their visions and messages hint at a cache of knowledge alledgedly hidden from the faithful, which the hierarchy would rather keep to itself.

Church writers of the early centuries traced the fundamental lines of a theology of spiritual mysticism, in which visions, apparitions, and interior locutions all had a legitimate place. In 1402 the respected French theologian and church reformer Jean Gerson penned a treatise that has served as a point of reference up to the modern age. *On Distinguishing True from False Revelations* struck a classic balance between prudence and passion when it came to claims of revelations and prophecies. Gerson believed that evaluating the authenticity of such experiences was a crucial task for the church. For one thing, he said, the ordinary faithful could become scandalized if popular revelations turned out to be mere "fantasies and illusions." Yet distinguishing a true mystical experience from a false one was not an easy task, and required training and experience. Above all it presumed a relationship between a mystic and a spiritual adviser, and a willingness on the part of the visionary to be guided by the church's traditional wisdom in such matters. In that sense, Gerson said, humility was the first necessary sign of authenticity. A person who boasted of being chosen for private revelations should be suspected of fraud, whereas someone who out of spiritual modesty "gently rejects" what he or she had experienced is more likely to be telling the truth. A second sign of spiritual credibility is moderation, Gerson said. He was particularly wary of what he considered fanatical religious practices of his time—excessive fasting or lengthy prayer vigils, which in his view weakened the brain and opened it to "every demoniacal illusion." A third sign of legitimacy is patience, which in some cases meant endurance of ridicule and insults. A fourth classic sign is agreement with Scripture and doctrine. That ruled out not only revelations that contradicted Scripture but also those that were empty and foolish. Here Gerson took issue with "superfluous tales of fantastic apparitions and the time wasted on them." If a miracle lacked any devout purpose or meaning, he said, it should be suspected or rejected, "as it would have been if Christ had flown through the air, and as with all sacrilegious stunts of magicians." The fifth and crowning sign of mystical authenticity, according to Gerson, is charity or divine love. He warned that such love should be chaste. Passionate feelings and carnal love could insinuate themselves in those who embrace devotional practices, he said, and "the more violent a passion is, the more easily it leads to a fall."

Even when church authorities followed such criteria, Gerson warned, they would not have an easy time differentiating between true and false revelations. They would do well, he said, to remember the biblical king Solomon, who tried to know divine matters by human effort alone and lamented: "It is deep, very deep: Who can find it out?" Like Solomon, Gerson said, the investigators of private revelations had to take care not to fool themselves or be fooled. The safest course was never to make hasty judgments, unless it was clear that deception was involved. But even when at first glance nothing false or foolish was apparent, it was wise to await the outcome of events. And here Gerson added a final admonition: the possibility that what appeared to be supernatural was really "preternatural," a manipulation of the laws of nature by the devil: "For a demon can sometimes start out with many truths, and in the course of time when he has persuaded people, then he adds what is deceptive."

Through the centuries other theologians have proposed similar criteria for judging private revelations. Following the classifications established by Saint Augustine, the church has traditionally divided mystical visions and other experiences into three categories: intellectual, imaginative, and corporeal. An intellectual vision involves perception of a higher truth or concept without the aid of a visual stimulus. An imaginative vision works through an image that is produced only in the imagination. A corporeal vision is actually perceived through the eyes and can leave physical effects. In the tradition of spirituality, the "intellectual" visions are considered by far the most compelling, even though they do not involve the dramatic sensory manifestations often associated with mystical experience. Indeed, because they are not mediated by the senses or even by language, they strike the visionary almost as a direct intuition from God, a dynamic burst of understanding that can arrive in an instant. For example, Saint Ignatius of Loyola was praying one day on the steps of a monastery when he suddenly envisioned the Holy Trinity as a harmonically intoned musical triad, a perception that arrived with such force that it caused him to break into uncontrollable sobbing.

In the modern age reports of private revelation tend to focus on visions and apparitions. The church's history, however, shows that the supernatural can express itself in many other ways. In his 1962 book *The Theology of Christian Perfection*, Dominican Father Antonio Royo Marín of Spain enumerated and classified a wide range of mystical phenomena, including auditory locutions, or the hearing of mystical voices; the "reading into hearts," or the ability to know what is in the mind and conscience of another person; and hierognosis, or the unexplained perception of the presence of sacred objects. In addition Royo Marín listed a number of physical prodigies that accompany mystical experience, such as the stigmata, in which an individual inexplicably manifests lesions that correspond to the crucifixion wounds of Christ; the sweating of blood or the crying of tears of blood; and the "odor of holiness," a perfume-like emanation from a person's body.

Another such traditional supernatural facility was bilocation, or the ability to be physically present in two different places simultaneously. Perhaps the most famous reported case of bilocation occurred in 1774, when Saint Alphonsus de' Liguori, then a bishop in southern Italy, celebrated Mass in the small village of Arienzo. After the liturgy, he fell into a prolonged spiritual trance, and his vicar-general told people not to disturb him. When he finally came to a day and a half later, he saw the worried looks on the faces of his household staff and asked them what was wrong. They told him how long he had been transfixed. To their astonishment Alphonsus replied that he had been to Rome to visit Pope Clement XIV, who had just died. His aides thought he had simply been dreaming, until a messenger brought news of the pope's death, which had occurred at the very moment Alphonsus regained consciousness. Later, multiple witnesses claimed to have seen the saint in Arienzo and in Rome during the same time frame.

While unusual, such gifts are not unheard of today. Maria Esperanza de Bianchini, a Venezuelan mystic who claimed apparitions of the Virgin Mary in 1984, was also said to have the gifts of bilocation, healing, locutions, reading into hearts, the odor of sanctity, and the stigmata. After a Mass in 1990, witnesses said, she levitated. In 2010, six years after her death, church officials began gathering documentation for her sainthood cause.

Theologians like Royo Marín were cautious when it came to assessing wondrous signs like bilocation or levitation. Citing the arguments of Saint Thomas Aquinas, Royo Marín said the concept that a person could truly be physically present in two places at once seemed to violate the very laws of human nature and the laws of the physical world—something God would never allow. Levitation, on the other hand, was viewed as a potentially supernatural sign, but one that is subject to falsification. In his classic work on beatification and canonization, Cardinal Prospero Lambertini wrote in the eighteenth century that reports of levitation should be carefully investigated to rule out trickery. He accepted the idea that defiance of gravity could be a holy sign, one that anticipated the glorified bodies of the universal resurrection. But he also observed that levitation was not beyond the power of angels or demons, who retain influence in the physical world.

That was one reason Royo Marín and others have deemed intellectual visions superior to the others: they are less susceptible to diabolical manipulation. The elevation of the soul and an intense perception of truth are phenomena over which demons have no control. Corporeal and imaginative visions, on the other hand, offer the devil a wide opening. Royo Marín cataloged the devil's playlist: inducing visions, falsifying ecstasy, producing heat or light in a body, causing feelings of tenderness, curing strange diseases that the devil has himself induced, creating stigmata, simulating levitation and bilocation, causing persons or objects to disappear from sight, producing false locutions, and making bodies incombustible when exposed to flames.

The golden rule when investigating such visions, therefore, has always been Jesus's dictum in the Gospel of Saint Matthew: "Beware of false prophets, who come to you in sheep's clothing, but underneath are ravenous wolves. By their fruits you will know them." For the person experiencing them, authentic mystical visions are characterized by several features: an initial feeling of fear followed by an overwhelming perception of love, a sense of inner peace, deep humility, and an igniting of spiritual energies. A demonic influence, on the other hand, typically produces a preliminary sensation of pleasure and power, but that is soon followed by internal anguish and behavior that is prideful or arrogant.

For a long time the Vatican has tended to leave the discernment of visions and revelations to bishops and their theological experts. It operated on the principle that these matters were best dealt with—and contained, if necessary—at the diocesan level. The less involvement by Rome, the better—a strategy for which there is a historical explanation. At the Fifth Lateran Council of 1512–17, following a rash of "divine messages" associated with political upheaval in Europe, Pope Leo X had barred preachers from publicly divulging such prophecies and reserved their approval to the Holy See. This marked an unusual exercise of direct papal authority in the realm of the mystical. But fifty years later, the pendulum had swung back. In 1563 the Council of Trent established a new framework for discerning miracles and other supposed supernatural events, placing the main responsibility with bishops and diocesan experts. That approach has been the operative policy ever since, for a purely practical reason: the Vatican simply did not have the manpower to sift through evidence of private revelations and the hundreds of messages reported by visionaries each year.

By the late twentieth century, however, clearer guidance from Rome was needed. In 1974 the members of the Congregation for the Doctrine of the Faith met at the Vatican to take a new, more comprehensive look at presumed apparitions and revelations. Several new developments worried them. One was that, given the speed of modern communications, news of alleged prophecies and divine messages was spreading around the world faster than local bishops could judge their authenticity. Moreover, investigations were now taking longer—in part because the modern mentality and the demands of science required more rigorous vetting. There was a third factor, one that reflected a worrisome trend in the Catholic Church after the Second Vatican Council:

bishops themselves were often unfamiliar with the classic church writings on mystical phenomena, and when faced with a reported vision had no idea how to go about evaluating it.

In 1978 the Vatican prelates accordingly devised a brief set of norms and circulated them privately among the world's bishops. Whenever a new revelation or apparition was reported in his diocese, each bishop was instructed to judge it according to both positive and negative criteria. The positive signs would include:

+ Verification of the reported facts, at least to the point of "moral certitude" or great probability
+ The personal qualities of the subject or subjects, including their moral honesty, their psychological health, their "docility toward ecclesiastical authority," and their capacity to return to a normal life of faith after the supernatural event
+ The absence of doctrinal error in any messages received
+ Healthy devotion and spiritual fruits that flow from the event, including prayer, conversion, and acts of charity

The negative criteria, which should serve as warning signs, were:

+ Manifest factual errors or dishonesty in the accounts of the revelation or apparition
+ Doctrinal errors attributed to God, the Virgin Mary, or saints
+ Evidence of a search for profit
+ Gravely immoral acts committed by the subject or his or her followers
+ Psychological disorder or psychopathic tendencies in the subject, or signs of psychosis or collective hysteria among witnesses

The Vatican's presumption was that if a bishop uncovered serious doubts or evidence of fraud, he would clearly express his negative verdict and, if necessary, make certain that the Catholic faithful in his care would not fall under the sway of the visionaries.

On the other hand, if a bishop weighed the evidence and came to a favorable conclusion, he was to proceed with caution, initially by allowing some public devotion regarding the vision, using a formula like "for now, nothing stands in the way" to indicate the church's ongoing vigilance. Eventually, when enough time had passed, and if the spiritual fruits had continued, the bishop could express a final judgment on the authenticity and supernatural character of the event.

While the new Vatican norms offered bishops a framework for evaluation, they remained confidential and, as the years went by, were largely forgotten. Many bishops found the Vatican's approach too theoretical. The standards may have appeared clear enough on paper, but claims of divine messages and visions rarely fell into neat categories of "positive" and "negative." More often they involved a complicated mix of pious fervor, faulty recollections, and contradictory testimony. Often, judgment seemed to depend on the spiritual leanings of the bishop himself. Some bishops considered private revelations a nuisance and referred disparagingly to devotees as "apparition chasers." Others seized on such phenomena with relish, eager to give their imprimatur. In a few instances bishops who tried to curb devotional enthusiasm for a local visionary were second-guessed by neighboring bishops, which led to a dangerous split in allegiances among the Catholic faithful.

Meanwhile, as the third millennium approached, reports of the supernatural reached epidemic proportions. Throughout the 1990s Vatican officials were increasingly disturbed at the abundant accounts of visions, apparitions, and divine messages in outlying Catholic communities on every continent. A preparatory document for the Synod of Bishops for America in 1996 declared: "Within the church community, the multiplication of supposed 'apparitions' or 'visions' is sowing confusion and reveals a certain lack of a solid basis to the faith and Christian life among her members."

Vatican officials began to speak out on their concerns. Cardinal Francis Arinze, a Nigerian who headed the Vatican's Congregation for Divine Worship and the Discipline of the Sacraments, expressed Rome's misgivings in a speech widely circulated on YouTube: "It is a negative sign when some Christians follow reported seers or visionaries. They follow them, they feed daily on their writings and utterances, but they won't read the Gospels, they won't read the Catechism of the Catholic Church, they won't read the documents of the pope.

"It's very difficult to know in practice if a reported apparition is really from God, or if it is only the fruit of somebody's overfertile imagination, somebody's pious ideas, somebody who does not distinguish between reality and dream. . . . It is very difficult to know when they are the result of deceit of the devil."

One fact was certain, Cardinal Arinze declared: whenever a private revelation caused division in the church, "it's not from heaven!"

By 2011 Pope Benedict recognized that many bishops did not have the training or the prudence needed to evaluate and, if necessary, quietly defuse the wondrous signs that kept erupting in their dioceses. He ordered the 1978 norms reissued and widely circulated, along with a new introduction that cited his specific concerns and reservations. Benedict said private revelations could have "a certain prophetic character" and in that sense "should not be treated lightly." They could also be useful in leading Catholics to the truths of faith revealed by Christ in the Gospel, or by giving rise to new forms of piety. But that was as much as the pontiff was willing to concede, and he returned emphatically to a point he had been making for years: that the faithful needed to understand the essential difference between private revelations and the word of God as revealed in Scripture. The role of private messages or visions or prophecies, he insisted, was not to complete or add to scriptural teachings. Nor did they demand a response of faith—Catholics were free to ignore them, even when approved. Indeed, he said, when the church "approved" a private revelation, it was not endorsing any specific supernatural claim, but simply decreeing that its message contained nothing contrary to faith and morals.

An eventual judgment by the church on revelations generally falls into one of three categories. For those that prove to be false, the Latin term *constat de non supernaturalitate* is used, meaning that authorities have determined that the events are in no way supernatural, and are most likely attributed to fraud—or to the devil. A more neutral, but still negative, verdict is *non constat de supernaturalitate*, meaning that authorities believe there is not enough evidence to establish that the events are supernatural. When a private revelation is deemed credible, the church uses the term *constat de supernaturalitate*, declaring that the event is of a supernatural character, and therefore worthy of belief.

But even after all the recent norms and cautionary instructions from the Vatican, the most common "judgment" of the church is no judgment at all. Rather than officially pronounce on every supernatural claim, authorities often maintain a prudent silence and try to avoid the publicity that a positive or negative decree would inevitably generate.

When it comes to specific prophecies, the Vatican tries to walk a fine line between credence and caution. On one hand, the Catholic Church teaches that Christians should avoid an "unhealthy curiosity" about knowledge of coming events, rejecting all forms of divination to foretell the future. Pursuits such as consulting horoscopes, astrology, and palm reading, as well as recourse to clairvoyance and mediums, can be sinful, depending on how seriously they're taken. They are considered forms of paganism and, as the Catechism of the Catholic Church puts it, they "conceal a desire for power over time, history, and, in the last analysis, other human beings."

Yet the same catechism also teaches that "God can reveal the future to his prophets or to other saints." Over the centuries, in fact, the church has recognized prophecy as a legitimate gift of the spirit, by which a person possesses divinely inspired knowledge of future events or awareness of hidden aspects of past and present events. Because it comes from God, prophetic knowledge is presumed to be for the good of humanity and therefore should be manifested to others. That's the theory, in any case. In practice, however, the Vatican has done little or nothing to broadcast prophetic statements, even when pronounced by saints, because that would inevitably be viewed as an endorsement. As with other private revelations, the Vatican regards prophecies as useful but unnecessary to the faith, so it does not want to be seen as promoting the messages of selected seers.

There's another reason for the Vatican's reticence. Quite often in history the most famous prophecies have focused on the church itself—its coming trials, the fate of future popes, and possible deceptions and failings at the highest levels. The predictions of seers like Maria Divine Mercy in Ireland are not taken seriously by Vatican officials, mainly because they can't accuse a sitting pope of being an impostor and still remain credible mystics in the eyes of church authorities. In the past, however, visionaries have prophesied all manner of mayhem at the Vatican; some have been condemned, some have been canonized, and some have experienced both censure and acclaim, depending on who is in power in Rome. Falling in and out of official favor is an occupational hazard for prophets, a fact that's well illustrated by the vicissitudes of the remarkable German mystic Anne Catherine Emmerich.

One of ten children of a poor farming family in western Germany, Emmerich joined an Augustinian religious order in 1802, at the age of twenty-eight. Her life in the convent was marked by strict observance of rules—indeed, she was so scrupulous in her spiritual and penitential practices that her behavior drew the attention of her superiors and the reproach of other nuns. She also suffered ill health, passing from moments of great pain to religious ecstasies. When her convent was closed during a period of political repression, Emmerich moved to a private home, where her illness soon confined her to bed. By this time she was exhibiting the stigmata, the wounds of the crucifixion in her hands and feet, which were pronounced genuine by church examiners. A reddish cross appeared through the skin of her breastbone. She was said to have extraordinary knowledge of the diseases that afflicted specific individuals and prescribed effective remedies for those who came to her bedside. She claimed to see the souls in purgatory and to speak with Jesus. Eventually the government sent its own investigating commission, which suggested fraud was involved but was never able to produce evidence of deception. About this time she received an unusual visitor, the German romantic poet Clemens Brentano, who for the next five years conversed with Emmerich and wrote down the particulars of her visions and prophecies. When she died in 1824 at the age of forty-nine, her well-attended funeral had an unusual postscript: a rumor spread that her corpse had been stolen from the cemetery in Dülmen. Twice her grave was reopened, and both times the coffin and body were found intact.

Emmerich might have faded from public memory had it not been for Brentano, who spent several years collating the notes from their conversations. In 1833 he published *The Dolorous Passion of Our Lord Jesus Christ According to the Meditations of Anne Catherine Emmerich*, a book that added detailed episodes to the Gospel account of Christ's suffering and death. As someone who claimed to have been spiritually "present" at the Passion, Emmerich was able to describe the events from an eyewitness perspective:

> No sooner had Pilate pronounced sentence than Jesus was given up into the hands of the archers, and the clothes which he had taken off in the court of Caiaphas were brought for him to put on again. I think some charitable persons had washed them, for they looked clean. The ruffians who surrounded Jesus untied his hands for his dress to be changed, and roughly dragged off the scarlet mantle with which they had clothed him in mockery, thereby reopening all his wounds; he put on his own linen under-garment with trembling hands, and they threw his scapular over his shoulders. As the crown of thorns was too large and prevented the seamless robe, which his Mother had made for him, from going over his head, they pulled it off violently, heedless of the pain thus inflicted upon him. His white woolen dress was next thrown over his shoulders, and then his wide belt and cloak. After this, they again tied round his waist a ring covered with sharp iron points, and to it they fastened the cords by which he was led, doing all with their usual brutal cruelty.

Emmerich described how the Romans wanted Jesus's cross to be more prominent than those of the two thieves who were crucified on either side of him, so they lengthened it with an additional piece of wood. Her vision of the crucifixion was clinical: "His chest was torn with stripes and wounds, and his elbows, wrists, and shoulders so violently distended as to be almost dislocated; blood constantly trickled down from the gaping wounds in his hands, and the flesh was so torn from his ribs that you might almost count them." Nearly two centuries later Hollywood director Mel Gibson would find her account so visually moving that he borrowed several elements for his 2004 movie, *The Passion of the Christ,* including Emmerich's vision of Judas tormented by demons after his betrayal of Jesus.

In a second volume prepared by Brentano, *The Life of the Blessed Virgin Mary,* Emmerich's visions added details to Mary's life that struck some as excessive. She spent several hundred words describing her coiffure at her wedding, extending even to the little plaits that were interwoven with silk and pearls. A later biography of Emmerich based on Brentano's journals included several other striking claims by the mystic nun: for example, that the sun had no heat and was peopled by holy spirits, or that the moon had "fields and thickets where animals roam." At times she put a strange spin on biblical passages, as when she declared that, because of God's curse, Noah's son Ham became the progenitor of "the black, idolatrous, stupid nations."

Anne Catherine Emmerich's most ominous prophecies, however, concerned the future church. She envisioned great tribulations, with the true church undermined by a "black counterfeit church," a pope "surrounded by traitors," and bishops "weak and wavering" in cowardice. Saint Peter's Basilica would be destroyed, and a new church constructed in its place that would host all manner of abominations: "No angels were supervising the building operations. In that church, nothing came from high above. . . . There was only division and chaos. It is probably a church of human creation, following the latest fashion." While Emmerich herself was sometimes said to have minimized the importance of her visions, she was quoted by Brentano as warning that church figures who ignored her prophecies "will have to render a severe account of their negligence."

In the late 1800s, after Emmerich's visions were more widely circulated, German church experts began assembling evidence to support her sainthood cause. They received encouragement from Pope Pius IX, who requested an Italian translation of her prophecies. The documentation was eventually forwarded to Rome, where it remained in the files for years. In the 1920s authorities at the Vatican took a closer and more critical look at the Emmerich-Brentano writings. They questioned the orthodoxy of certain elements, found that Brentano had taken literary liberties with the material, and some even suspected he had fabricated many of the passages, utilizing maps of the Holy Land, travel guides, and pilgrims' accounts. The Holy Office, charged with defending Catholic doctrine, suspended the sainthood cause in 1928.

It wasn't until 1973, after a request from a German bishop, that Pope Paul VI reopened the sainthood process for Anne Catherine Emmerich. Still, the cause lacked momentum and again seemed stuck in the bureaucratic machinery at the Vatican. In 1979 German bishops petitioned the recently elected Pope John Paul II and asked him to move the cause forward. The Polish pope, who had a mystical bent and was already familiar with the writings of Emmerich, was happy to oblige. At this point the Vatican's sainthood experts, faced with thousands of pages of questionable visions, prophecies, and scriptural embellishments, decided to take the simplest course of action: it would disregard her writings entirely. "It is absolutely not certain that she ever wrote this. There is a serious problem of authenticity," said Jesuit Father Peter Gumpel, who studied the issue for the Vatican's Congregation for Saints' Causes. Emmerich would accordingly be judged on the basis of her personal holiness, not her literary output. When John Paul II beatified her in 2004, he made no reference to the visions that had propelled her to fame.

The Vatican disclaimer, however, did not specifically condemn the Emmerich-Brentano writings, which set the stage for a remarkable revival of her prophecies in 2013, the Year of Two Popes. The resignation of Pope Benedict XVI and the election of Pope Francis left many conservative Catholics disoriented and displeased, and before long some of them began examining Anne Catherine Emmerich's prophecies about the rise of the "black counterfeit church." It seemed to them that her dire predictions were now being played out at the Vatican in uncanny detail: "Then I saw the connection between the two Popes. . . . I saw the fatal consequences of this counterfeit church; I saw it increase; I saw heretics of all kinds flocking to the city. I saw the ever-increasing tepidity of the clergy, the circle of darkness ever widening."

Indeed Emmerich had foreseen an exhausted true pope set aside by the forces of the "new" church, a prophecy that to Catholic traditionalists was a close enough correlation to the situation of the retired Pope Benedict: "I see the Holy Father in great distress. He lives in another palace and receives only a few to his presence. . . . I fear the Holy Father will suffer many tribulations before his death, for I see the black counterfeit church gaining ground, I see its fatal influence on the public. The distress of the Holy Father and of the Church is really so great that one ought to pray to God day and night."

And later: "I saw many pastors cherishing dangerous ideas against the church. . . . They built a large, singular, extravagant church which was to embrace all creeds with equal rights: Evangelicals, Catholics, and all denominations, a true communion of the unholy with one shepherd and one flock. There was to be a Pope, a salaried Pope, without possessions. All was made ready, many things finished; but in place of an altar were only abomination and desolation."

To most Catholics and non-Catholics Pope Francis represented a welcome change, a pope who had set aside the church's judgmental policies of the past and reached out to people with a simpler message of Christian salvation, mercy, and forgiveness. But while his gestures and comments were winning him a new audience, a Catholic conservative minority began to see him as potentially dangerous—the kind of figure described by Anne Catherine Emmerich as one who would bring "division and chaos."

The modern Catholic Church proclaims that faith and reason are in harmony, a principle underscored by the teaching of recent popes and by the Vatican's own scientific activities. Because religious prophecies can challenge that harmony, Vatican experts are cautious when it comes to assessing claims of supernatural phenomena. But in the Vatican's view, pseudoreligious prophecies are much worse, for by co-opting Christian beliefs and inserting them in bizarre apocalyptic scenarios, they can make religion itself look foolish.

On a September morning in 2012, two visitors traveled up a steep, winding road to the Mount Graham International Observatory in southern Arizona. They spent several hours at the site, treated to a tour of telescopes that operate in optimal viewing conditions at 10,700 feet above sea level. The visitors had a special interest in one particular facility known as the Vatican Advanced Technology Telescope, a six-foot-wide honeycombed mirror that produces an unusually sharp image. Built in 1993 with donor funds at a cost of nearly $5 million, the Vatican telescope on Mount Graham has explored the Andromeda Galaxy, measured gravitational forces in deep space, and, closer to home, tracked objects orbiting beyond Neptune. A Jesuit priest on duty showed the visitors the telescope, as well as control rooms where images are relayed and studied on computer screens. He noticed that their questions were a little odd; they kept returning to the topic of unidentified cosmic objects and extraterrestrials. The priest sent them on their way to tour other non-Vatican facilities at the observatory.

Several months later Vatican officials were surprised and annoyed at the publication of a six-hundred-page sensationalist tome titled *Exo-Vaticana: Petrus Romanus, Project L.U.C.I.F.E.R. and the Vatican's Astonishing Plan for the Arrival of an Alien Savior*. The book suggested that the Vatican's astronomers were scanning the heavens with a telescope named "Lucifer" in anticipation of an approaching extraterrestrial deity. Its authors, the evangelical Christian writers Cris Putnam and Thomas Horn, were the two men who visited Mount Graham in 2012. On a rational or scientific level, the book was easily dismissed. But as the ultimate Vatican conspiracy theory, it soon attracted a following among prophecy fanatics. Published soon after the resignation of Pope Benedict, it managed to tie together the "last pope" prophecies, UFOs, and the End Times into one big cabalistic plot. The book's main thesis was that the Vatican possessed hidden knowledge about extraterrestrial intelligence and was using it to prepare for the arrival of spiritually superior aliens—yet the authors warned that this might all in fact be a "gigantic setup," because the godly aliens could turn out instead to be Satanic powers bent on destruction. The Vatican, therefore, has "wittingly or unwittingly set itself up to be the agent of mass end-times deception regarding 'salvation, from above,'" they said. The story line was beyond science fiction but it got an unexpected boost in 2014, when the "last pope" Francis remarked, tongue in cheek, that if an expedition of Martians arrived tomorrow and asked to be baptized, he wouldn't turn them away. The pope's humorous aside was soon being spun as another warning sign of an apocalypse that would arrive from outer space.

Among the *Exo-Vaticana* "revelations" were purported statements made by Jesuit Brother Guy Consolmagno, a leading Vatican astronomer. Consolmagno had once suggested that nonhuman intelligent creatures were no strangers to the Bible. As an example, he pointed to the reference to creatures known as "Nephilim," which the Book of Genesis ambiguously describes as a race that appeared on earth alongside humans. He said this seemed to indicate that the writers of the Bible were willing to entertain the possibility of a different kind of intelligent being. Consolmagno has become famous for daring to confront the deeper religious questions posed by the possibility of nonhuman intelligence and extraterrestrial life. As the Jesuit astronomer would later discover, however, speculation about Nephilim was a subject on which prophecy-mongers could capitalize. It played into the popular sci-fi fantasy theme that looks to extraterrestrials as either futuristic saviors or doomsday-dealing foes, powers capable of redeeming or destroying the human race.

The Vatican has no official church teaching on aliens or on mystical experiences outside our solar system. But it has maintained an astronomical observatory since the late 1700s, a fact that often surprises people, given that in the 1600s the Roman Inquisition had put the pioneering astronomer Galileo Galilei on trial for heresy and banned some of his writings. In fact the Vatican has had a long-standing interest in the science of astronomy, in part because of papal efforts to reform the solar calendar in the sixteenth century. The first papal observatory was set up in 1789 in a medieval tower in the Vatican Gardens. It was later moved and passed into the hands of the Italian state, but was officially refounded by Pope Leo XIII in 1891, who built a new observatory atop the Vatican hill, behind Saint Peter's Basilica. Pope Leo, who was known for his openness to modern thinking, wanted to counter the image of a church hostile to science. Jesuit priests, who had established themselves as the church's best and brightest when it came to scientific research, were put in charge of the observatory, and before long they were cataloging stars, searching for comets, and collecting meteorites. In 1935, when artificial nighttime light made viewing difficult in Rome, the observatory was moved to the papal villa in Castel Gandolfo, about fifteen miles south of the city. By the 1980s increasing light pollution forced the pope's astronomers to invest in the Arizona facility and work there for a good part of the year.

In recent decades the Jesuit astronomers at the Vatican have made a name for themselves by hosting seminars on black holes and galaxy collisions, as well as more philosophical conferences on science and faith. Inevitably discussions about astrobiology have led to the topic of extraterrestrial life and all its theological implications. In 2008 the director of the observatory, Jesuit Father José Gabriel Funes, made headlines when he said Christians should consider alien life as "extraterrestrial brothers" and a part of God's creation. Intriguingly Funes seemed to imply that any eventual alien race might not need the kind of redemption that God brought to human beings. He cited the Gospel parable of the shepherd who left his flock of ninety-nine sheep in order to search for the one that was lost, and said: "We who belong to the human race could really be that lost sheep, the sinners who need a pastor." Other intelligent beings, he said, "might have remained in full friendship with their creator." That kind of talk has disturbed tradition-minded Catholics, who suspect that the stargazing Jesuits have lost their religious bearings.

The headquarters of the Vatican Observatory outside Rome can be reached in one of two ways. The main building opens onto a busy square in the town of Albano, and is entered through a nondescript gate. By far the more scenic access is through the grounds of the papal farm that stretches to nearby Castel Gandolfo. A gravel road winds beneath tall pines, past fields with grazing cows and henhouses decorated with terra-cotta roundels. At the end of the road stands a complex with modest offices, a library, and exhibition cases full of ancient telescopes and meteorite chips. It is here that Brother Guy Consolmagno does his thinking and writing during the months he spends away from the Mount Graham facility.

"People trying to reconcile science with supernatural signs make some fundamental mistakes. First, they think that both science and religion are big books of facts that you have to believe, and these two books are supposed to agree. But science is not a big book of facts. Science is a conversation about the data, and how to understand them. Religion is even less a big book of facts. It's the exploration of a relationship with God."

Consolmagno perched on a stool in a small and sparsely furnished office. A sixty-two-year-old native of Detroit, he wears a bushy beard that has turned gray during his two decades at the observatory. His path to the Jesuits and to astronomy was the result of two elliptical orbits that intersected at the age of thirty-seven. As a young man he studied planetary science at the Massachusetts Institute of Technology and later lectured at the Harvard College observatory. He'd "always been a nerd," he explained, and astronomy seemed a perfect fit. Consolmagno returned to MIT for postdoctoral work in 1983, when he had a "what am I doing with my life?" crisis. He would wake up at three o'clock in the morning and wonder: *Why am I wasting my time looking at the moons of Jupiter when people are starving in the world?* And he couldn't find an answer. Astronomy suddenly seemed self-indulgent and useless, so he quit academia and joined the Peace Corps, asking to be sent wherever he would be most useful. He was posted to Kenya, and three months later he found himself at the University of Nairobi—teaching astronomy to young African graduate students. He would sometimes take a telescope to nearby villages and let local residents gaze at the stars. "They would look at Jupiter and go, 'Aaaaah!' And that's when I realized why you do astronomy. Because we're human beings and we're hungry for more than food," he explained.

Consolmagno returned to the United States after his tour of duty in Africa and taught at a college in Pennsylvania. He'd been mulling over the idea of joining the Jesuits for years, and in 1989, after breaking up with his girlfriend, he entered the order and professed vows as a brother two years later. In 1993 he took on his assignment at the Vatican Observatory. Since then much of his research has focused on meteorites, asteroids, and other small bodies in the solar system, and he even has an asteroid named after him: 4597 Consolmagno. Unlike most of his Vatican confreres, Consolmagno has a relatively high public profile as a speaker and an author. His 2011 stargazing primer, *Turn Left at Orion*, became one of the most popular of all astronomy books. A coffee-table volume, *The Heavens Proclaim*, gave an overview of the Vatican's astronomical endeavors and landed him on *The Colbert Report*, where he was asked, predictably, about aliens. Rather than run away from such questions, Consolmagno has embraced them, partly because he believes they touch on some fundamental issues about God, humanity, and the universe. In 2014 he and Jesuit Father Paul Mueller published a book provocatively titled *Would You Baptize an Extraterrestrial?* He does not consider that merely a rhetorical question.

"The joke answer is, 'Only if they ask.' And that's meant to raise a smile. But it also means that you have to be in communication, they have to be intelligent enough to ask and to know what baptism means," Consolmagno said. He acknowledged that potential aliens might not necessarily share the salvation history of human beings. But if they have intellect and free will, he explained, they would have confronted the issue of sin and therefore "need redemption from their own mistakes." Beyond that, he added, "you're hypothesizing in the absence of data, because we don't know. We don't know whether the second person of the Trinity arrives in other places, in other guises."

While that kind of open-mindedness might stimulate a thoughtful discussion at one of the Vatican Observatory's scholarly conferences, it also excites the imaginations of nonacademics, including those who wouldn't hesitate to promote the arrival of aliens as the final chapter in human history—a chapter that, according to the prophecy promoters, has already been written, and therefore can be foretold by reading the "signs."

Consolmagno dismissed *Exo-Vaticana* as an amateurish blend of inaccuracies and fantasies undeserving of attention. To take just one detail, consider the "Lucifer" telescope that features so prominently in the supposed search for an alien savior: First, it's a camera and spectroscope that doesn't belong to the Vatican, but to a group of European institutes at a separate Mount Graham facility; second, naming the device "Lucifer" was essentially an inside joke by its German manufacturers, who were acknowledging funding assistance provided through a government official named Teufel—the German word for "devil." (In the wake of the wild speculation about "Lucifer," the astronomers now prefer to call the instrument "Lucy.")

But beyond such bizarre Vatican conspiracy theories, the alien–End Times connection does have a wider following in popular culture, among people who imagine aliens either as the ultimate threat or as a conduit to the divine. That's created a lucrative opening, Consolmagno said, for those who "make their living feeding off the paranoia of others" and who hype the search for supernatural clues. It's a tendency that, in his view, demonstrates a weak confidence in one's own religious beliefs.

"The main problem is a lack of faith, the fear that our understanding of our religion will not survive radical changes in the way we understand the universe. If you presume that the arrival of an alien will rock your foundations, then you've got pretty shaky foundations."

In that sense the Vatican's astronomers believe faith should not impose preconceived notions on the exploration of the universe, as that would involve placing limits on the creative freedom of God. Aliens, if they exist, may have a different relationship with the Creator. "We have to be open to however God actually did create this universe, not the way that we want him to," Consolmagno observed. And that means astronomy, even Jesuit astronomy, should be looking to expand scientific understanding, not trying to prove some divine plan.

Sign seekers, on the other hand, want an interpretive key, some piece of secret knowledge that can unlock all the answers. But that's not how things work, Consolmagno said. "If I were to see such a sign, I wouldn't trust it. Because first of all I know how fallible my science is. People are looking for certainty, and they're looking for certainty *right now*. And the two things that science never gives you are certainty and certainty right now. Those are lies, and anyone who promises those things to you is trying to sell you something. Secondly, I know enough about God to know that's not how God operates. Whoever's giving me that sign, it's not God. It's not just me saying this. That's what Jesus says about false prophets—if you're looking for that kind of certainty, it's because you don't have faith."

Acknowledgments

I am indebted to the many people, at the Vatican and elsewhere, who so willingly spoke to me during my research for this book, often on topics that invite misunderstanding. The realm of miracles, apparitions, and prophecies extends beyond church documents and official teachings, and its exploration required much assistance and guidance. Cardinal José Saraiva Martins and Monsignor Robert Sarno explained in detail the subtleties of Vatican investigations of miracles and the theological principles involved, and for that I am very grateful. Father Paolo Molinari, even in sickness a few months before his death, took the time to enlighten me on the evolving notion of miracles. I thank Nazzarreno Gabrielli for his candid accounts of exhuming the bodies of saints and his perspective on the value of relics. Father Giandomenico Mucci, with great warmth and a fine sense of humor, led me across the tricky landscape of apparitions and personal revelations in the church's history. I was greatly aided by exorcists in Italy, including Father Francesco Bamonte, who took time from their busy schedules to explain their ministry, and in Indiana by Father Michael Maginot, who shared details of a very strange case of possession. My gratitude goes to Father Mihály Szentmártoni, who helped me understand that the concept of the miraculous has found many expressions in the church's tradition of spirituality. I want to acknowledge the generous cooperation of the three young *miracolati* in Kansas, who believe that they owe their lives to the intercession of a saint, and to the kind hosts of the Emil Kapaun museum in Pilsen, Kansas, who opened the facility after closing hours and took me through each room, explaining every artifact of the priest's life. Thanks, too, to Francesco Grana and Katherine Wilson for helping me understand Naples and its patron, Saint Januarius. To all the others who offered their time and expertise, including those who preferred not to be named, goes my gratitude.

My research was informed by the published work of many authors and journalists. Classic sources are noted in my book. Documentation on Medjugorje, provided in works by Ivo Sivric and Donal A. Foley, was very helpful. Other sources, while too numerous to list here, included works by Father Gabriele Amorth, Tarcisio Bertone, Bill Briggs, Peter Brown, Alexis Carrel, Leonard Cheshire, Saverio Gaeta, Jane Garnett and Gervase Rosser, John H. Heller, Stanley L. Jaki, Aaron Kheriaty and John Cihak, René Laurentin, Jean Lhermitte, Walter McCrone, William L. Maher, Jacques Martin, Don Mullan, Salvatore Perrella, Arthur Tonne, Roy Wenzl and Travis Heying, Ian Wilson, Kenneth Woodward, and Émile Zola. I drew upon Catholic News Service and its unparalleled coverage of Vatican affairs, as well as reporting by Peter Finney Jr. of the New Orleans *Clarion Herald*, Patrick Downes and Anna Weaver of the *Hawaii Catholic Herald*, the Baltimore *Catholic Review*, and the *Catholic Anchor* of Anchorage.

My thanks goes to Daniel L. Johnson, Richard Thavis, and Cindy Wooden for their help in reviewing the manuscript, and to all those who offered encouragement and suggestions, including Michelle Boorstein, Robert Duncan, David Gibson, and Phoebe Natanson.

I thank my agent, Kristine Dahl of International Creative Management, for her unerring guidance and support, and Rick Kot, my editor at Viking, and his assistant, Diego H. Nunez, for their careful and always excellent work.

Index